Years of Liberalism and Fascism – Italy 1870–1945

D1332429

Years of Liberalism and Fascism – Italy 1870–1945

David Evans

Hodder & Stoughton

A MEMBER OF THE HODDER HEADLINE GROUP

Orders: please contact Bookpoint Ltd, 130 Milton Park, Abingdon, Oxon OX14 4SB.
Telephone: (44) 01235 827720. Fax: (44) 01235 400454. Lines are open from 9.00–6.00,
Monday to Saturday, with a 24 hour message answering service. You can also order
through our website www.hodderheadline.co.uk

British Library Cataloguing in Publication Data
A catalogue record for this title is available from the British Library

ISBN 0 340 850 388

First published 2003
Impression number   10 9 8 7 6 5 4 3 2 1
Year   2007 2006 2005 2004 2003

Cover photo shows Benito Mussolini; © AKG London and Milizia Voluntaria Sicurezza
Nazionale 1941; © MORA ROMA.

Produced by Gray Publishing, Tunbridge Wells, Kent
Printed in Great Britain for Hodder & Stoughton Educational, a division of Hodder
Headline Plc, 338 Euston Road, London NW1 3BH by J. W. Arrowsmith Ltd, Bristol

Contents

∽ LIST OF TABLES ∽

↩ LIST OF MAPS ↩

↩ LIST OF DIAGRAMS ↩

∾ LIST OF CHARTS ∾

∾ LIST OF ILLUSTRATIONS ∾

↬ LIST OF PROFILES ↫

Preface: How to use this book

This book covers the history of one country over a period of 100 years – Italy. As far as modern European history is concerned, Nazi Germany and Communist Russia have long been the most popular periods of study and this means that the histories of other European nations have been largely ignored. Although France is our neighbour, an ally in two world wars and a partner in the EEC, the history of that country is seldom taught. Italy fares a little better but few syllabuses offer an opportunity for broad-based and in-depth study of the country but instead concentrate narrowly on selected periods – the *Risorgimento* and the years of Mussolini's Fascist dictatorship. Generally therefore our knowledge of Italy and of things Italian is sparse. It is hoped that this book will go some way towards correcting that.

Although the introduction of a two-tier system of examinations, Advanced Subsidiary and Advanced Level (AS and A2) have brought some changes in syllabus content and methods of assessment, the historical skills required to succeed in the examinations remain largely the same. These are the skills needed to analyse, evaluate, interpret and use different types of historical sources, the ability to use historical concepts to develop an argument, to communicate clearly and write concisely and with relevance. To these has been added a synoptic dimension and the ability to prepare well-planned coursework which we will consider later.

1 ⌐ USING SOURCES

We study history in order to find out about the past. It is necessary to discover not merely what happened but also to consider why it happened, who was responsible and what were the consequences. To do this it is necessary to find evidence. On almost every historical topic there is a vast amount of source material that can be used to build up an overall and balanced picture. It is not therefore surprising that the use of sources in A-level examining has increased considerably. Sources may be primary or secondary. Primary sources may take the form of written documents, eye-witness accounts, films and photographs; secondary sources may be written accounts based on research, interpretations and opinions, illustrations, maps, diagrams, cartoons and sometimes statistics. Different sources provide different types of evidence and the first task of a historian is to assess their usefulness by judging their reliability. Is the source genuine? To what extent is it biased?

Many types of sources are used in AS and A2 examinations. Questions may be based on a single source, two sources or many (multi-) sources. Some may be original or primary sources written or photographed by people who witnessed the event at first hand. Others may represent the views of historians who, after completing their research and enjoying the advantages of hindsight, will detail their conclusions in books. Historians often disagree with each other and will challenge interpretations, evaluations and conclusions reached. They will point out errors, inconsistencies and conflicting points of view. The documentary exercises that accompany the chapters in the book are of the types currently used by the examination boards. They are designed to help you develop the skills needed to assess evidence and help you comment on their value and reliability. The questions have been chosen to test your ability to:

● demonstrate understanding by showing your ability to recall/select the most relevant historical knowledge and apt terminology needed to answer questions based on sources
● evaluate and interpret primary and secondary source material of various types
● extract the relevant information needed to answer the question
● distinguish between fact, opinion and fiction
● detect bias, be aware of gaps and inconsistencies in the source material, place it in context
● compare and reach conclusions based on the evidence provided by the sources
● draw conclusions about the value of the sources based on the academic expertise of their authors.

2 ﹏ ANSWERING SOURCE-BASED QUESTIONS

The documents you may be asked to consider may be extracts from books and documents as well as visual material such as pictures, illustrations, maps, cartoons and statistics. The books may be academic texts, memoirs or diaries. Pictures may take the form of photographs or artists' impressions. Statistics may appear in numerical form or in graphics such as column graphs, bar graphs and pie charts. If the questions are structured, presented as a series of questions, the chances are that the marks for the questions will be progressive with the highest mark reserved for the last, usually most demanding, question. You will need to consider the mark allocation and provide lengthier and more detailed answers as the questions become more difficult. Take care to note if your answer has to be derived from the source only or if you are invited to use your own background knowledge.

Understanding the source

Before you begin to answer the questions read the source(s) carefully. If there are words you do not understand, you may be able to work out their meaning from the context of the text. You may be asked to explain a particular word or phrase. If this is the case, a simple dictionary definition may or may not be sufficient. It is usually necessary to explain the meaning within the context of the source. Keep your answer as brief as possible and if the question can be answered with one or two words, there is no need to write a whole sentence. Unless you are specifically asked to do so, do not include your own additional background knowledge. This type of question can be time consuming since there is a temptation to waste a great deal of time providing unnecessary detail.

Considering the attribution or authorship of a source

In considering the authorship of a source, or provenance as it is sometimes called, you should bear in mind:

- who actually wrote the source. Did he or she actually witness the events him or herself or did they produce the work as a result of consulting other peoples' works – research?
- was the author a knowledgeable person. Was he or she possibly an academic with a reputation for existing work in that particular field. Is the information provided reliable and well founded or the author merely expressing a personal opinion possibly based on guesswork?
- did the author have a particular reason or motive for writing in that way? In other words, was he or she biased or even possibly lying. Remember, authors write for money (royalties) and the more sensational or controversial they are the more likely it is that their books will sell well!

Comparing sources

Some questions will require you to compare sources and comment on their similarities and differences. The sources may be taken from the works of authors who share the same view but more likely from the works of authors who have differing views or place differing emphasis on aspects of an historical topic. Here it is essential that you understand what the authors are getting at so that you can identify the differences in their viewpoints and arguments. Often such differences will be immediately obvious but sometimes it is necessary to 'read between the lines' in order to discover a meaning that is not immediately obvious. More difficult is the ability to detect a nuance – a very slight degree or shade of difference. Here again, consider the attributions to the sources since these may make the reasons for the differing views and emphasis immediately obvious.

Testing the reliability of a source

Sources will usually reflect the opinions of their authors – their bias and prejudices. Some sources will be propaganda clearly designed to make a specific impression on the reader and influence his or her thinking. Remember that propaganda often includes blatant and intended false-hoods. Photograph-type sources should be considered similarly. It used to be claimed that 'the camera does not lie' but today we are aware that photographs can be faked and that cameramen can give a false impression simply by altering the angle of their camera. Of course, cartoons are almost inevitably biased since they are intended to represent the view of the newspapers in which they appear.

Evaluating a source

When it comes to finally evaluating a source, ask yourself the following questions:

- Is the source of significant or only limited value?
- Is the source the product of genuine academic research or is it mere trivia?
- Does the source show deficiencies – are there gaps in the detail provided, are there obvious errors or inconsistencies?
- To what extent does the source show bias or merely represent the unsubstantiated views and opinions of the author? Is the source blatant propaganda?
- Just how valuable is the source to an historian studying that particular topic?

3 ⌐ ANSWERING ESSAY QUESTIONS

Types of questions

Most history essay questions fall into one of three categories. These are:

- questions that require you to investigate the causes, events and consequences and will tend to start with phrases such as 'Account for …' and 'For what reasons …'
- questions that require you to consider the relative importance of factors. These will be introduced by such phrases as 'How important …', and 'To what extent …'
- questions that require you to discuss issues or develop an argument. These are likely to begin with such phrases as 'Do you agree that …', 'With what justification can it be claimed that …' and 'Comment on the view that …'. They may also end with 'How valid is this assessment of …' or simply 'Discuss'.

Examples of all the questions detailed above are provided at the end of the chapters.

Requirements of a good essay answer

It is essential that before you start answering a question you make absolutely sure that you have read the question correctly and decide upon your approach. Failure to do this is one of the main reasons why students fail to achieve their expected grades. You may be advised to prepare an outline or skeleton answer. This is sound advice but remember that it can be very time consuming. A good answer should aim to achieve:

- balance – you should make sure that you are aware of all aspects of the question and do not emphasise some to the detriment of others.
- breadth – you should show a sound depth of knowledge based on your recall of your lesson notes and your own reading.
- depth – you should provide support for your argument and make sure that it is based on accurate and relevant factual evidence.

It is usual to divide an essay into three parts – introduction, development and conclusion.

Introduction. This is really where you set the scene. Your introduction should outline your intended approach and briefly state your argument. Try to relate your introduction to the wording of the question. A word of warning; some feel that writing the introduction is a good opportunity to impress the examiner with a fine turn of phrase which takes the form of a dramatic or flamboyant statement. This can be overdone and may prove counter-productive!

Development. This is the main section or body of your answer. In it you refer to the points mentioned in your introduction, develop your argument and provide explanations with supporting evidence. Make sure that the factual detail you include is accurate and avoid irrelevance or flannel. Sometimes good answers can be surprisingly short whilst, on the other hand, lengthy answers can be repetitive and lacking in focus. Take the trouble to write paragraphs that are well constructed and correctly spelt and punctuated. In spite of the shortage of time, try to avoid allowing your handwriting developing into an illegible scribble.

Conclusion. Once again refer to your plan or introduction and make sure that all the points you intended to raise have been adequately dealt with. This is an opportunity to bring together the factual content, issues and argument used and reach a conclusion. This should be brief and should not merely be a summary of what you have already stated in the development of your answer. You should make the examiner aware that your argument is complete and that you have reached a conclusion.

An essay likely to gain high marks should:

- use accurate and relevant historical knowledge
- be well focused throughout
- follow an evaluative/analytical approach
- include evidence of a developed and well-supported argument
- contain a reasonable number of accurate dates
- be clearly written using sentences and paragraphs
- contain few spelling mistakes and errors in punctuation and grammar.

Examiners are not impressed by:

- irrelevance, verbiage, flannel and chatty-type answers
- answers that merely repeat notes
- 'I'll tell you all I know'-type answers. Such answers are badly focused, largely narrative in content and cover all aspects of the topic being considered whether they are relevant or not
- answers in which the essential issues raised by the question are dealt with in the final paragraph
- answers that contain significant omissions
- inaccurate or generalised dates such as 'In the 1930s...'
- poor standards of literacy and slovenly and sometimes near illegible hand-writing
- the incorrect spelling of frequently used historical terms – *dopolavoro*, *transformismo*, *squadristi* – or historical names – D'Annunzio, Depretis, Farinacci, Giolitti
- the use of slang or witticisms.

4 ⌁ SYNOPTIC QUESTIONS

The word 'synoptic' comes from the Greek *synopsis* and means to take an overall or general view. Synoptic-type questions will require you to draw together your knowledge of an extended period of time, usually 100 years, and be able to show your understanding of the political, economic, cultural, social and religious characteristics of the period. Of necessity, such questions tend to be very broad-based and may follow an on-going theme. You will be required to use a range of historical skills and concepts in order to present an argument. To do this, you will need to:

- **recall** – identify from the broad factual content of your study that which is relevant to the question
- **communicate** – show clearly your mastery of that knowledge and that you can explain it in a clear manner
- **understand** – indicate that you have a clear understanding of the important developments of the period
- **interpret** – provide evidence of your ability to evaluate different types of sources
- **explain** – evaluate different interpretations of historical events
- **identify** – show evidence of your ability to recognise cause, change and continuity
- **access** – indicate the importance of events, individuals, ideas and attitudes in their historical setting
- **make judgements** – provide historical explanations and evaluate evidence (see above under 'USING SOURCES').

The questions may be structured, take the form of an open-ended essay or be based on a range of sources. The sources may be primary or secondary and cover many areas of historical debate. Topics covered in this book may be used for synoptic questioning and we will consider these at the end of Chapter 13.

See pages 238–9

In your examination, it is absolutely essential that allow yourself sufficient time to answer the required number of questions. Rushed final answers and answers written in outline do not earn high marks!

5 ⌁ COURSEWORK ASSIGNMENTS

Coursework requirements and the nature of assignments vary from one examination board to another. With some, it is possible for students to undertake an assignment decided and marked by the centre but moderated by the examination board. Alternatively, it is possible to work on an assignment based on a topic nominated by the examination board. The assignment is then marked and moderated by the examination board concerned. The usual objectives to be examined are:

- the ability to recall, select and deploy historical knowledge and communicate that knowledge in a clear and efficient way
- the ability to present historical explanations that show an understanding of appropriate concepts and arrive at substantiated judgements
- the ability to evaluate and use a range of sources
- the ability to explain and interpret historical events
- an awareness of historiography – a knowledge of differing interpretations of historical events and development by leading historians.

6 ⌁ MAKING NOTES

Advice sections that appear at the end of each chapter are intended to help you develop your skills of research and analysis based upon the content and themes explored in the chapters. The guidelines below will help you break down the information by asking questions about the various elements:

- locate the relevant section of the chapter and refer to the written or visual evidence provided
- skim-read the section in order to gain an overall picture of the main areas of argument or interpretation. This focuses your attention on the relevant material and ensures an effective understanding
- using the questions, organise your notes on the main themes covered in the chapters, leaving out the detail that adds nothing to your understanding of the main points identified.

You are also encouraged to make use of the bibliography in order to carry out further research and so develop your own ideas and form judgements.

Bibliography see page 241

✎ ACKNOWLEDGEMENTS ✎

The Publishers would like to thank the following for permission to reproduce the following material in this book:

R.N.L. Absalom, for an extract from *Mussolini and the Rise of Italian Fascism* by R.N.L. Absalom (1995) used on page 78; Addison Wesley Longman, for extracts from *Italy since 1800, A Nature in the Balance? (The Present and the Past)* by R.N.L. Absalom (1995) used on pages 156, 237; Edward Arnold, for extracts from *Mussolini* by R.J.B. Bosworth (2002) used on pages 109, 141, 191, 222–3; Cambridge University Press, for an extract from *A Concise History of Italy* by Christopher Duggan (1994) used on page 236; The Centre for Educational Studies, University of Wales, Aberystwyth, for an extract from *File on Fascism* by D. Mansel Jones (1990) used on page 137; Columbia University Press, for extracts from *European Historical Studies 1750–1970* by B R Mitchell used on pages 149, 153, 156, 157, 160; Constable and Robinson Ltd, for extracts from *Mussolini* by Jasper Ridley used on pages 69, 94, 116, 175; Greenwood Publishing Group, for an extract from *My Autobiography* by Benito Mussolini (1970) used on page 71; The Independent, for an extract from *Mayor in Battle to Halt Mussolini Revival* by Kate Goldberg (25 July 2002) used on page 223; Lawrence and Wishart, for an extract from *Lectures on Fascism* by Palmiro Togliatti (1976) used on page 155; Longman, for an extract from *Mussolini and Italy* by C. Bayne-Jardine (1965) used on page 51; John Murray (Publishers) Ltd., for an extract from *Fascist Italy* by John Hite & Chris Hinton (1998) used on page 132; Oxford University Press, for an extract from *History of the Great War* by C.R.M.F. Crutwell (1982) used on pages 44–5; Palgrave Macmillan, for an extract from *International Historical Statistics, Europe 1750–1988* by B.R. Mitchell (1992) used on page 134; Penguin Books Ltd, for an extract from *A History of Contemporary Italy: Society and Politics 1943–1988* by Paul Ginsborg (1990) © Paul Ginsborg 1990 used on page 232; Scribner, for an extract from *The Origins of the Second World War* by A.J.P. Taylor (1996) © 1961 A.J.P. Taylor used on page 222; Weidenfeld & Nicholson, for extracts from *History of the Italian People* by Giuliano Procacci (1973) used on pages 47, 49 and for an extract from *The Nature of Fascism* by Stuart J. Woolf (1981) used on page 83.

The Publishers would like to thank the following for permission to reproduce the following copyright illustrations in this book:

© Associated Press pages 108 (above right), 158, 174, 232; © Bettmann/Corbis pages 21, 38, 70 (above), 103, 108 (centre), 185, 216 (below); © Corbis pages 54, 68 (above), 68 (below), 79, 97 (above), 97 (below), 192; © Hulton Archive pages 71, 99 (above), 107, 108 (below centre), 130, 220; © Hulton-Deutsch Collection/Corbis pages 7, 45, 80, 99 (middle), 99 (below), 100, 108 (below left), page 108 (below right), 216 (above); © Hulton Getty page 182 (below); © The Imperial War Museum pages 106, 182 (above), 217 (left); © Keystone, Paris page 108 (above left); © Moro Roma pages 15, 16, 17, 37, 55, 63, 91, 123, 134, 143, 180, 214, 233; © PA News page 103 (right); © Popperfoto pages 68 (below right), page 70 (below), 100 (below), 108 (above centre), 136; © *Punch* pages 31, 33, 72, 175; © Purnell & Sons Ltd page 217 (right); © *South Wales Echo & Express* page 198; © Topham Picturepoint pages 93, 182 (middle).

Every effort has been made to trace and acknowledge ownership of copyright. The publishers will be glad to make suitable arrangements with any copyright holders whom it has not been possible to contact.

The Birth of Modern Italy

INTRODUCTION

Historians have not served Italy particularly well. To many, the only aspects of that country's history worth studying are those that relate to either the *Risogimento* or the years of Mussolini's Fascist state. This is largely because, whilst there have always been Italians, there has not always been an Italian nation. Indeed, apart from flamboyant rulers such as the Medicis and Borgias, irascible Popes and Michelangelo, Raphael and other famous artists and sculptors of the Italian Renaissance, the leading figures in Italian history have tended to be regarded as colourless. In reality, this is far from the truth.

Today, some 1500 years after its demise, many Italians look back to what they consider to have been the greatest period in their country's history – the heyday of Imperial Rome. The Roman Empire, which at its greatest extended from Britain in the north to Egypt in the south and from Portugal in the west to the banks of the River Tigris (modern day Iraq) in the east, preserved the civilisation of the Ancient World. Its conquering legions also brought justice and peace, '*Pax Romana*'. The emblem of a Roman magistrate was the *fasces*, an axe in a bundle of rods. This was later to be the symbol of the Fascists, the supporters of Benito Mussolini. The Italian dictator also promised to rekindle memories of the glory of Ancient Rome by restoring the ruins of such buildings as Vespasian's great amphitheatre, the Colosseum. Rome grew powerful and wealthy on the spoils of its conquests. It was during this period that the Christian church first established itself in Rome. St Peter's authority for founding the church in Rome is based upon Jesus Christ's pronouncement, 'Thou art Peter, and upon this rock I will build my church.' In AD 337 during the reign of the Emperor Constantine, Christianity became the official religion of the Roman Empire. The title 'Pope' was not given to the head of the Church until AD 384. As leaders of a worldwide or Catholic Church, the Popes were to become not only spiritual leaders but also temporal or worldly rulers and important political figures. They were to have a lasting influence in Italian affairs. The glory of Ancient Rome was not to last. Threatened by barbarian invaders, by AD 476 the Empire had collapsed. For centuries, the Italian peninsula was made up of a number of states on the fringe of what was then called the Holy Roman Empire. Kingdoms and empires rose and fell and, by the middle of the thirteenth century, many of the states had fallen under foreign domination. This situation lasted until Napoleon Bonaparte's victorious campaign in Italy in 1796. It was during this time that Italians first experienced a sense of national

Fasces, see page 82

identity and there appeared the first of many patriotic associations, such as Mazzini's Young Italy. After the French Emperor's defeat in 1815, the country lapsed back into its former condition. In 1848, there were uprisings against Austrian rule in Milan and Venice but these were crushed. In Sardinia-Piedmont, the king, Carlo Alberto, granted his people a **constitution** that was to survive.

constitution rules defining a system of government

The following year Count Metternich, the Austrian Chancellor, correctly summed up the situation when he wrote, '*Italien ist ein geographischer Begriff*' – 'Italy is a geographical expression.'

1 ⌐ ITALIAN UNIFICATION

The Italian *Risorgimento*, or revival, and the achievement of unification is regarded as being the achievement of Giuseppe Mazzini (1805–72), the revolutionary thinker and so-called 'apostle of Italian republicanism', the heroic patriot and adventurer Giuseppe Garibaldi (1807–82), the Piedmontese aristocrat and statesman Count Camillo Cavour (1810–61) and Victor Emmanuel II (1820–78), King of Sardinia-Piedmont. There were numerous barriers to be overcome before national unity could be achieved. There were long-standing regional differences and the conflicting self-interests of the rulers of the states. Mountain ranges such as the Apennines made communication difficult and the road and railway systems were inadequate and hindered their efforts. There were different schools of thought about the means by which unification should be achieved and the form of government to be adopted afterwards. Most immediate was the opposition of Austrian Habsburgs who still largely dominated the north of the country and the hostility of Pope Pius IX who was intent on safeguarding his interests and lands, the Papal States. The 1850s and 60s saw the emergence of Piedmont as the state most likely to champion the cause of unification. The scheming Cavour, the Piedmontese prime minister, succeeded in involving his country in alliances and wars which ensured the backing of other powers, particularly neighbouring France. In 1859, he won the support of Napoleon III for a war against Austria. The consequence was a number of upheavals that resulted in Lombardy and other states overthrowing their **autocratic** regimes and joining Piedmont. Meanwhile, Garibaldi's successes in Sicily and the Kingdom of Naples brought the unification of the Italian states even closer and, by 1860, Tuscany, Modena, Parma, Naples and most of the Papal States had united with Piedmont. On 10 March 1861 at a ceremony in Turin, Victor Emmanuel took the title 'King of Italy'. There remained only Venetia and Rome. In 1866, Italy received Venetia as a reward for joining Prussia in a war against Austria; in 1870, Italian troops took advantage of Napoleon III's involvement in a war with Prussia and occupied Rome. This meant that after being situated firstly in Turin and then in Florence, Italy at last had Rome as its true capital city. Although the unification of Italy was complete, a great deal of work remained to be done to make the integration of the Italian people a reality. As the Piedmontese statesman Massimo d'Azeglio

autocratic rule by one man

stated, 'Now that we have made Italy, it is necessary for us to create Italians.' Italians faced a problem of identity.

2 ⌒ THE CHALLENGES FACING THE NEW ITALY

The new Italian state had been created and now it was necessary to sweep away the old political, economic and social structure and replace them with alternatives that were acceptable to all the interested parties. This was not to be easily achieved since old loyalties and prejudices remained. Across the country as a whole, levels of poverty and illiteracy were the worst in Europe and there were also other long-standing domestic difficulties to be overcome.

A *Italy – the north–south divide*

The regional differences between the north and the south were enormous. Northern Italy was the most densely populated and enjoyed a wide range of advantages over the southern half of the country. The bulk of the nation's raw materials were in the north, and most industrial development was concentrated around Milan, Turin and Genoa. Whilst the north had a developing system of roads and railways, the whole of the south was served by less than 100 kilometres of railtrack. Although carried out on a much smaller scale, agriculture in the north had made greater progress and benefited from better soil and a more favourable climate than was the case in the south. Compared with the prosperous north, southern Italy, known as the *Mezzogiorno*, was backward and underdeveloped. In Italian, the term *Mezzogiorno* refers to the strength of the midday sun. There the hot climate had eroded the topsoil and made what remained arid and too poor for the cultivation of crops. In that region there was virtually no industry and, still using primitive farming methods, the peasant workers struggled to make a living from their fields, vineyards and olive groves. Even worse, absentee landlords, who showed little concern for the condition of their labourers and failed to see any reason to improve farming methods, owned the large estates, the *latifundia*. The aristocracy, professional middle-classes and skilled artisans were more abundant in the north where they enjoyed a sophisticated lifestyle and much higher standard of living than those in the south.

The living standards of many of the southern peasantry seldom rose above subsistence level. Across the country as a whole, some 77% of the Italian people were unable to read and write. Even so, the north enjoyed better education facilities than the south where few peasants received any formal education and consequently over 87% were illiterate. It is not surprising that those living in the south felt disadvantaged and their reaction to their poverty was to increasingly engage in banditry and violence. From a political viewpoint, Italians in the south resented domination by the north and the fact that they had been forced to

> **KEY ISSUE**
>
> *Reasons for the differences between northern and southern Italy.*

MAP 1
Italy – regional differences

THE NORTH	THE SOUTH
Because of the influence of Piedmont, the north was politically dominant.	Little political influence. The south resented domination by the north.
Concentration of the aristocracy, professional people and skilled artisans.	Largely a region of rural peasantry.
Reasonable living standards.	Widespread poverty and low living standards.
Considerable industrial development.	Little industrial development.
Nearly 1750 kilometres of railways.	Barely 100 kilometres of railways.
Agriculture – good soil, favourable climate meant higher production levels.	Agriculture – hot climate, erosion, poor soil meant low production levels. Estates often owned by absentee landlords.
Improving education standards but still 70% of population illiterate.	Low education standards with less than 18% of children attending primary school. Over 87% illiteracy rate.
Law and order largely maintained.	Banditry and lawlessness. Activity of the Mafia.

CHART 1
Italy – regional differences

accept systems imposed by Piedmont. Since the **franchise** was subject to literacy and property qualifications, few in the south had the right to vote compared with the more affluent north.

franchise the right to vote

B *Law and order*

The period after 1870 witnessed an increase in crime and civil disorder. Across Italy generally there was disquiet at the lack of government action to reduce poverty and improve social conditions. Many were also disappointed by the extent of the political corruption in the country. In the south, socialist and **anarchist** groups encouraged the peasants to take matters into their own hands and remedy the situation. There were times when the situation threatened to get out of hand and the military had to be sent in to deal with the widespread violence and restore order. Sicily was the scene of the greatest lawlessness and it was there that the Mafia was the most active.

See pages 17–18

anarchist one who believes that an ideal society is one without government and is prepared to use terror to achieve his aims

The Mafia or *Cosa Nostra*, originated in Sicily and was one of numerous secret societies that existed in Italy. This network of criminals was not new but had existed in one form or another for centuries. During the nineteenth century it dominated Sicilian social life and recruited its membership from all classes and backgrounds. Its members, the *Mafiosi*, sought self-enrichment by intimidating the peasantry. It issued decrees, fixed land rents and practised extortion that took the form of running protection rackets. Its members, who were often involved in revenge murders and **vendettas**, were protected by a self-imposed code of silence. Later, Italians who emigrated abroad took the practices of the Mafia with them. This was particularly true of the many who left for the United States.

vendettas on-going feuds between families or gangs

C *The State and the Church*

The Pope, the spiritual leader of the Roman Catholic Church, ruled over an area of central Italy, the Papal States. Between 1861 and 1870, these lands were forcibly taken from him. The Law of Guarantees of 1871 granted the Pope sovereignty over the area immediately around St Peter's Church in Rome, the Vatican City, and a country residence at Castel Gandolfo. He was exempt from taxation and given an annual maintenance grant of three million lire. The Vatican was allowed to appoint its own representatives in other countries. The Law gave the government the right to veto any temporal laws, the right to inspect **seminaries** and made Roman Catholic clergy subject to the laws of the Italian state. The Law of Guarantees was passed without consulting the Papal authorities. The Pope, Pius IX, reacted by refusing the government grant and threatening to **excommunicate** those responsible for the loss of his temporal power. He declared himself 'the prisoner of the Vatican' and for the next 50 years no pope ventured outside its walls. To make matters worse, in June 1870, Pius IX, who had earlier denounced liberal principles, assembled the First Vatican Council and declared the dogma of papal infallibility. The Council stated that when 'the Roman

KEY ISSUE

Papal hostility to the Italian State.

seminaries colleges for training Catholic clergy

excommunicate expel from the Catholic Church

PICTURE 1
St Peter's Church and the Plazza San Pietro in the Vatican

ex cathedra from the Pope's throne

Pontiff, speaks *ex cathedra* on matters of faith and morals … he is possessed of that infallibility with which the Divine Redeemer wished His Church to be endowed.' Put simply, henceforward all the Pope's religious pronouncements were to be considered divinely inspired and consequently they had to be accepted and obeyed by all Roman Catholics.

The doctrine had the effect of widening yet further the breach between the Church and the State. Pius IX actively encouraged Catholics not to co-operate with the new regime and forbade them to participate in politics. He ordered them not to stand as candidates or vote at elections. In spite of this, a means of co-existing together had to be found but the hostility between Church and State was to continue until 1929.

See pages 120–4

D *Financial problems*

Following unification, the financial affairs of all the former independent states became the responsibility of the central government. This meant that the burden of their indebtedness, which was considerable, now fell upon the Italian kingdom. There was a need to find substantial sums of money to spend on the army and navy, pay for a programme of public works and improve the transport system, particularly the railways. In 1862, there was a major shortfall between government income and expenditure that meant there was insufficient funds to meet their requirements. The government had no choice but to increase taxation and raise new loans. In 1868, a duty was imposed on milled corn, the grist tax. For many, particularly in the south, this led to a further fall in living standards. The increase in the price of bread meant that many existed at subsistence levels and some even faced starvation.

POPE PIUS IX (1792–1878)

Giovanni Maria Mastai-Ferretti was born at Sinigaglia in 1792. He had first hoped to enrol in the Papal guard but was refused admission because of his epilepsy. Instead, he turned to the study of theology. After being ordained a priest, he became the apostolic delegate to Chile and was the first pope to visit the American continent. He became a cardinal in 1840 and, six years later, was elected pope. '*Pio Nono*', as he was known, came to office with a liberal reputation.

This was confirmed when he declared an amnesty for political prisoners in the Papal States and carried through several reforms. However, when he refused to become involved in the war with Austria in 1848, his popularity plummeted. He was forced to leave Rome and live at Gaeta until a French army was sent to restore his authority. With his liberal reputation in tatters, Pius IX followed a more reactionary line and in 1860, Italian troops again occupied the Papal States. Pius IX now became vigorously involved in spiritual matters and in putting forward new church dogmas. In 1864, he issued the *Quanta Cura* and with it a syllabus of eighty errors. These included condemnation of modernism, liberalism, socialism and communism. Finally in 1870, Italian soldiers marched into Rome itself and the city became the capital of the new nation. He never accepted the loss of the Papal States and refused to co-operate with the Italian government. In 1870, he proclaimed the dogma of papal infallibility. In 1876, he said, 'It is an error to believe that the Roman Pontiff can and ought to reconcile himself to and agree with progress, liberalism and contemporary civilisation'. He died in 1878.

PICTURE 2
Pope Pius IX (1792–1878)

A new Italy had been created and it was now necessary to sweep away the former political, economic and social structure and old fashioned attitudes. This was not to be easily accomplished. Between 1870 and 1914 weak leadership and frequent changes of government led to political instability. The problem was that many politicians lacked the idealism demanded by the dawning of a new age in Italian history. In order to gain office and win promotion, deputies were prepared to be manipulative and openly resorted to bribery and corruption. Political scandals and even the rigging of elections were commonplace. This caused people to lose faith in their politicians who, instead of planning reforms and a strategy to deal with the economic and social problems that faced the country, showed a lack of principle and worked solely to enhance their own interests.

3 ⌁ STRUCTURED AND ESSAY QUESTIONS

A *This section consists of questions that might be used for discussion (or written answers) as a way of expanding on the chapter and testing your understanding of it.*

1. What did Metternich mean when he referred to Italy as 'a geographical expression'?
2. Why did people refer to southern Italy as the *Mezzogiorno*?
3. On what did the power and the influence of the mafia depend?
4. To Roman Catholics, what was the significance of the dogma of papal infallibility?
5. In what sense might Pope Pius IX claim to be 'the prisoner of the Vatican'?

B *Essay questions.*

1. 'Mainly the result of the indifference of absentee landlords.' How valid is this explanation of the poverty in southern Italy?
2. To what extent was the Papacy responsible for the breakdown in relations between the Church and State in Italy during the 1870s?

4 ⌁ MAKING NOTES

The chapter you have studied is an introduction to a 100-year period of Italian history. Its aim is to provide a background that considers the condition of Italy in 1870 and the nature of the problems faced at that time by the Italian people. In order to make sure that you have a broad understanding of those problems, copy and complete the following chart:

Problem	Effects on the Italian people
Poverty of southern Italy	
Lawlessness	
Political corruption	
Government indebtedness	
Lack of a national education system	

Years of Liberalism and *Transformismo,* 1870–1915

2

INTRODUCTION

As we have seen, the problems of unification did not end in 1870. The nation had massive debts, few natural resources, little industry, apart from that concentrated in the north, and inadequate transport facilities. It's people, who were the most heavily taxed in Europe, were also the most poverty stricken and illiterate. In the countryside, the desperately poor and those out to avoid compulsory military service contributed to a high level of brigandry and lawlessness. Some 100,000 regular soldiers were sent to the worst regions in an effort to maintain law and order.

1 ～ THE GOVERNMENT OF ITALY

After unification, Italy became a constitutional monarchy. The hereditary sovereign had the right to summon and dissolve parliament and appoint and dismiss ministers. The form of government was based on a written constitution and the right to make laws was passed to an elected assembly. The constitution also guaranteed the rights and freedoms of individual citizens. The parliament consisted of two chambers, the *Camera dei Depitati,* the Chamber of Deputies, and the *Senato,* the Senate. The most important was the Chamber of Deputies since it contained the representatives elected by the people. The electoral system was the same as that introduced in Piedmont in 1848. Age, property and educational qualifications determined the extent of the franchise and consequently, out of a population of some 28 million, less than half a million had the right to vote. Between 1870 and 1876, the government of Italy was liberal in the sense that it was dominated by Deputies drawn from the centre-right – moderate liberals and socialists who tended to come from a similar type of background. In reality, the political system was extremely confused if indeed a system existed at all! Although some Deputies used party labels, most were liberals of one type or another. At election times, genuine political contests were rare since the majority of Deputies were re-elected without opposition. With political parties having no chance of being strong enough to form majority governments, the governments of the day were coalitions made up of factions. This led to political instability and to some extent explains why, between 1870 and Italy's entry into the First World War in 1915, the country had 23 different governments. As ministry followed ministry, parliamentary life was sometimes reduced to a

1871	Rome capital of Italy
1876	Depretis forms first of his three governments
1877	Coppino's Education Law
1878	Death of Victor Emmanuel II Leo XIII elected Pope
1882	Electoral Law – extension of franchise
1887	Crispi prime minister
1891	Pope Leo XIII's encyclical Rerum Novarium
1895	Italian Socialist Party formed
1898	Riots in Milan
1900	Umberto I assassinated. Succeeded by Victor Emmanuel III
1904	General strike
1912	Electoral Law – vote extended to all males over 30
1914	'Red Week'

TABLE 1
Date line of events in Italy prior to the First World War

KEY ISSUE

Reasons for political instability.

shambles. Members of the Chamber of Deputies represented local or factional interests and were not prepared to subordinate these to the overall interests of the nation. With corruption and intrigue commonplace, a bribe, position or offer of promotion was sufficient to tempt Deputies to switch loyalties and move from one faction to another. In such circumstances, there seemed little chance of rapid progress being made towards the establishment of democratic government. Instead, a system known as *transformismo* developed. In practice, *transformismo* meant government by contrivance and duplicity. **Radical** Deputies who did not conform were bribed and so transformed into loyal supporters of the regime. In this way, prime ministers were able to bring together groups of able and influential Deputies, regardless of party loyalty, to run the country. A master manipulator of this style of government was Agnostino Depretis.

radical a person in favour of thorough-going reform

1869–1873	Giovanni Lanza	1898–1900	Luigi Pelloux
1873–1876	Marco Minghetti	1900–1901	Giuseppe Saracco
1876–1878	Agostino Depretis	1901–1903	Giuseppe Zanardelli
1878	Benedetto Cairoli	1903–1905	Giovanni Giolitti
1878–1879	Agostino Depretis	1905–1906	Alessandro Fortis
1879–1881	Benedetto Cairoli	1906	Sidney, Barone Sonnino
1881–1887	Agostino Depretis	1906–1909	Giovanni Giolitti
1887–1891	Francesco Crispi	1909–1910	Sidney, Barone Sonnino
1891–1892	Antonio Di Rudini	1910–1911	Luigi Luzzatti
1892–1893	Giovanni Giolitti	1911–1914	Giovanni Giolitti
1893–1896	Francesco Crispi	1914–1916	Antonio Salandra
1896–1898	Antonio Di Rudini		

TABLE 2
Prime Ministers 1869–1916

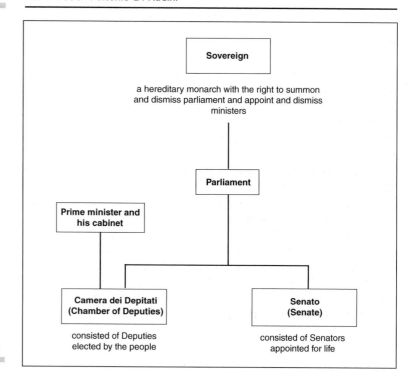

DIAGRAM 1
System of government pre 1922

2 ✎ AGOSTINI DEPRETIS AND *TRANSFORMISMO*

As a young man, Agostino Depretis (1813–87) had been a member of Mazzini's republican Young Italy movement. He entered the Piedmontese parliament in 1848 and for a time led the opposition to Cavour. Following a change of heart, he became a supporter of Cavour and the monarchy. After holding several government positions, as leader of the moderate left he became prime minister three times during 1876–8, 1878–9 and 1881–7.

A *Transformismo*

Depretis managed to stay in power by taking advantage of *transformismo*. He used this to ensure that governments maintained a majority in the Chamber of Deputies by entering into deals, agreeing compromises and manipulating political factions to sustain a coalition. Government reshuffles occurred regularly and Depretis was known to purposely provoke government crises in order to reshuffle his government and get rid of unwanted ministers. He was not above involvement in conspiracy and corruption and used his political skills to avoid problems instead of attempting to solve them. During this period public disquiet grew regarding the state of Italian politics and the behaviour of their Deputies. However, Depretis did pass several significant measures during his premierships.

B *Domestic reforms*

In 1877, an Education Law, the Coppino Law, was passed which aimed to provide much needed compulsory education for children aged between six and nine. Good in intent, lack of teachers and facilities often made the law impossible to enforce. Penal reforms included the abolition of imprisonment for debt and a limited right to strike. The hated grist tax on the grinding of corn, first introduced in 1869, was finally abolished in 1879 but, even so, the price of bread continued to rise.

> **Q**
> *How corrupt was the Italian parliamentary system?*

A step towards greater democracy came with the Electoral Law of 1882. The amount of property and the level of education needed to qualify to vote were reduced and the age qualification lowered from 25 to 21. The requirement to be able to read and write remained and this particularly penalised those in the south where educational opportunities were few and illiteracy high. Altogether these changes increased the size of the electorate from just less than half a million to over two million but this still represented only 7% of the population. Depretis also took steps to try to reduce corruption and allow minority groups greater representation but the results of these measures were minimal.

✎

In 1878, Victor Emmanuel II and Pope Pius IX both died. The King had earlier caused annoyance by choosing to continue with his former House of Savoy title, Victor Emmanuel II, when as the first king of a united Italy he should have styled himself Victor Emmanuel I. His son, Umberto, who regarded himself as truly the first king of Italy, succeeded him. The new Pope, Leo XIII, was more moderate in his views than his predecessor, Pius IX. Even so, he was not prepared to acknowledge the Kingdom of Italy and feared the growing impact of socialism on Italian politics. To some extent, he was to prove himself a moderniser and showed interest in the condition of the poor and working classes. Nicknamed 'the working men's Pope', he was to be leader of the Roman Catholic Church for the next 25 years. In his latter years, Depretis became increasingly unpopular for the failures of his foreign policy rather than his direction of Italian domestic policy. He died in office in 1887 and was succeeded by his most vocal critic, Francesco Crispi.

See pages 27–9

3 ✍ FRANCESCO CRISPI – REFORMER TURNED REACTIONARY

Francesco Crispi (1819–1901) was born in Sicily into a family of Albanian origin. After working as a lawyer in Naples, he took part in the Sicilian revolt in 1848. Expelled from his homeland, he travelled to Piedmont and there made a modest living as a journalist. Forced to leave Piedmont because of his republican views, he eventually made his way to London where he met Mazzini. On his return to Italy, he took part in the expedition to Sicily in 1861 where he served as Garibaldi's right-hand man. Later in the same year, he was elected as a Deputy to the Italian parliament. At first he retained his staunch republican sympathies but then changed his allegiance to the monarchy. In a letter to his former **mentor**, Mazzini, he wrote, 'The monarchy unites us; the republic would divide us.' For the best part of a decade his political career was blighted by scandal following the disclosure that he was a bigamist. By 1887, his reputation had recovered sufficiently for him to be appointed a minister in Depretis's government. Later that year, at the age of 70, he succeeded him as prime minister. He held this position twice – between 1887–91 and 1893–6. A person with a great belief in his own ability and who exuded self-confidence. Crispi was an admirer of the German Chancellor Otto von Bismarck and was known on occasion to seek his advice. He was also liable to be impetuous.

mentor a tutor or wise councillor

A *Crispi's domestic policies*

As prime minister, his domestic policy largely followed the lines of Depretis and he seemed intent on repeating the faults of his predecessor. His Communal and Provincial Administration Law granted the various regions of Italy a greater degree of self-government and reduced the level of government interference in local affairs. A measure was also introduced to improve levels of sanitation and hygiene that helped to improve public health. His Minister of Justice, Giuseppe Zanardelli, introduced measures that further liberalised the penal code and an attempt was made to heal the breach with the Papacy. This came to nothing. Crispi's last years in office coincided with a severe downturn in the nation's economy.

B *Economic recession*

In common with other European countries, Italy began to face severe competition from overseas. Imports of grain from North America and cheap cotton goods from the Far East had an adverse effect on both Italian agriculture and the textile industry. As a result, landowners and manufacturers demanded action from the government. Crispi's reaction was to increase the **tariffs** imposed on imported goods and so make home produced goods more competitively priced. The tariff on bread virtually doubled to 50 lire a tonne and had the effect of increasing the price of bread for the urban areas that had previously benefited from the cheap grain imports. Although well intended, the consequences of the tariff policy were calamitous. France, an important trading partner, was upset and retaliated by imposing tariffs on Italian imports. The volume of Italian exports to France fell dramatically and this particularly affected those dependent on the export of wine and citrus fruits. The trade war triggered an economic recession. A drastic fall in their already meagre incomes caused even greater hardship for the Italian peasantry. Many peasants were forced to leave the land and seek employment in the towns where slum conditions and dire poverty led to outbreaks of cholera. Some went further and sought a solution to their problems by emigrating abroad. During the period 1881–90, some 992,000 Italians emigrated and this rose to a startling 1,580,000 between 1891 and 1900. During the first decade of the twentieth century, this figure more than doubled to 3,615,000.

Emigration began in a relatively small way with peasants leaving Italy to find seasonal employment elsewhere in Europe – usually in France, Switzerland and Austria. At first, permanent emigrants looked mainly to North and South America. In 1871, an Italian census gave the number of Italians living abroad as 400,000. As the number of emigrants rose, many became victims of unscrupulous travel agents who charged inflated fares and provided poor accommodation. Even worse, once at their destination, they found themselves as badly exploited as they had been at home. Homesickness took its toll and many returned home. Whilst some were unskilled, some tried to follow their traditional occupations and worked in domestic service, as waiters in cafés and bars. Some became hairdressers, street organ grinders and music teachers. By 1922, there were over 20,000 Italian emigrants in Britain. Nearly 2000, who came from Bardi in the Ceno Valley, made their home in the Valleys of South Wales where they ran cafés. Such names as Bracchi, Berni, Conte, Carpanini and Fulgoni became commonplace and, even today, in South Wales the common name for a café is a Bracchi.

KEY ISSUE

Government's measures for dealing with overseas competition.

---

tariffs duties imposed on imported goods

1861–70	27,000
1871–80	168,000
1881–90	992,000
1891–1900	1,580,000

TABLE 3
Emigration from Italy 1861–1900

There were other disastrous consequences. Companies and banks began to experience difficulties, and bankruptcies became increasingly common. The collapse of one bank, the *Banca Romana*, proved particularly embarrassing for the government since it showed that even during an economic depression government corruption was continuing to flourish. This bank had earlier acquired the right to issue its own banknotes and it now became apparent that 60 million lire had been issued illegally and without official sanction. The bank itself had used much of this money and some had been made available as interest free loans to leading politicians including Crispi! With the people as a whole suffering because of the recession, this **sleaze** in high places led to a political storm and public protests.

sleaze disreputable behaviour

See pages 17–18

As disquiet increased, Crispi reacted by passing a decree that strengthened and extended the powers of the prime minister. This resulted in him assuming virtual total responsibility for all domestic and foreign policy decisions. The man who started his premiership as a liberal was becoming increasingly **authoritarian**. In spite of this, he managed to survive but his reputation had been damaged beyond repair. As with Depretis, in the end it was not just Crispi's handling of domestic affairs but also his mismanagement of foreign affairs that led to his downfall. In 1891 he resigned following a defeat in the Chamber of Deputies.

authoritarian putting one's own authority above the rights and liberty of the people

4 ⌐ ANARCHISM AND SOCIALISM – YEARS OF DISCONTENT AND UNREST

One of the most disturbing aspects of life in Italy during the 80s and 90s was the increase in violence and terror. At the time of the death of Depretis in 1887, the country was in sorry state. As the situation further deteriorated, an increasing number of people became convinced that the solution to their problems lay in the views of the Russian-born anarchist Mikhail Bakunin (1814–76) and the German-born socialist Karl Marx (1818–83). Bakunin believed in the absolute freedom of the individual and that it was necessary to overthrow existing forms of government and institutions in order to achieve such freedom, He wrote, 'Freedom, morality, and the human dignity of the individual consists precisely in this; that he does good not because he is forced to, but because he freely conceives it, wants it and loves it.' Marx, on the other hand, believed in the inevitability of a class struggle in order to overthrow the **capitalist system**.

capitalist system an economic system in which the ownership the means of production is in the hands of private individuals

Although both men believed in revolution, their views otherwise differed and this brought them into conflict.

A *The emergence of Italian socialism*

From the start, the Italian socialist movement was broad based but fragmented and liable to break up into small splinter groups. Whilst most were moderate reformers, there were also extremist groups, such as syndicalists, who championed the cause of revolution. As in other European countries, Italian socialists depended on the support of the industrial proletariat and working class associations. Unfortunately, out of a population of 25 million less than 4 million were employed in industry.

There was little collaboration between different groups of workers and consequently trade unions were slow to develop. The total membership of the various workers' associations was less than a quarter of a million. Radical leaders such as the lawyer Filippo Turati, the political philosopher Antonio Labriola and the writer and poet Felice Cavallotti tended to be more theorists than firebrand revolutionaries. They were moderates who wished to use the parliamentary system to bring about social reform. They had to cope with extremists such as the **syndicalists** who would have nothing to do with democratic government and championed the cause of revolution. In 1891, the first regional workers' organisation, a *Camera del Lavoro*, Chamber of Labour, was set up. The following year, as a result of a congress held in Genoa, a new political organisation, the *Partito dei Lavoratori Italiani* or Italian Workers' Party, was formed. There were several different strands in the campaign to establish an Italian Socialist Party. Filippo Turati (1857–1932), a Milanese lawyer from a well-to-do family, was one of the leaders who favoured moderation or change without violence. Andrea Costa (1851–1910) led the Revolutionary Socialist Party and, in 1882, was the first Socialist Deputy to be elected to the Italian Parliament. A supporter

syndicalists left-wing extremists who favour direct action as a means of overthrowing the capitalist system

PICTURE 3
Identity card used by members of the Italian Socialist Party

of the idea of a Christian-type Socialism was Camillo Prampolini (1859–1930) who preached that Jesus Christ had been the first Socialist and used biblical texts to support his argument. The leading campaigner for women's rights was Anna Kuliscioff (1857–1925). Born Anja Rosenstein of Russian-Jewish extraction, she abandoned her medical studies to become an active revolutionary. Her activities made it necessary for her to flee her homeland and live in exile in Italy. Finally, in 1895, the Italian Socialist Party, the *Partito Socialista Italiano (PSI)*, was formed. Its reform programme was ambitious and included the extension of the franchise to all adult men and women, religious equality, a more humane penal system, an eight-hour working day, old age pensions, accident insurance and free school meals. They also sought to pay Deputies in the hope that it would make them less open to bribery. By 1913, the Italian Socialist Party had the support of 20% of the electorate.

ITALIAN ANARCHIST REVOLUTIONARIES

PROFILE

PICTURE 4
Errico Malatesta (1853–1932)

ERRICO MALATESTA (1853–1932)

Errico Malatesta was born in 1853 at Capua near Naples. Whilst studying medicine at Naples university, he became interested in left-wing politics and joined the International Working Men's Association. An associate of Bakunin, he worked to spread anarchist propaganda throughout Italy. He was first arrested in 1873 and again the following year. In 1877, Malatesta was involved in an armed uprising in the province of Benevento. Once again he was arrested and spent a year in prison before being brought to trial. Now constantly under police surveillance, he made his way to Egypt. Expelled and then banned from Switzerland, he went to London where he worked as an ice-cream seller and part-time mechanic. He secretly returned to Italy where he set up an anarchist weekly newspaper, *La Questione Sociale*. Back in Italy, Malatesta was arrested and sentenced to three years imprisonment. On his release, he went to South America and lived briefly in Buenos Aires. He spent the next eight years in London and there wrote the pamphlet *L'Anarchia*, Anarchy. He then returned to Italy yet again. Arrested, he was sent to a penal settlement but managed to escape. He next travelled to the United States where a fellow anarchist who disagreed with him shot him in the leg. After the First World War, Malatesta went back to Italy where he took part in demonstrations and ran the newspaper, *Umanita Nova*. Harassed by the police, Malatesta retired to run a small workshop from which he did electrical repairs. He died in 1932, aged 79.

ANNA KULISCIOFF (1857–1925)

Born at Moskaja in the Crimea, Anja Rosenstein, who later changed her name to Anna Kuliscioff, was the daughter of a prosperous Jewish merchant who had converted to Christianity. Aged 18, she left Russia to study medicine at Zurich in Switzerland and it was there she first came into contact with left-wing revolutionaries and anarchists. She read Marx, Engels and Bakunin avidly. Kuliscioff returned to Russia where she became involved in revolutionary activity until the attention of the tsar's secret police forced her to flee abroad. She first went to France but, on being expelled, moved to Tuscany in Italy. There she lived with a fellow revolutionary, Andrea Costa, and bore him a daughter. For a time, she worked on the socialist newspaper *Avanti*, and then began to campaign for women's rights. She countered the claim that women did not deserve the vote because they did not fight by stating, 'It is true that women do not fight like soldiers but unfortunately they produce soldiers'. In 1898, Kuliscioff was arrested for being involved in the riots in Milan. Then, in 1911, she formed the Socialist Committee for Female Suffrage and famously said, 'Married women are nowadays the most miserable beings. There are two forms of sexual slavery – prostitution proper and mercantile marriage.' Continuing her work as a doctor, she became ill with tuberculosis. After the war, Kuliscioff opposed Fascism and described Mussolini as 'a scoundrel dressed like a gentleman'. At her funeral, following her death in 1925, *squadristi* thugs attacked her cortège.

PICTURE 5
Anna Kuliscioff (1857–1925)

B Disorder and violence

The activities of both anarchists and some socialist extremists involved the use of terror. In Naples, the attempted assassination of King Umberto and his wife Cairoli shocked the nation whilst at Pesaro, on the Adriatic coast, an attempt was made to raid the armoury at a local barracks. There were also bomb outrages in Florence and Pisa. The situation was further inflamed by increasing evidence of corruption in high circles and the failure of the government to take any determined action. To start with, the situation improved slightly under Crispi but this was not to last. An outbreak of disorder in Sicily led to troops being sent to the island where they put down the troubles with extreme ferocity. Many of those involved were executed or received excessive prison sentences. News of these events drove the peasantry to take even more extreme action. The workers' at the marble quarries in the Carrara district rioted, bombs were thrown in Rome, Leghorn and Rimini and an attempt was made on the life of Crispi. The Prime Minister's reaction was to ban all socialist workers' associations but again the measures backfired since they aroused even greater sympathy for the socialists and support for the movement increased. Whilst landowners and

Q

Why was the Catholic church so hostile to the Socialists?

capitalists urged the government to take a stronger line against those responsible for the outrages, King Umberto attempted a more conciliatory approach when he used his powers to reduce the sentences imposed on the Sicilians. At least Pope Leo III, safe within the Vatican, approved of the measures taken against the socialists!

In 1891, there were more riots in Rome and another attempt on the King's life. As the country edged closer towards a complete collapse of law and order, the poor harvest of 1898 increased the misery of the peasants and there were uprisings at Apulia in the south. However, General Luigi Pelloux went to the area and restored order without any undue use of force. Later in the same year there was widespread rioting in Romagna and Tuscany. In May 1898, a major crisis occurred in Milan.

C *The Milan riots of May 1898*

In May 1898, after further increases in the price of bread, anti-government feeling reached boiling point when demonstrations and riots took place in the streets of Milan, the capital of Lombardy. The situation

MAP 2

1898 – Italy in crisis

rapidly got out of hand and there were fierce clashes between the demonstrators and the forces of law and order. Military units under General Fiorenzo Bava-Beccaris were sent to the city where he ordered his troops to open fire on the crowd. Even cannon were used and as a result, 80 civilians were killed and a further 450 injured. It was later claimed that there were inadequate police in the city to deal with the situation since many had been diverted to deal with troubles elsewhere. Further, it was said that if better trained troops had been used, the casualties would have been far lighter. Once peace had been restored, the military courts passed lengthy prison sentences on the ring-leaders. Afterwards there was public condemnation of the brutal methods used by Bava-Beccaris against the civilian population of Milan and this increased when he received the Grand Cross of the Order of Savoy for his services to the country.

In July 1898, Crispi's government resigned and was replaced by an administration led by General Luigi Pelloux. With several other senior army offices included in his government, it became known as the 'Cabinet of Generals'. To start with, Pelloux followed a **conciliatory** line but before long further outrages and pressure from landowners, businessmen and sections of the upper and middle classes forced him to become more reactionary. A number of new measures were introduced, one of which empowered the government to ban any organisation whose activities were considered a threat to the national security. Opposition to the measure in the Chamber of Deputies and a refusal by the High Court to allow the law to be passed by Royal Decree forced Pelloux to dissolve parliament and call an election. Unfortunately for Pelloux, the new parliament was no more amenable to his policy than its predecessor. His attempt to run the country along military-style authoritarian lines had failed and in 1900 he resigned. He was succeeded by Giuseppe Saracco. The new century opened with yet another tragedy.

> **conciliatory** willing to bring together, make friends

L R. COMMISSARIO STRAORDINARIO

In virtù dei poteri conferitigli

DECRETA

Da domani e fino a nuovo ordine. è vietata nell'intera Provincia di Milano la circolazione delle Biciclette, Tricicli, e Tandems o simili mezzi di locomozione.

I Contravventori saranno arrestati e deferiti ai Tribunali di Guerra.

Le truppe e gli agenti della forza pubblica sono incaricati dell'esecuzione del presente Decreto.

R. Commissario Straordinario
f. BAVA BECCARIS

THE GENERAL COMMISSIONER
By virtue of the power invested in me
A DECREE
From tomorrow a new order prohibits the entire Province of Milan from using bicycles, tricycles and tandems and other similar means of transport.. Offenders will be arrested and tried before Military Courts. The troops and agents of the authorities are the people responsible for carrying out the new decree.

PICTURE 6
A decree issued by Bava-Beccaris to the people of Milan in 1898. The decree gives some idea of the repressive measures introduced by Bava-Beccaris

D *The assassination of King Umberto I*

Umberto I, sometimes referred to as 'The Good King', had always taken an interest in the condition of his people. He had actively supported the provision of free elementary education, the widening of the franchise and the need to improve communications. He was also responsible for making Italy the first country to abolish capital punishment. Although not directly involved in the measures taken to deal with the social unrest in his country, he had personally decorated Bava-Beccaris. These events had played into the hands of the anti-monarchists and the King faced increased hostility. On 28 July 1900, Umberto arrived at the town of Monza, a few kilometres from Milan, where he was to present prizes at an athletics meeting. The following morning he was assassinated by Gaetano Bresci. Tuscan-born Bresci had earlier emigrated to the United States and during his time there had become associated with an anarchist group based in New Jersey. He returned to Italy with the intention of avenging the victims of Milan.

Umberto was succeeded by his son, Victor Emmanuel III. The new king was to rule Italy for the next 46 years during a period that included both the Fascist era and the Second World War.

5 ⌐ GIOVANNI GIOLITTI – POLITICAL OPPORTUNIST WITH HIS OWN BRAND OF *TRANSFORMISMO*

During the period 1900–14, Giovanni Giolitti (1842–28) dominated Italian politics. He had earlier been prime minister in 1892 but had been forced to resign the following year because of his involvement in a banking scandal. He returned in 1903 and was to lead his country on four more occasions: 1903–5, 1906–9, 1911–14 and 1920–1. Even during the periods he was out of office, he still remained influential since he continued to control many Deputies in the Chamber who owed their position to his earlier **patronage**.

See page 21

patronage backing (often money) given by a supporter in high places

A *Giolittismo*

A wily politician, Giolitti proved himself to be the master of the Italian political system. As with his predecessors, Depretis and Crispi, he was essentially a manipulator. He was prepared to engage in bribery and corruption but unlike them, he had a broader vision of what was needed to restore the fortunes of Italy. Giolitti aimed to unite the Italian people by reducing class differences, balancing the demands of various political and social groups and so draw them to the centre ground in Italian politics. To this end, he sought the co-operation of the socialists and Catholics and showed a willingness to work with other parties and adopt their ideas. In a sense, he was a contradiction in that he was prepared to use corrupt means to achieve his liberal aims. The southern radical, Gaetano Salvemini, went as far as to call him the 'master of the

Q

In what ways did Giolitti's approach to politics differ from that of Depretis and Crispi?

GIOVANNI GIOLITTI (1842–1928)

Giovani Giolitti was born in Mondovi, Piedmont, in 1842, the son of a court official. He studied law at Turin university and was elected a Deputy to the Italian Parliament in 1882. Between 1889–90, he served as finance minister in Crispi's government. Appointed prime minister in 1892, he was forced to resign the following year because of his involvement in a banking scandal. He returned later in the year and, in all, was to serve as prime minister on five occasions. In spite of his willingness to engage in corruption and other illegal practices, he was responsible for the introduction of many much needed reforms. Giolitti tried to bring socialists into his government and encouraged the re-entry of Roman Catholics into politics. He favoured the creation of an Italian overseas empire but opposed Italian entry into the First World War in 1914. He resigned and became leader of the opposition. In 1920, he was again returned to office but, in common with other politicians, he refused to condemn Fascist brutality and, in 1920, he encouraged Fascist deputies to join his administration. He resigned the following year but remained a Deputy. He did begin to openly oppose Mussolini in 1924, and in his final speech in the Chamber, in 1928, he called for resistance to the Fascists. By that time it was far too late. He died during the same year.

PICTURE 7
Giovanni Giolitti (1842–1928)

underworld'. Some historians have referred to his particular form of *transformismo* as *giolittismo*.

His first problem when he re-assumed office in 1903 was to deal with mounting industrial and civil unrest which ended in a general strike. To avoid arousing public hostility, he involved the military but only sparingly. He used the occasion to appeal to Italians to reject political extremism and went as far as to offer socialist Deputies an alliance. They declined. His approach did not please the industrialists and land-owners.

B *Giolitti's reforms*

Giolitti was fortunate that his early years in office coincided with a period of boom and industrial expansion. Rapid industrial development reduced unemployment, and Italy's trade with the rest of the world more than doubled. This was particularly beneficial for its traditional food exports as well as textiles, machinery and its rapidly developing motor industry. It was during this period that the future Italian car giants were founded – Fiat (then known as *Societa Aninima Fabbrica Italiana di Automobili*) in 1899, Lancia in 1906 and Alfa Romeo in 1910. In 1904, the Italian railway system was nationalised and this resulted in better public services and improved transport facilities for manufacturers and exporters. As the nation's finances improved, so Giolitti worked to ensure that some of the new-found prosperity would be spent on social reform and to the benefit the poorer classes.

Q

To what extent might Giolitti's electoral reforms represent a major step towards establishing democratic government in Italy?

See page 11

artisans a skilled craftsmen or workers

KEY ISSUE

The reasons for the popular discontent that led to the events of 'Red Week'.

A range of new laws were passed to regulate working hours and conditions covering the employment of women and children. Factory conditions were to be supervised and steps were taken to encourage accident prevention. The fact that half a million Italians, mainly from the south, were emigrating annually suggested the need for urgent agricultural reforms. Giolitti's government authorised increased expenditure to provide water and improved communications in rural areas. Old age pensions and health insurance were introduced, the tax on salt removed and public holidays legally enforced. Education still remained a problem. In spite of Michele Coppino's measures of 1877, over half the population remained illiterate. In 1911, the responsibility for education was taken from local communities who had clearly failed in this respect and passed to the provincial authorities. In addition, more money was made available. In the same year, it was at last agreed to pay Deputies. This was, by chance, the same year that British Members of Parliament were first paid! The Electoral Law of 1912 extended the franchise to all men over the age of 30, literate or not, as well as to all men of any age serving in the armed forces. This increased the size of the electorate to nearly nine million. Symbols were added to ballot cards to make sure that illiterates were able to vote for the candidate of their choice with certainty.

Giolitti's reforms did not please everyone. To the radical left, they did not go far enough; to the right, they went too far. Like the upper classes, the middle classes, that had grown to include increased numbers civil servants, professional people, businessmen, shopkeepers and others with commercial interests and hard working **artisans**, were alarmed by the concessions made to the socialists. They began to doubt the wisdom of Giolitti's policies and questioned if liberalism any longer served their best interests. In March 1914, disagreement about Italy's involvement in the First World War led to Giolitti resignation. He wrongly assumed that he would be quickly restored to office but this was not the case. He remained in the political wilderness for six years but returned as prime minister in 1920 to face the problems of post-war Italy.

Giolitti was replaced by Antonio Salandra (1853–1931), a moderate on the traditional right in Italian politics. With the economy edging towards recession, the workers faced wage cuts and the growing possibility of unemployment. In addition, the moderate socialists were finding it increasingly difficult to keep their extremists, the so-called *barricadieri*, in check. For Salandra, it was not a good time to take office. A wave of hostility from those opposed to militarism and a wide range of demands from the radical left immediately faced him. As tension rose, there were demonstrations and riots and the syndicalists called for a general strike. These events finally culminated in what became known as 'Red Week'.

C 'Red Week', June 1914

On 7 June 1914, violent scenes occurred in Ancona and Romagna when strikers confronted strike-breakers hired by local employers. The left-wing press encouraged them, particularly Benito Mussolini, the editor of a Milan-based socialist newspaper *Avanti*. The situation rapidly deteriorated as rioters took to the streets in Ancona and then formed a local **commune**. In Bologna, shops were looted and telegraph lines and railway tracks destroyed. There were instances when soldiers were besieged in their barracks and Romagna went as far as to declare itself an independent republic. More than 100,000 soldiers had to be called into action before order was restored. Although these events were of great concern to the government and caused unease amongst the public at large, the revolutionary movement lacked good leadership and organisation. Once the authorities employed strong-arm tactics to disperse demonstrators and arrested their ring-leaders, the workers backed down and the general strike collapsed. Order was restored but a residue of bad feeling remained and it was clear there would be more battles to be fought in the future. Another reason for the failure of the workers to achieve their aims was the fact that catastrophic events were happening elsewhere as Europe edged ever closer towards war.

> **commune** a town or region that declares self-government

See pages 36–40

6 ⌒ THE CHURCH AND THE STATE – THE ON-GOING CONFLICT

In 1878, Leo XIII was elected pope following the death of Pius IX. The new pope, more a man of the world with a greater understanding of the realities of political life, faced difficult problems in Italy and beyond. At first he remained as opposed to the Italian State as his predecessor but he came to realise that self-imposed political isolation risked making the Church even more remote from the everyday lives of Italians. He gradually changed his stance and allowed Catholics to become more directly involved in politics. He was concerned at the advance of anarchism and socialism. Whilst Marx had earlier expressed the view that religion was 'the opium of the people', Bakunin had described religion as 'collective insanity'. Leo XIII loathed both these Godless political philosophies and feared that they would grow to challenge Catholic teaching and make it less relevant to the people. In his **encyclical** *Rerum Novarum* of 1891, he was critical of both capitalism and socialism when he wrote:

> **encyclical** a circular letter sent by the Pope to all his bishops

> a small number of very rich men have been able to lay upon the toiling masses of the labouring poor a yoke little better than slavery itself.'
>
> 'To remedy these wrongs the socialists wrongly work on the poor man's envy of the rich and are striving to do away with private property and contend that individual possessions should be the common property of all …

Like Pius IX, Leo XIII did not really approve of liberalism but appreciated the value of many of the reforms passed by Crispi and Giolitti. The increasing popularity of socialism and the lawlessness in Italy, particularly the events in Milan in 1898, disturbed him greatly. He died in 1903 and was succeeded by Pius X.

7 ∽ STRUCTURED AND ESSAY QUESTIONS

A *This section consists of questions that might be used for discussion (or written answers) as a way of expanding on the chapter and testing your understanding of it.*

1. To what extent might the Electoral Law of 1882 be considered 'a step towards greater democracy'?
2. In what ways did Crispi's decision to introduce tariffs adversely affect the Italian economy?
3. What are the aims of anarchists?
4. To what extent might the measures taken against the Milan rioters in 1898 be considered excessive?
5. How far reaching were the reforms introduced by Giolitti?
6. How valid were the criticisms made by Pope Leo XIII in his encyclical *Rerum Novarum*?

B *Essay questions.*

1. 'A time when political life was reduced to a shambles.' How valid is this assessment of Italian politics during the period 1870–1915?
2. To what extent might *transformismo* be considered 'government by contrivance and deception'?
3. To what extent might attempts to introduce parliamentary democracy in Italy between 1870 and 1915 be considered a failure?

8 ∽ DOCUMENTARY EXERCISE ON THE PROBLEMS OF ITALIAN LIBERALISM

Study the source below and answer the questions which follow:

SOURCE

From Modern European History *by the British Historian K. Perry, 1976.*

The history of Italy in this period represents in general a most melancholy spectacle. The high hopes of the *Risorgimento* were confounded and unity seemed to bring few real benefits to the Italian people. One factor causing disillusionment was the failure to develop effective parliamentary institutions. Power remained in the hands of two coalitions of parties, the Left and the Right, but there was no essential difference between these groupings, and therefore no possibility of constructive debate or alternation of power. In practice, a few politicians avid for office kept themselves in power by the technique of *transformismo*. They disregarded party labels and made bargains … to create a parliamentary majority. The chief practitioners of this method were Depretis, Crispi, and Giolitti, who was perhaps the most skilful of the three.

1. *What is meant by*
   (a) *'a most melancholy spectacle'? (5 marks)*
   (b) *'they disregarded party labels'? (5 marks)*
2. *How did Italian politicians use 'the technique of* transformismo'
to create a parliamentary majority? (10 marks)
3. *How highly does the author of the source regard developments in*
Italian politics during this time? Explain your answer. (15 marks)

9 ⌐ MAKING NOTES

Read the advice section about making notes on page xix of the Preface.
Now make notes about the policies of three Italian prime ministers
mentioned in this chapter under the following headings:

	Political changes	Economic policy	Social policy
Agostino Depretis			
Francesco Crispi			
Giovanni Giolitti			

Great Power and Imperial Ambitions – Italian Foreign Policy 1870–1914

TABLE 4
Date line of events in Italian foreign policy

INTRODUCTION

In 1870, Italy, a backward country with few resources and only partly industrialised, could hardly have been considered a candidate for great power status in Europe. However, its leaders did not see it that way. Victor Emmanuel II declared, 'Italy must not only be respected, she must make herself feared'. Italians regarded their country as an equal of Britain, France and Germany and as having an important role to play in European affairs. Clearly the German Chancellor Bismarck doubted this when he commented that Italy had 'poor teeth for such a large appetite'.

1 ⌐ ITALY'S FOREIGN POLICY AIMS

In spite of its domestic problems and frequent changes of government, Italy's foreign policy aims were followed with some consistency. Acquiring overseas colonies and military success would be popular with the nationalist extremists at home and also help to silence the government's critics. Italy's foreign policy aims were governed by four considerations:

a) Italy's need to gain equal status and prestige with other European powers;

b) it need to settle the issue of *Italia Irredenta* – the future of territories along its north-east border where the people spoke Italian but lived under Austrian rule;

c) the need to become an imperial power and so gain colonies that would provide access to much needed raw materials and lucrative markets. For obvious economic reasons, industrialists and those with commercial interests supported *grandezza*, a drive for colonies. Italy's leaders regarded with some jealousy the vast overseas empires of Britain and France;

d) the need to acquire additional living space since the country was becoming overpopulated. Already thousands of Italians were emigrating in search of a better life for themselves and improved opportunities for their children

National figures (millions)	Growth of major cities (thousands)		
		1850	*1900*
1852 24.4	Rome	175	463
1881 28.5	Genoa	120	235
1911 35.4	Milan	242	493
	Naples	449	564
	Palermo	150	228

TABLE 5
*The population of Italy
Source:* European Historical
Statistics, *B. R. Mitchell,
Macmillan 1980.*

2 ～ ATTEMPTS AT COLONISATION IN AFRICA

Italy had largely been a spectator during the early stages of the 'Scramble for Africa', that period from the middle to late nineteenth century when European powers such as Britain, France, Germany, Portugal and Belgium carved up that continent into colonies. It was late in the day that Italy made a bid for those few territories that remained.

> **Q**
> *What advantages did Italy hope to gain through the acquisition of African colonies?*

A *Tunisia*

Italy first looked to Tunisia in North Africa then a Turkish possession. Unfortunately, it had rivals. For some time, the British had been dominant in the area but this had declined as French influence grew. In 1871, an Italian expedition was sent to Tunisia with the hope of **annexing** the country but the move was opposed by Britain and France. At the Congress of Berlin in 1878, Britain agreed that Tunisia should fall under French influence in return for French agreement to their acquisition of Cyprus. In 1881, the issue was finally put beyond doubt when, by the Treaty of Bardo, Tunisia was declared a French **protectorate**. The Italian protests that followed were ignored. As relations between the two countries deteriorated so the Italian government showed its displeasure by joining the existing alliance between Germany and Austria–Hungary. In 1882, the Dual Alliance of 1879 became the Triple Alliance. It proved to be an unhappy arrangement since Italy was clearly the junior partner. Although the treaty was renewed in 1891 and 1892, it was very much disliked by Italians.

annexing joining to or taking possession of

protectorate a country under the guardianship of another state

B *Eritrea and Abyssinia*

Italy next turned its attention to the Horn of Africa. As early as 1869, an Italian company had acquired a trading station at Assab on the Red Sea. During 1885, Italian troops occupied the port of Massawa and then pressed inland into the hinterland beyond. This led to border incidents and their progress was finally checked by the Abyssinians. At Dogali in 1887, an irregular native force succeeded in wiping out 500 well-equipped Italian troops. At home, this humiliation led to the removal of Depretis. Dogali was but an omen of worse to come. During a dispute over rights of succession to the Abyssinian throne, the Italian authorities decided to back Menelek. Afterwards, Italy and Abyssinia agreed the

See page 178

Treaty of Uccialli (1889) and consequently Italy claimed Abyssinia as a protectorate. Menelek challenged this claim. Whilst the Abyssinian emperor was an unreliable and sometimes treacherous ruler, the Italians may also have been guilty of some dishonesty. The dispute was over the interpretation of Article 17 of the Treaty of Uccialli.

> The Italian version read – 'The Emperor consents to use the Italian government for all business he does with all the other Powers and Governments';
>
> The Abyssinian version read: 'The Emperor has the option to communicate with the help of the Italian government for all matters that he wants with the kings of Europe'.

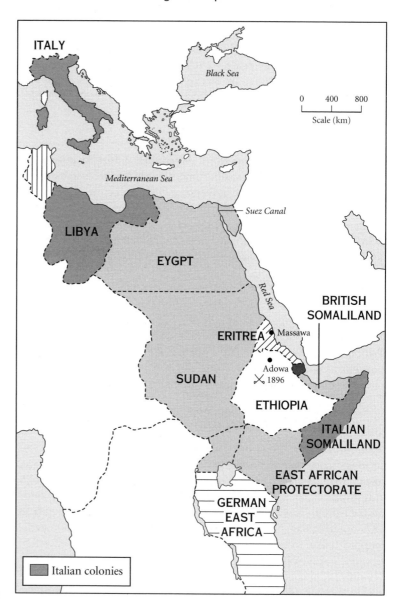

MAP 3
Italy's African colonies by 1914

Whilst all the European powers supported the Italian version, Menelek tried to find a diplomatic solution but failed. He next claimed that he had been cheated and rejected the terms of the treaty outright. He boasted that the Italians were 'burrowing into the country like moles' and claimed 'With God's help I will get rid of them'. In 1895, forces under General Oreste Baratieri used Eritrea, now an Italian colony, as a springboard for another attempt to invade Abyssinia. Menelek was well prepared with an army of nearly 200,000 men, many of them armed with rifles earlier provided by the Italians! Baratieri's army was disorganised and its officers did not even have maps of the area. On 1 March 1896, at the Battle of Adowa, the Italians were annihilated. Forced to flee in confusion, they left behind some 5,000 dead including 2,000 Askari, Eritreans fighting for the Italians. Some 70% of the invading force was killed, wounded or captured. Afterwards, by the Treaty of Addis Ababa that replaced the terms agreed at Uccialli, Italy had to accept Abyssinian independence and also had to pay 10 million lire in reparations before Menelek would agree to release captured prisoners. This disaster brought to an end, at least for the time being, not only Italy's colonial ambitions but also Crispi's political career. A Tripartite Pact between Britain, France and Italy in 1906 recognised the independence of Abyssinia. However, in the event of further difficulties, the three powers agreed defined areas of influence for themselves. Menelek protested at the implications of this agreement.

> ### KEY ISSUE
> *The impact of the humiliation at Adowa on Italy.*

See page 178

C *Tripoli and Cyrenaica*

By 1911, the only regions of North Africa not colonised by the great powers were Tripoli and Cyrenaica. Although nominally still under Turkish control, Italians had been settling there for some time. The Italian annexation of that country had long been expected. The only opposition came from Germany and this was largely due to Italy's obvious lack of enthusiasm for its membership of the Triple Alliance. In October 1911, the Italian government sent an ultimatum to Turkey demanding that country's agreement to their occupation of Libya and Cyrenaica. A declaration of war and the dispatch of soldiers followed. In Italy, the war was supported by the nationalist press who used it as an excuse to encourage an orgy of patriotism. The popular Gabriele D'Annunzio also used his poetry to add to the nationalistic fervour. The war, which unexpectedly lasted for a year, was an uninspired conflict. In 1912, the Treaty of Lausanne finally brought the war to an end. Again Italians greeted news of their victory with unrestrained **euphoria**. Unfortunately the acquisition of Libya did not answer Italy's needs. They were to gain little benefit from the control of a country that was largely desert and offered few attractions. Even worse, it was likely to place yet another financial burden on the Italian government.

euphoria a great feeling of well-being

3 ～ *ITALIA IRREDENTA*

Italia Irredenta, 'unredeemed Italy', is the name given to the various regions on Italy's north-east border that remained under Austro-Hungarian domination after the Austro-Prussian War of 1866. These lands – the South Tyrol, Trentino, Istria, Fiume, Trieste and parts of the Dalmatian coast – were largely inhabited by Italian-speaking peoples. The Trentino, whose population included 370,000 Italians, was a province that extended well into Italy and was regarded as a threat. *Irredentists* were part of an Italian nationalist movement that campaigned for the annexation of these lands where there were frequent clashes between Italian workers and Austrian officials. In 1903, there were major anti-Austrian demonstrations in Istria. Although nationalist agitation continued, *irredentists'* claims were ignored. Nevertheless the three countries promised to follow a policy of peace and friendship, and not to be part of any armed conflicted.

MAP 4
Italia Irredenta

4 ～ ALLIANCES AND TREATIES

A *The Triple Alliance, 1882*

See page 27

In 1882, Italy joined the Triple Alliance and so became the third member of the previously arranged Dual Alliance (1879) between Germany and Austria–Hungary. Italy's decision was the outcome of its resentment of the establishment of a French protectorate over Tunis and the fact that it gave it security against any possible French attack. It also wanted the support of more reliable allies in its quest for colonies. Since Germany and Austria–Hungary were both monarchies, the treaty strengthened the hand of Victor Emmanuel II in his struggle against Italian republicanism and it also restricted the activities of Austrian Catholics who had been secretly plotting to restore the power of the Papacy. On the other hand, the treaty made Italy an ally of its erstwhile enemy Austria, a country with which it still nurtured a grievance over the issue of *Italia Irredenta*. The Triple Alliance listed eight articles. Simply explained, they were:

I.   The three countries involved promised peace and friendship and not to enter into any alliance against one another.

II.   In the case of Italy, if, without provocation, France attacked it, the other two powers were bound to go to its assistance. Italy was to reciprocate if Germany was attacked by France.

III.   If one or two of the Alliance members were, without provocation, attacked or involved in a war with two or more of the other Great Powers, the other two would go to its assistance.

IV.   If one of the other Great Powers should threaten one of the Alliance members and this should end in war, the other members of the Alliance would remain neutral or, should they see fit, go to the aid of their ally.

V.   If the peace of any one of the Alliance members should be threatened, the three would consult with each other and decide on the appropriate measures to be taken.

VI.   The Alliance members agreed to keep the terms of the treaty secret.

VII.   The terms of the treaty were to remain in force for five years.

VIII.   The treaty was to be ratified within three weeks or sooner.

From the point of view of Germany and Austria–Hungary, Italy's membership of the Triple Alliance meant that it would no longer be in a position to form an alliance with either Britain or France or to support Russia in any future war with Austria–Hungary.

B *Closer ties with Britain*

Since Britain supplied coal and iron essential to the Italian economy, it was important for Italy to maintain friendly relations with Britain. It was at Italy's insistence that the signatories of the Triple Alliance powers also made a 'Ministerial Declaration' in which they stated that the Alliance 'was not in any way directed against England'. Although this was

THE JUNIOR PARTNER.

The German Emperor (*the head of the Firm*). "LOOK HERE, UMBERTO, ALL WE CAN SAY IS, IF YOU DROP ANY MORE IN 'ABYSSINIANS,' WE MAY HAVE TO DISSOLVE PARTNERSHIP."

PICTURE 8
In a Punch *cartoon of 1896, Wilhelm II and Franz Josef, the German and Austrian Emperors, threaten to dissolve the partnership (The Triple Alliance), if Umberto is responsible for any more blunders like the failure of his Abyssinian venture*

not included when the treaty was renewed in 1887 and 1890, the Italian government made it clear that it would not support its Triple Alliance allies in any war against Britain. In 1887, as a result of a Mediterranean Agreement, Italy, Britain and Austria–Hungary jointly undertook to maintain the ***status quo*** in the Mediterranean, Adriatic, Aegean, Black Sea and the Balkans. In a move clearly aimed to hinder possible French and Russian expansion. At the same time, Britain agreed to support Italian aims in Tripoli in return for Italian support in Egypt. In 1907, the British king, Edward VII, met the Victor Emmanuel III at Gaeta.

status quo maintaining the existing situation

C *Improved relations with France*

As we have seen, rivalry over Tunisia, a tariff war and French support for the Papacy led to tension between the two countries, but relations began to improve by the mid-1890s. The Franco–Italian Convention of 1896 resulted in Italian recognition of the French protectorate over Tunisia in return for certain political and commercial privileges. Two years later, a commercial treaty brought to an end the damaging trade war. As the result of a secret agreements made in 1900 and 1902, Italy and France agreed to recognise their respective ambitions in Tripoli and Morocco and Italy promised to remain neutral in any future war that involved France and would not assist Germany in the events of a French attack. To all intents and purposes, this virtually ended Italy's commitment to the Triple Alliance. In 1906, Italy supported France and Britain against Germany at the time of the Moroccan crisis and at the subsequent conference at Algeciras. As final evidence of the improved relations between the two powers, in 1903 Victor Emmanuel III visited Paris and the following year President Loubert of France was welcomed to Rome.

D *Agreements with Russia and Austria*

In 1909, following the crisis caused by the Austrian annexation of Bosnia, Italy concluded the *Racconigi* Agreement with Russia.

THE *RACCONIGI* AGREEMENT, 1909

By the terms of the agreement, in what would appear to be aimed at Austrian ambitions in the region, Italy and Russia promised to work to preserve the *status quo* in the Balkans. Further, neither country would enter into an agreement with a third country regarding plans for the area without first involving the other. Russia agreed to show 'benevolent neutrality' with regard to Italy's ambitions in Tripoli and Cyrenaica. In return, Italy agreed to support Russian plans to open the Dardanelles to her shipping.

Some days later, Italy also reached an agreement with Austria–Hungary that, on the face of it, would appear to contradict the *Racconigi* arrangements. Both countries agreed not to enter into agreements with any other nation without the knowledge of the other. In the events prior to the outbreak of the First World War in 1914, Italy did do its utmost to restrain the warlike intentions of Austria–Hungary, but without success.

SHOCK TACTICS.

EUROPA (*to Italy, who has temporarily discarded the barrel-organ in favour of the bombardon*). "IF YOU GO ON LIKE THAT, YOUNG MAN, YOU'LL GET YOURSELF DISLIKED."
ITALY. "WELL, THAT'S BETTER THAN NOT BEING NOTICED AT ALL."

PICTURE 9

A Punch cartoon of May 1912 shows Europe's (Europa) concern at Italy's increasingly aggressive foreign policy. Italy is shown as having abandoned her traditional barrel organ in favour of a bombardon, a loud brass tuba

5 ⌐ STRUCTURED AND ESSAY QUESTIONS

A *This section consists of questions that might be used for discussion (or writing answers) as a way of expanding on the chapter and for testing your understanding of it.*

1. For what reasons did the attempted Italian invasion of Abyssinia in 1895–6 end in disaster?

2. Why were many Italians against their country's membership of the Triple Alliance?

3. Why was *Italia Irredentia* such a controversial issue to Italians?

4. To what extent did relations between Italy and France fluctuate during this period?

5. Would it be accurate to say that Italy and Britain maintained friendly relations throughout this period?

6. With what justification might Italy have considered herself to be a great European power by 1914?

B *Essay questions.*

1. 'Mainly driven by its desire to become an imperial power.' How valid is this assessment of the aims of Italian foreign policy during the period 1870–1914?

2. To what extent had Italy succeeded in establishing friendly relations with the major European powers before 1914?

6 ⌐ MAKING NOTES

Read the advice section about making notes on page xix of the Preface: How to use this book, and then make your own notes on the following aspects of Italian foreign policy:

1. *Foreign policy aims.*
   (a) Who were considered to be the major European powers in 1870?
   (b) Britain and France apart, which other European countries were colonial powers?
   (c) Reasons for Italian emigration abroad during this period?

2. *Italian attempts to colonise Africa.*
   (a) Why was the outcome of the Congress of Berlin (1878) such a disappointment to Italy?
   (b) How did Menelek manage to outwit the Italians in 1895–6?
   (c) Why was the Italian campaign against the Turks in 1911 described as 'an uninspired conflict'?

3. *Italia Irredenta.*
   (a) What is meant by the term *Italia Irredenta*?
   (b) Which territories comprised the *Italia Irredenta*?
   (c) Why did Italy consider it had a right to claim these territories?

4. *Alliances and treaties.*
   (a) Reasons for Italy's decision to join the Triple Alliance in 1882?
   (b) To what extent might Britain have been considered a Mediterranean power?
   (c) The difficulties in the relations between Italy and France during the period 1870–1914?
   (d) The advantages gained by Italy from the *Racconigi* Agreement of 1909?
   (e) On the evidence of the state of international relations in 1914, in the event of a war would Italy have appeared more likely to side with Germany or France?

Italy and the First World War

INTRODUCTION

There was no single cause for the Great War that started in Europe in the summer of 1914. The war was the outcome of the suspicion, rivalry and enmity that existed between the major European powers. The historian A.J.P. Taylor has described the events that led to the conflict as 'war by time-table'. The European rivalries that existed at the time led to the creation of a system of alliances – the Triple Alliance of 1882 of Germany, Austria–Hungary and Italy and the Triple *Entente* of 1907 that included France, Russia and Britain. In such a situation, it was always likely that any provocative act might lead to a crisis. The impulsive German Kaiser, Wilhelm II, described as having 'the touchiness of a prima donna and the conceit of a spoilt child', was not the best suited to dealing with the difficulties of confrontation. The twentieth century started ominously with an armaments race between Britain and Germany as each tried to keep ahead of the other in naval construction. In the Balkans, Austria–Hungary and Russia competed to extend their influence as the Turkish Empire collapsed. As a result of Franco–German rivalry over Morocco, a crisis arose in 1905 when the solidarity shown by the *Entente* members forced the Kaiser into a humiliating climb down. Another crisis came in 1908 when Austria–Hungary annexed Bosnia. This led to an unsettled situation in the Balkans and the growth of Pan-Slavism. A second crisis over Morocco occurred in 1911 and again the Germans were forced to back down. The unrest in the Balkans led to two wars in 1912 and 1913 that further increased the tension in that region.

It was the assassination of Archduke Franz Ferdinand, heir to the Austrian throne, at Sarajevo in Bosnia on 23 July 1914, that finally set Europe on course for war. The assassins were members of a Serbian secret society, the *Ujedinjenje Ili Smrt* (Union or Death) better known as the Black Hand, that had crossed into Bosnia to commit the murder. In the ensuing exchanges between Austria–Hungary and Serbia, the German Kaiser offered the Austrians his unconditional support, a so-called '**blank cheque**'. On 28 July 1914, Austria–Hungary declared war on Serbia and this brought the alliance system into play. Two days later, Russia began to mobilise and Germany demanded that its military preparations should cease. The next day, Germany declared war on Russia. Germany next demanded a French promise not to become involved in the war. With no such guarantee forthcoming, on 3 August, Germany declared war on France. The following day, German troops, having been denied free passage across the country, invaded Belgium.

See pages 30–1

blank cheque freedom to act as one thinks best

1882	Triple Alliance agreed
1905	First Moroccan crisis
1907	Triple *Entente* agreed
1908	Bosnia annexed by Austria–Hungary
1911	Second Moroccan crisis
1912	First Balkan War
1913	Second Balkan War
1914	Giolitti declared for Italian neutrality
	Start of the First World War
1915	Treaty of London
	Italy joined the war on the side of the Allies
1915–16	Battles along the River Isonzo
1917	Battle of Caporetto
	Cardona replaced by Diaz
	Orlando became Italian prime minister
1918	Battle of Vittorio Venito
	Austrian surrender

TABLE 6

Date line showing Italy's involvement in the Great War

By the Treaty of London of 1839, Britain, together with other major European powers including Prussia and Austria, had guaranteed Belgian independence, demanded the withdrawal of German troops. The Germans ignored the ultimatum and consequently, on 4 August 1914, Britain declared war on Germany. The peoples of the nations involved were led to believe that the war would be short and victory easily won. For them, disillusionment was to be swift and traumatic. Italy had played very little part in these events but now that the major European powers were at war, decisions had to be made.

1 ➢ ITALIAN INVOLVEMENT IN THE WAR

There were some Italians who thought that the difficulties between Austria–Hungary and Serbia would come to nothing and that the crisis would soon be over. Claudio Treves, a leading Socialist, expressed the view that there would be no major European war since it would not be in the interests of the capitalist classes of the great powers and that fear of revolution would cause their leaders to negotiate a settlement. A former prime minister, Luigi Luzzatti, was of the opinion that war had to be avoided since it would lead to 'the destruction of lives, wealth, culture, civilisation … and would debase and debilitate Europe'. Even Giolitti, still among the most influential Italian politicians, refused to believe that 'Europe would fall prey to the folly of war'. Once these predictions proved false, Italian politicians had to consider two issues.

A *Italy's dilemma – neutralists versus interventionists*

Firstly, they had to decide whether or not to become involved in the war or remain neutral; secondly, should they decide to enter the war, on which side should they fight – for the Triple Alliance or the Triple *Entente*? Public opinion was hopelessly divided. There were those who tended to support the view that Italy should fulfill its obligations to the Triple Alliance of which it had been a member and supported for over 30 years. General Cadorna, chief-of-staff of the Italian army, went as far as to begin to mobilise for a war with France and encourage the King to send an Italian army to the River Rhine to support the Germans! Others, whilst they admired Germany, found it impossible to side with their other partner, the arch-enemy Austria–Hungary. These, mainly *Irredentalists*, were quick to champion the slogan 'No blood, no money, no complicity with the Habsburgs'. Memories of the Italian failure to gain Tunisia caused some nationalists to still regard France as the main enemy. They also saw involvement in a war as an ally of Germany as a convenient way of increasing the prestige of Italy. For these reasons, they first backed Italian intervention on the side of their Triple Alliance partners. Religious ties meant that some Italian Catholics had sympathy with Catholic Austria and looked for the restoration of Papal power in their own country. On the extreme left, there were syndicalists,

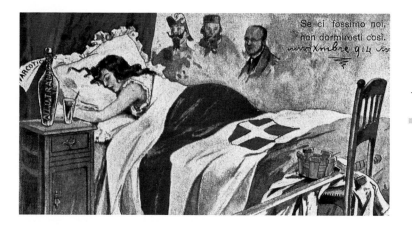

PICTURE 10
A postcard of 1915 shows Italy asleep as she enjoys her neutrality. At her bedside, the heroes of the Risorgimento *say – 'If it were us you would not be sleeping'*

republicans and anarchists who encouraged entry into the war on any side since it might create circumstances favourable to revolution and the overthrow of the hated monarchy. War, they hoped, would be 'the fuse, the explosion, to blow away capitalism'. From the government's point of view, war did have some appeal since it might unite the country and divert attention from the major economic and social problems facing the country. Whilst some dithered, the moderate Socialists, Liberals and other parties of the centre stood largely for non-intervention and this was confirmed by a speech made by Giolitti at the end of 1914.

B *Giolitti and Italian neutrality*

On 5 December 1914, the former prime minister, Giovanni Giolitti, delivered a speech to the Italian Chamber of Deputies in which he revealed that, in 1913, a whole year before the crisis following the assassination at Sarajevo, the Marquis di San Giuliano, the Italian foreign secretary, had sent him a telegram informing him:

> Austria has communicated to us and to Germany her intention of taking action against Serbia, and defines such action as defensive, hoping to bring into operation the **casus foederis** of the Triple Alliance.

He had replied:

> If Austria intervenes against Serbia, it is clear that a *casus foederis* can not be established. It is a step which she is taking on her own account, since there is no question of defence, inasmuch as no one is thinking of attacking her.

This he claimed was proof that the murder of Archduke Franz Ferdinand was but an excuse and not a valid reason for the Austrian attack on Serbia since there was clear evidence that such a move had been

KEY ISSUE

Giolitti's reasons for not supporting the Triple Alliance.

casus foederis coming clearly within the terms of the treaty

planned earlier. In view of these disclosures, Giolitti saw no reason for Italy to become involved in the war and concluded, 'I think it is right that in the eyes of all Europe it should appear that Italy has remained completely loyal to the observances of her pledges.' The members of the Chamber stood and loudly applauded him.

C *A volte-face – Italy's change of mind*

Within a few days of Italy's declaration of neutrality, the country's leaders went through a remarkable change of mind. The Nationalists, led by Enrico Corradini, suddenly began to champion the need for intervention on behalf of the *Entente* powers. Some went as far as to suggest

PICTURE 11
*Gabriele D'Annunzio
(1863–1938)*

See pages 54–6

GABRIELE D'ANNUNZIO (1863–1938)

Born in 1863 at Pescara on the Adriatic coast, the son of a wealthy landowner of Dalmatian origin, Gabriele D'Annunzio was educated at the universities of Prato and Rome. He began writing for the newspaper *Tribuna* in 1881. In 1883, he married the aristocratic Maria Hardouin di Gallese and afterwards worked to maintain the lifestyle of his extravagant wife. In 1887, he was elected to the Chamber of Deputies but failed to win re-election three years later. Always living beyond his means, in 1910, he fled to France to escape his creditors. Already notorious for his many love affairs, in Paris he began a much publicised tempestuous relationship with the actress Eleonora Duse. This was to be the subject of his first novel, *Il Fouco* (The Flame of Life). Now associated with the likes of the actress Sarah Bernhardt and the artist Romaine Brooks, it is said that he 'lived like a dandy and was a symbol of decadence'. He next wrote *Le Martyre de Saint Sebastian* for his mistress Ida Rubinstein. In the book he claimed that Saint Sebastian had both male and female sex characteristics. The Roman Catholic Church banned the work. A poet as well as a novelist, many of his books were salacious and consequently very popular. Prior to the First World War, he returned to Italy where, as an open and exaggerated nationalist, he again became involved in politics and campaigned for his homeland's involvement in the war on the side of the Allies. He joined the Italian armed services and, in turn, served as a soldier, sailor and airman. During the course of the war he lost an eye. However, his most famous exploit came after the war. Outraged by the fact that Italy had been denied Fiume in the post-war treaties, he raised a force to occupy the port where he established an illegal government. For a while, he became an associate of Benito Mussolini but this did not last. In 1924, he was made Prince of Monte Nevoso. In old age, suffering from a nervous disorder and blindness, he lived as a recluse. He died in 1938.

that in order to gain the lands of 'unredeemed Italy', Italy should wage war against Austria–Hungary on its own, a purely Italian war, without involving the Allies or Germany. In the meantime, an approach was made to the Austrians to see if they would agree to surrender these territories if Italy promised to remain neutral. The offer the Austrians rejected out of hand.

The views of the Nationalists were popularised by the Italian press and consequently began to win the popular support of the people. Amongst those who helped to spread such views were Benito Mussolini, a former socialist who was now the editor of pro-interventionalist newspaper, *Il Popolo d'Italiana*, and the popular poet and writer of erotic novels, Gabriele D'Annunzio. The Nationalists also benefited from the quality of Allied propaganda which far excelled that of Germany and Austria–Hungary.

See page 30

Article 1. A military convention shall be immediately concluded between the General Staffs of France, Great Britain, Italy and Russia. This convention shall settle the minimum number of military forces to be employed by Russia against Austria–Hungary in order to prevent that power from concentrating all its strength against Italy... On her part, Italy undertakes to use her entire resources for the purpose of waging war with France, Great Britain and Russia against all their enemies.

Article 3. The French and British fleets shall render active and permanent support to Italy.

Article 4. Under the Treaty of Peace, Italy shall obtain the Trentino... as well as Trieste... all Istria...

Article 5. Italy shall also be given the province of Dalmatia...

Article 8. Italy shall receive entire sovereignty over the Dodecanese Islands...

Article 9. ...in the event of total or partial partition of Turkey, she ought to obtain a just share.

Article 11. Italy shall receive a share of any eventual war indemnity corresponding to their efforts and sacrifices.

Article 13. In the event of France and Great Britain increasing their colonial territories in Africa at the expense of Germany... Italy may claim some equitable compensation...

Article 14. Great Britain undertakes to facilitate... a loan of at least £50,000,000

Article 16. The present arrangement shall be held secret.

CHART 2
Articles from the Treaty of London, 26 April 1915

D *Italy decides for the Allies*

If Italy could be brought into the war on their side, it would clearly be to the advantage of the Allies. It would open another battlefront and place additional demands on Austria–Hungary since that country was already engaged in a war with Russia on the Eastern Front. It would also secure bases in the Mediterranean from which the Allies could more easily wage war on Turkey. Italy, however, would have to be tempted. In April 1915, the Allies and Italy secretly negotiated the Treaty of London, the *Patto di Londra*. At the time, Italy was in a position to drive a hard bargain for her involvement and won promises of both territorial and financial concessions once the war was over.

Although the Allies eventually agreed to Italy's demands, there would be obvious difficulties to overcome later. For an example, some of its territorial claims were levelled at Slav rather than Austrian lands and clearly Italy would have to make a major contribution to the winning of the war to merit such rewards.

Although the Socialists, republicans and pacifists remained largely opposed, the increase in the popular clamour for war-orchestrated by the Nationalists and the inflammatory war mongering by d'Annunzio and Mussolini made their position increasingly difficult. Anti-war demonstrations by peasants and workers were broken up but similar actions taken by interventionists were encouraged by the police and backed by the military. On 23 May 1915, Prime Minister Antonio Salandra formally announced that, in view of public opinion and pressure from Nationalists and militarists, his country would not be joining the Central Powers. Instead, he declared Italy's support for the Allies. In a speech to the nation, he said:

Q *Did the Allies Italy bribe Italy into entering the war on their side?*

> I address myself to Italy and the civilized world in order to show not by violent words but by exact facts and documents, how the fury of our enemies has vainly attempted to diminish the high moral and political dignity of the cause which our arms will make prevail ... The horrible crime of Sarajevo was exploited as a pretext a month after it happened – this was proved by the refusal of Austria to accept the very extensive offers of Serbia ... if there had been a possibility of mediation being exercised, it would not have interrupted hostilities, which had already begun... The truth is that Austria and Germany believed that until the last days that they had to deal with an Italy, weak, blistering, but not capable of ... enforcing by arms her good right ... In the blaze thus kindled internal discussions melted away, and the whole nation was joined in a wonderful moral union, which will prove our greatest source of strength in the severe struggle that faces us ...

Italy declared war on Austria–Hungary on 24 May 1915. Unknown to the Italians, General Conrad von Hotzendorff, chief of the Austrian general staff, had been urging the Emperor Franz Josef to agree to a

pre-emptive offensive against Italy in order to dissuade it from joining the Allies. The Emperor refused and declared that Italy's neutrality had to be respected. Salandra, fearing that his declaration might bring a hostile reaction from Italy's former allies, ordered Cadorna to mobilise the army. Within days, units of the Italian army were deployed to defend their country's borders with Austria–Hungary. Italy did not declare war on Germany until mid way through 1916. The conflict that Italy had joined was seen by some as 'the last war of the *Risorgimento*' – the war that would finally bring together all Italian-speaking peoples.

> **pre-emptive** to attack first in order to forestall an enemy's action

E *Italy's readiness for war*

Military expenditure had not been a priority of Eduardo Daneo, the Italian Finance Minister. Referring to it as 'unproductive', he refused the demand for £24m that the War Minister, Vittorio Zapelli, claimed was necessary to prepare the armed services for war. In the end, he allocated barely a third of that sum. The Abyssinian and Libyan wars of 1896 and 1911 gave some indication of the shortcomings of the Italian army. The soldiers had shown themselves to have low morale and to be lacking in resolve and fighting spirit; they had also been badly led and inadequately equipped. To what extent had matters improved by 1915? Certainly sums of money had been spent on the army but this fell short of the sum required. For soldiers, conditions of service were poor and their training methods outdated. Volunteers that joined the regular army were generally of poor quality and these were soon to be joined by largely unwilling conscripts – poorly educated peasants from the countryside and militant workers from the industrial regions. Such men were soon to face the harsh demands of trench warfare and rigors of a winter campaign fought in the inhospitable Alps. How would such men fare under the leadership of General Cadorna, a man who only a short time previously had wanted them to be mobilised to fight against France on the Rhine? Equally important, were the Italian people ready to face the demands and appalling sacrifices that the war would demand of them?

> **Q** *How prepared was the Italian army for war?*

	Italy	Austria–Hungary
Population	35 m	50 m
Men under arms in 1915	75 m	81m
Divisions at the front	35	25
Fleet – various warships	36	28
Fleet – submarines	12	6
Merchant fleet	1.75 m tonnes	1 m tonnes
Aircraft	58	120
Military expenditure 1913–14	£10 m	£22 m

TABLE 7
Military potential – Italy and Austria–Hungary compared

KEY ISSUE

The difficulties of waging war along Italy's north-east frontier.

2 ⌐ ITALY AT WAR

The common frontier between Italy and Austria–Hungary stretched for some 650 kilometres from the Swiss–Italian border to the Gulf of Venice. For most of this distance it ran along the Alps and, anticipating Italy's entry into the war, the Austrians had strongly fortified their side of the frontier so that it was virtually impregnable. To the east, the frontier more or less followed the course of the River Isonzo to the point where it joins the Adriatic Sea. Although the local terrain is criss-crossed by rivers and valleys, here the Alpine slopes are more gentle. Along nearly the whole length of the front, the Austrians almost invariably held the high ground and this meant that any Italian offensive would be fought uphill. The exception was the 30-kilometre coastal strip close to where the River Isonzo entered the sea. At the start of the war, Cadorna had 35 divisions at his disposal, 10 more than the Austrians had. The Austrians, on the other hand, had the advantages of high ground and vastly superior artillery. The Italian general appreciated that the area most suitable for military operations was to the east along the River Isonzo and it was there that he soon decided to concentrate his main effort. Although on the face of it the easiest option, the river was liable to flood and during the years 1915–18 the rainfall was to be particularly heavy. During the forthcoming two and a half years, the Italians were to fight no less than 11 'Battles of the Isonzo', suffer horrendous casualties and advance barely 11 kilometres. As we shall see, although the battles along the Isonzo tended to merge with each other, some historians have given the most significant individual names.

A *1915 – the opening campaigns*

At the start of the war General Cadorna boldly launched an offensive along the whole front line and the Italian armies gained some success almost everywhere. However, when the offensive was renewed in October, the Austrians were better prepared and were able to take advantage of

> **THE EVACUATION OF THE SERBS – AND OUTSTANDING ITALIAN ACHIEVEMENT**
>
> In September 1915, across the Adriatic Sea in the Balkans, the remnants of the Serb army was having a hard time as, harassed by the Austrians and their new allies, the Bulgarians, they tried to fight their way to the Dalmatian coast. The Serbian soldiers were accompanied by columns of civilian refugees. In order to assist their evacuation, the Italians occupied the ports of Durazzo, Valona and Giovanni de Medua and provided shipping to get them across the Adriatic Sea to the Italian mainland. They also protected and provided humanitarian aid for the hard-pressed refugees. In all, some 260,000 Serbs were rescued by the Italian navy in an operation that was to be one of their outstanding achievements of the war.

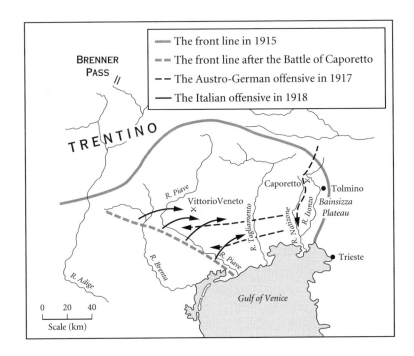

The front line in 1915

The front line after the Battle of Caporetto

The Austro-German offensive in 1917

The Italian offensive in 1918

BRENNER PASS

TRENTINO

R. Piave

Caporetto   Tolmino

VittorioVeneto   Bainsizza Plateau

R. Tagliamento

R. Natizone

R. Isonzo

R. Brenta

R. Piave

Trieste

R. Adige

Gulf of Venice

0   20   40

Scale (km)

MAP 5
The Italian Front, 1915–18

their enemy's shortage of shells. It was from this point that Cadorna concentrated on a narrower sector along the Isonzo. During 1915, the first four Battles of the Isonzo were fought. These offensives resulted in 250,000 casualties and very little gain. Fortunately, severe winter conditions brought the fighting to an end and granted the soldiers some respite.

B *1916 – failures on the Isonzo and declining morale*

1916 witnessed a further five Battles of the Isonzo. With the onset of spring, Cadorna, who was planning another series of offensives, received news that the Austrians were massing their forces to the west in the Trentino. Accordingly, he cancelled his own plans and moved troops to reinforce his defences there. Once the Austrians had failed to achieve a breakthrough, he reverted to his original plans. His offensives achieved little and once again the Italian armies suffered heavy casualties. The onset of the second winter of the war brought major problems. The rivers in the Isonzo valley flooded, swept away bridges and turned the system of trenches into a morass of clinging mud. Soldiers in forward positions high up in the snow-covered Alps endured terrible hardship. The shortage of munitions was further aggravated by strikes and acts of industrial espionage on the home front by left-wing militants determined to force their country's withdrawal from the war. The movement of available supplies and munitions to the front was handicapped by the adverse weather conditions. Overall, the events of the year had a damaging effect on both front-line soldiers and civilians at home who were themselves suffering acute shortages.

C *1917 – disaster and humiliation at Caporetto*

The entry of the United States into the war in April 1917 boosted the morale of the Allies generally and revived the flagging Italian war effort. On the other hand, a Bolshevik revolution in Russia later in the year forced that country's withdrawal from the conflict. This released German and Austrian armies from the Eastern Front to fight elsewhere and encouraged those elements who thought that revolution at home might lead to Italy's withdrawal from the war. Meanwhile, in the northeast three more battles were fought along the River Isonzo. With little success to show for their efforts, morale declined still further and this brought with it disillusionment and defeatism. In spite of their reversals, France and Britain urged the Italians to attempt yet another offensive in order to gain the high ground on the Bainsizza plateau to the east of the Isonzo. After some initial progress, the offensive had to be called off again because of a shortage of munitions. The Italian high command was also concerned at news provided by prisoners and Austrian deserters that units of the German army had been sent to reinforce the Austrians. In late October came an Austrian offensive that was the final battle of the Isonzo. It became known as the Battle of Caporetto.

THE BATTLE OF CAPORETTO

The Battle of Caporetto began on the morning of 24 October 1917. Following a five-hour artillery bombardment, the Austrian and German troops under the command of the German General Bernhard von Bulow were immediately successful and advanced along the whole front. By advancing southward along the River Natizone, to the west of the Isonzo, they took the Italians by surprise, outflanked their positions, forced a 20-kilometre gap in the Italian lines and captured the town of Caporetto. Cadorna had no choice but to withdraw his armies and try to reform along a defensive line further to the west along the River Tagliamento. The retreat was far from orderly and the Italians fled in panic. Totally demoralised, thousands of soldiers threw away their weapons, deserted and made their way homewards. In his *History of the Great War*, C.R.M.F. Cruttwell describes the chaos:

> 400,000 soldiers were going home, with the determination that for them at least the war was ended. The reports of their behaviour are most curious.
> Having broken contact with the enemy, they were in no hurry; they stopped to eat and drink and pillage. One observer notes their air of 'tranquil indifference', another that while they had all thrown away their arms, they kept their gas masks; nearly as many civilians were fleeing more wildly, from the face of the enemy, blocking what remained of the road space with their carts and household goods.

Unable to hold a line along the River Tagliamento, Cadorna was forced to retreat further and by 9 November he had managed to restore some order and established a new defensive line along the River Piave. Here, although outnumbered, the Italians stood and managed to hold their ground against repeated efforts to dislodge them. The courage shown on the Piave was in complete contrast to the previous evident loss of nerve witnessed earlier. Fortunately for the Italians, all was not well with the Austrians and Germans. The speed of their advance was unexpected. As a result their lines of communication were extended and this left them without adequate supplies. This meant that they could not take full advantage of the situation and this helped Cadorna. The lull in the fighting allowed the Italians breathing space and gave time for the high command to restore order and discipline. Importantly too, British and French units arrived to reinforce the line.

KEY ISSUE

The impact of the disaster at Caporetto.

The Battle of Caporetto proved costly for the Italians. 300,000 of their soldiers were taken prisoner and 40,000 killed or wounded. In addition, 3,000 heavy guns fell into enemy hands. General Cadorna was held responsible for the humiliation and was replaced by General Armando Diaz. There were also repercussions on the home front where Paolo Boselli, who had replaced Antonio Salandra in 1916, resigned in favour of Vittorio Orlando.

Q

Was Cadorna a scapegoat for Caporetto?

GENERAL COUNT LUIGI CADORNA (1850–1928)

Born at Pallanza in 1850, Luigi Cadorna was the son of one of Italy's most illustrious generals, Count Raffaele Cadorna, who had fought with distinction in the Crimean War and the wars of the *Risorgimento*. He became chief of staff and set about modernising the structure, training methods and weaponry of the Italian army. He had barely begun his task when the war started. General Cadorna was given command of the Italian armies confronting the Austrians along his country's Alpine frontier. During the period 1915–17, he directed the numerous battles fought along the River Isonzo. His plan was to advance in stages in order to gain limited objectives. After each offensive, he paused before moving forward again. Even so, during the eleven Battles of the Isonzo, the Italian armies endured heavy casualties and advanced less than 10 kilometres. Bearing in mind that he lacked adequately trained soldiers and had a shortage of guns and munitions, he proved himself a competent general with sound military judgement. His fault was that he could be aloof and arrogant. There was lack of contact

PROFILE

PICTURE 12
General Count Luigi Cadorna (1850–1928)

between Cadorna and his commanders. According to the military historian Ronald Seth, this had the result 'of imprisoning Cadorna in an ivory tower by which he was denied all knowledge of both officers and men to the war in general and their own problems in particular.' He would not tolerate failure and, during the 19 months before the Battle of Caporetto, he dismissed no less than 217 generals and nearly 600 other senior officers. He showed little interest in the condition of his soldiers and at times appeared to disregard the high casualty rates suffered by the men under his command. Although he was largely the victim of circumstances, he was held responsible for the disaster of Caporetto (1917) and was dismissed and allowed to retire.

D *1918 – Caporetto avenged – the Battle of Vittorio Veneto*

The first change of fortune came in June 1918 when the Italians, still supported by French and British units, repulsed an Austrian offensive along the River Piave. Then, on 24 October, after some months of hesitation and on the anniversary of Caporetto, the cautious Diaz launched his own offensive at Vittorio Veneto. Without German assistance, the Austrians were no match for the Allies who managed to advance 24 kilometres and capture the town of Vittorio Veneto. Totally demoralised, Austrian resistance crumbled. As their soldiers fell back, their retreat turned into a rout. After a 10-day campaign, the Allies had taken 300,000 prisoners and captured 5,000 guns. The battle marked the final collapse of the Austrian armies on the Italian Front and, two days later, on 2 November, an armistice was signed at Padua.

3 ✍ THE WAR AT SEA AND IN THE AIR

See page 42

The first sea operations involving the Italian navy came in September 1915 when, under the command of Admiral Paolo Thaon di Revel, some 260,000 Serbian soldiers and refugees were brought to safety across the Adriatic Sea. Afterwards things did not go so well when several cruisers were sunk by German submarines and, even worse, at home when two battleships, the *Benedetto Brin* and *Leonardo da Vinci*, were destroyed at their home bases as a result of acts of sabotage carried out by traitors. Whilst there were no major sea battles involving the Italian navy, there were several successful hit and run actions. During 1917, Italian torpedo boats ventured into the well defended port of Trieste and sank two Austrian battleships. In 1918, they enjoyed successes against Austrian shipping in the Adriatic.

At first, the Italian air force, the *Corpo Aeronautico Militare*, tended to use out-dated French fighter aircraft. At the start of they war, they had only 58 aircraft and 91 pilots which were mainly used for reconnaissance purposes. Even so, as the war progressed, its pilots won considerable success against the Austrians. Their leading ace was Francesco Baracca who shot down 34 enemy aircraft. Others with impressive combat records included Silvio Scaroni, Pier Piccio and Flavio Baracchini. During 1918, Italian designers produced the highly regarded Caproni CA heavy bomber and, later, the Pomilio PE fighter. The latter played an important role in the Battle of Vittorio Veneto.

4 ⌐ THE HOME FRONT

The domestic effects of this war, which had lasted beyond the most pessimistic estimates, were enormous, and their importance can hardly be calculated. We must not forget that in 1914 the Italian state was still young and delicate; only three years past its fiftieth anniversary; it was therefore bound to be seriously disturbed by the sort of tests it had to face.

From History of the Italian People *by Giuliano Procacci, 1968.*

It has been claimed that when Italy entered the war in 1915, precious few Italians knew what the war was about or what they were fighting for. Within the country, the differences between neutralists and interventionists continued and there were still those opposed to the war who openly campaigned for it to be brought to an end. As the war progressed, the powers of the government increased and the state became more authoritarian. Parliament was rarely consulted and, in order to avoid rumour and the spread of **defeatism**, the press subjected to strict censorship. In effect, the government in collaboration with the military and leading industrialists ran the country. In 1915, the country was both economically and militarily unprepared for war. Consequently, enormous demands were placed on Italian industry as it switched from peacetime to wartime production. Working hours were increased so that some laboured for up to 75 hours a week and women were employed in industry in greater numbers. The need to mobilise industry to meet the demands of war led to a need to set up an organisation to oversee war production in all the nation's factories. There was also a move towards centralisation as large companies and banks took over whole sections of the Italian economy. In some sectors of the economy production more than doubled. Government spending on the war meant that vast profits were to be made and the price of goods increased. Since jobs were plentiful and industrial wages high, this had little impact on factory workers. Even so, a black-market in scarce goods flourished and this allowed profiteers to make a good living. Soldiers home on leave from the front became aware of this and it added to their sense of grievance. During the course of the war, Italian morale varied according to successes on the battlefield. With no great victories to celebrate, it was particularly low during late 1916 and 1917

See page 40

defeatism a willingness to accept defeat as inevitable

at times when war-weariness led to disenchantment and defeatism. Such were the demands that Ministers for War did not last long and between 1915 and 1918 five different men held this position. By comparison, only two men held the post of Finance Minister. The German naval blockade was sufficiently successful to cause food shortages and during the summer of 1917, there were food riots in Turin. The Left did not help by persisting with its anti-war stance. Even though the Socialist Party's slogan was 'No support, no sabotage', there were those on the extreme Left who were prepared to act against their country's interests and actively engage in acts of sabotage. During 1917, they took advantage of the success of the Bolsheviks in Russia to campaign under the slogan – 'Not a man in the trenches next winter'. At one stage, the Pope urged Catholics to support an ending to the carnage and agree to a 'white peace' by which he meant a peace with no territorial gains at all. Strangely it was the disaster of Caporetto that re-galvanised Italy. In his first speech as the new Prime Minister, Vittorio Orlando told the Italian people 'the situation will not be discussed, it will be faced'. Afterwards Italian morale recovered and defeatism largely disappeared. Altogether, Italy mobilised 5,230,000 men that represented 14.4% of her total population. The balance sheet of the war left her with 650,000 dead, 947,000 wounded and a further 600,000 missing or prisoners-of-war. Of those mobilised, just over 39% became casualties. She also lost 846,333 tonnes of her merchant shipping. Between 1915 and 1918 the Italian people faced no great increase in personal taxation but received substantial loans from her allies – £459 million from Great Britain and £353 million from the United States. Even so, her gold reserves fell by £19m.

With the war over, as the euphoria of victory faded Italians waited anxiously to discover if the post-war peace conferences would honour the territorial gains promised by the Treaty of London in 1915.

5 ⌐ STRUCTURED AND ESSAY QUESTIONS

A *This section consists of questions that might be used for discussion (or written answers) as a way of expanding on the chapter and testing you understanding of it.*

1. Which groups in Italy wanted their country to remain neutral and not become involved in the war?
2. Would it be fair to say that Gabriele D'Annunzio was something of an eccentric character?
3. What aspects of the Treaty of London (1915) encouraged Italy's entry into the war?
4. In 1915, who was the better prepared for war, Italy or Austria–Hungary? (Refer to Table 7 on page 41).
5. For what reasons were the conditions on the Italian Front described as 'rigorous' and 'inhospitable'?
6. By the end of 1917, would it be fair to say that most Italians would have good reason to regret their decision to enter the war?

B *Essay questions.*

1. Was hatred of Austria the main reason why Italy entered the war on the side of the Allies in 1915?

2. 'Lacking in fighting spirit, they proved to be a liability to the Allies.' How valid is this view of the Italian contribution to the First World War?

6 ➭ DOCUMENTARY EXERCISE ON THE CONDITION OF THE ITALIAN ARMY DURING THE FIRST WORLD WAR

Study the source below and answer the questions which follow:

On the whole the Italian army, which had lost 600,000 men, had fought well, and the peasants flung into the trenches had done their duty with the same resigned determination that they had applied to their daily tasks as civilians. If one considers that, at least in the first two years of war, the Italian army was one of the least prepared and worst armed that fought on the various fronts in Europe, one cannot but feel respect for the tenacity and self-denial of the Italian soldier. At the outbreak of hostilities, the Italian forces lacked artillery, machine guns, trucks and officers. Officers had to be improvised with all haste, with results that may easily be imagined. As for the general staff and its commander until the defeat of Caporetto, General Cadorna, they were often unequal to the tasks they had to perform, and the incompatibilities of character between some of its main members certainly did not improve its efficiency. The defeat at Caporetto, which Cadorna blamed on the 'defeatism' that had wormed its way into the army, fostered by the 'reds' and 'blacks', was, rather, largely the result of lack of co-ordination between various armies.

From History of the Italian People *by Giuliano Procacci, 1968.*

1. *What is meant by*
   (a) *'incompatibilities of character'? (5 marks)*
   (b) *'defeatism'? (5 marks)*
2. *What evidence does the source provide of the readiness of the Italian army for war in 1915? (10 marks)*
3. *What does the author consider to be the reasons for the shortcomings of the Italian army? (10 marks)*
4. *How useful is this source to an historian studying fighting on the Italian Front during the First World War? (15 marks)*

7 ⌐ MAKING NOTES

Read the advice section about making notes on page xix of the Preface. Now consider the two important issues raised in this chapter: the reasons why Italy entered the war and how well its armies performed during the war. To be able to answer questions based on these issues complete the charts below.

VIEWS REGARDING ITALY'S ENTRY INTO THE WAR

Views of the neutralists.	
Views of the interventionists who favoured fighting on the side of France and Britain.	
Views of the interventionists who favoured fighting on the side of Germany and Austria.	

VIEWS REGARDING THE CONTRIBUTION OF THE ITALIAN ARMY TO THE WAR

Evidence to support the view that 'on the whole, the Italian army fought well'.	
Evidence to support the view that the Italian army had been a liability to the Allies.	

Post-War Italy – The Crisis Years, 1919–21

5

INTRODUCTION

In 1919, post-war Italy faced many economic and political problems. The cost of the war totalled some 148 billion lire – twice the amount of the government's total expenditure between 1861 and 1914! The nation's industries struggled to revert from wartime to peacetime production. Enforced wartime economies and saving now released money that Italians spent on all sorts of goods. Unfortunately, the economic boom this created was short lived. Neither industry nor agriculture could satisfy the increased demand for their products and this led to shortages, price rises and inflation. The amount of money in circulation in 1919 was ten times higher than that of 1914! Demobilised soldiers returning home found it difficult to adjust to a more humdrum domestic routine. Some either found it impossible or were disinclined to find work and joined together with the 150,000 wartime army deserters still in hiding to form marauding bands of brigands. As far as law and order was concerned, some rural localities became virtual no-go areas.

As it was soldiers returned home uncertain of what they had been fighting for, and not very proud of the way in which they had fought. Before questions could be asked about the regiments that broke and ran at Caporetto, Italians began to brag about the land they had won for Italy. All over Italy men opened litres of wine for the toast to victory. As the evenings grew colder so the arguments in the cafés grew warmer and, as time went on, tinged with bitterness. Why had Italy entered the conflict in 1915? The simple answer was that she wanted land. The returned soldiers and the café politicians all agreed that this was so.

From Mussolini & Italy *by C. Bayne-Jardine, 1966*

The pre-war problems of poverty and the north–south divide reappeared and recovery was hindered by shortages of coal and raw materials. People were not only hungry and disillusioned, they were soon to be humiliated by the terms of the peace settlement. Increasingly they turned to the parties of the Left – the Socialists and Communists – and there were protests, demonstrations and strikes, many of which became increasingly violent.

TABLE 8
*Date line showing events in
post-war Italy*

1 ⌐ THE PEACE SETTLEMENT

The peace conferences attended by the representatives of 32 countries opened in Paris on 18 January 1919. The Italian representatives were the prime minister, Vittorio Orlando and his foreign secretary, Sidney Sonnino. At Paris, separate treaties were agreed with each of the defeated countries. The most famous was that which involved Germany, the Treaty of Versailles. The treaty that was concerned with Austria, and was therefore of the greatest interest to Italy, was the Treaty of St Germain.

A *Differences of interpretation – the Treaties of London and St Germain*

An immediate problem was the fact that Italian claims were based on the Treaty of London agreed with France and Britain in 1915, whilst it was widely accepted that the terms of the peace treaties would be based on the ideas of the American President, Woodrow Wilson, as outlined in his Fourteen Points. The Treaty of London was a secret treaty and Italy and her allies had failed to inform Wilson of its terms. There had been opportunities – an Italian delegation had visited the United States in 1917 and Wilson had visited Rome on his way to Paris in 1919. The outstanding discrepancy between the Treaty of London and the 'Fourteen Points' was that the former was an ad *hoc* arrangement between the three powers concerned whilst Wilson's principles were regarded as an all-embracing basis for the post-war peace settlement. Briefly summarised, three of the most significant Points that concerned Italy were:

I. All diplomacy was to be conducted openly, no more secret negotiations.

IX. Italian frontiers to be adjusted along clearly recognised lines of nationality.

X. The various peoples of Austria–Hungary to be allowed to develop as individual nations.

Orlando and Sonnino were totally dissatisfied and insisted that their original claims should be settled in full. When no compromise was reached, the talks broke down and the Italian representatives walked out of the conference. This achieved nothing and the Treaty of St Germain was finally signed on 10 September 1919. In Italy, the interventionists were outraged and public opinion turned against France, Britain and the United States. The arrangements agreed at St Germain, referred to by Gabrielle D'Annunzio as 'a mutilated victory', were regarded as a betrayal of promises made in 1915 and scant reward for the efforts made by Italians during the war.

From the point of view of Woodrow Wilson, some of the territorial demands made by Italy infringed his view that self-determination must be the guiding principle in deciding new international frontiers. Granting her demands would not have been in accordance with the agreement

KEY ISSUE

The post war treatment of Italy – a 'mutilated victory'?

Based on the Treaty of London 1915	Agreed by the Treaty of St. Germain 1919
Trentino	Trentino and South Tyrol – agreed
Trieste	Trieste – agreed
Istria	Istria – agreed but excluding port of Fiume. The issue of Fiume was later settled by the Treaty of Rapallo, 1920 (see page 56)
Dalmatian Coast	Became part of the new Yugoslavia
Dodecanese Islands	Eventually ceded by Turkey in 1923 in return for payment
Share of Turkey if that country was partitioned	Although Greece was granted the . western part of Anatolia and Allied detachments were stationed on the east side of the Dardanelles, no allocation of Turkish land was made to Italy
A share of Germany's colonial territories	No allocation made to Italy. Instead former German colonies in Africa became mandates of Britain, France and South Africa. However, Italy was allowed to extend her Libyan territories and Britain gave her a small area of Somaliland.

CHART 3
Italy's post-war territorial claims

that Italian frontiers had to be drawn 'along clearly recognised lines of nationality' since it would have involved non-Italian peoples being forced to live under Italian rule. There were also other considerations. Italy was not able to bargain from a position of strength. Britain, and even more so France, had made considerably greater sacrifices in the war than Italy. In view of the fact that, after the Battle of Caporetto in 1917, British and French units had to be sent to bolster the Italian position along the River Piave, some considered that their Italian allies had become a liability. Neither Britain nor France were in a mood to be **magnanimous** and grant the Italians what they considered to be their rightful share of the spoils. It is also claimed that, at the conference table, Orlando, usually an intelligent and articulate man, failed to impress and present his case with sufficient vigour. He did not possess the obstinacy of the Frenchman Georges Clemenceau, the guile of David Lloyd George, the British Prime Minister, or the persuasiveness of the Serbian representative, Nicola Pasic, who presented his case well.

magnanimous show generosity

2 ⮑ THE ISSUE OF FIUME

If indeed the terms of the Treaty of St Germain represented 'a mutilated victory' to the Italians, it was the failure to gain Fiume (sometimes known as Rijeka), a port at the head of the Adriatic Sea, on the border between Italy and Croatia and formerly part of the Austro-Hungarian Empire, that caused the most disquiet and the greatest hurt. This is strange because, although Fiume had a sizable Italian population, Italy

PICTURE 13
Vittorio Orlando (1860–1952)

VITTORIO ORLANDO (1860–1952)

Born in 1860, Vittorio Orlando was raised in Palermo, Sicily. He became a professor of law and between 1903 and 1905 served in Giolitti's government as Minister of Education. In 1907, he was appointed Minister of Justice, a post he retained until 1909. A strong supporter of Italy's entry into the war, he became Minister of the Interior in 1916 and the following year was appointed wartime prime minister. His appointment, coming as it did after the debacle of the Battle of Caporetto, gave a boost to the nation's flagging morale. He was responsible for replacing Cadorna with Diaz and the following year the Italian army won a resounding victory over the Austrians at Vittorio Veneto. In 1919, he led the Italian delegation to the peace conferences in Paris but failed to gain all the territorial concessions promised by the Treaty of London in 1915. He walked out of the conference but returned later to sign the Treaty of St Germain. He returned home with his reputation undermined and resigned as prime minister in November 1919. Later that year, he was elected president of the Chamber of Deputies. An early supporter of Mussolini's Fascist government, he later withdrew his support after the murder of the prominent socialist, Giacomo Matteotti (see page 91). He resigned from the Chamber of Deputies in 1927 and afterwards devoted his time to lecturing and writing. In 1946, at the age of 76, he unexpectedly returned to politics and was elected president of the Constituent Assembly. The following year he was elected to the new Italian Senate but was defeated when he stood for the presidency of the Italian republic. He died in 1952.

did not originally claim it. At his rabble-rousing best, D'Annunzio declared, 'Fiume and Dalmatia belong to Italy by divine right as well as human law'. Fiume was one of the largest ports on the Adriatic Sea. It had strategic importance since it was the southern terminus of a railway line that led to Vienna and Budapest. Immediately after the war, the port was occupied by French, British and American troops. The arrival of Italian forces and the raising of the Italian flag over the city led to tension and there were incidents during which a number of French soldiers were killed and wounded. An international commission sent to Fiume decided that the port should be put under international control. For many Italians this decision proved the last straw and nationalists inflamed the situation by supporting D'Annunzio's view that if Italy failed to gain Fiume then their sacrifice would not have been worthwhile and their victory would be 'mutilated'.

A D'Annunzio's occupation of Fiume

In September 1919, the 'eccentric one-eyed poet and popular hero' led a force of some 2,000 so-called legionaries into Fiume and occupied the city. On his way to the city, he raided a military depot and **requisitioned** vehicles. On arrival in Fiume, General Luigi Pittaluga, commander of the Italian troops in the city, confronted D'Annunzio's force that comprised a mixed bag of ex-servicemen, self-styled patriots, students and all kinds of adventurers and rogues. With typical bravado, he challenged the general to shoot him first before turning his guns on his brother Italians. Pittaluga backed down and with a shout of 'Viva Fiume Italiana' welcomed him into the city. Elsewhere, the authorities took no action against him and Italians living in Fiume welcomed him as a liberator. The Italian press hailed his action as a triumph and some admirers tried to raise funds to support his venture. It is claimed that Benito Mussolini, editor of Il Popolo d'Italia raised over 3 million lire, though most of it went to supplement the funds of his political party and not to D'Annunzio. For more than a year, D'Annunzio ruled as 'Regent of Fiume'. In Fiume, he proclaimed a constitution, set up his own militia and even printed his own postage stamps. In his introduction to the new constitution, he wrote:

> The people of the free city of Fiume, ever mindful of its Latin fate and ever intent on realising its legitimate wishes, has decided to renew its governing principles in the spirit of its new life…offering them for fraternal election by those Adriatic communities which desire to put an end to all delay, to shake off oppressive subjugation, and rise up and be resurrected in the name of the new Italy.

requisitioned taken over by demand

PICTURE 14
D'Annunzio, Dante and Italy look at the Quarnaro

PICTURE 15
A postage stamp issued to emphasise the region's independence and earn revenue

He even went as far as to order the people to cut the heads off the eagles on the civic coat of arms since they represented the Austrian and not the Roman eagle! The men of his militia were the first to wear black uniforms, give the raised arm Roman salute and use enforced doses of castor oil to humiliate their opponents. All this, and much more, were later to be copied by Mussolini and his Fascists. From Fiume, D'Annunzio hurled defiance as he rounded on Italy's former wartime allies and insulted his country's Prime Minister, Francesco Nitti, by referring to him as a worthless coward. He skillfully used propaganda and political antics – parades, rallies, proclamations and emotive speeches – to maintain enthusiasm and keep his supporters in a state of continuous excitement. Some historians are of the view that he may have had ambitions to overthrow the Italian government and establish his own dictatorship. Gradually, Nitti began to exert pressure on him to withdraw. When in June 1920, Giovanni Giolitti returned for a fifth period in office, he negotiated a settlement with Yugoslavia over the issue of Fiume.

See pages 61–2

Q

What did D'Annunzio hope to achieve by the occupation of Fiume?

B *The Treaty of Rapallo, 1920*

In November 1920, Rapallo, a town south of Genoa and on the Ligurian Sea was the meeting place of Italian and Yugoslav delegates who had assembled in an effort to settle the issue of Fiume. At the meeting, Italy was represented by their Foreign Minister, Carlo Sforza, Ivanoe Bonhomi, the War Minister, and the distinguished general Pietro Badoglio. The Prime Minister, Giolitti, did not take part in the discussions but attended later to sign the final agreement. As a result of a **bilateral** settlement between Italy and Yugoslavia it was agreed that Italy should occupy the whole of Istria, Zara and a number of small islands in the Adriatic Sea – Cherso, Lussino, Lagosta and Pelagosa. The remaining islands and Dalmatia were to remain part of Yugoslavia. Fiume was to become an independent city under international control. The treaty was finally signed at the Villa Spinola on 12 November 1920. The treaty led to much improved relations between Italy and Yugoslavia and allowed both countries the chance to collaborate and expand their trading opportunities in the Balkans.

bilateral involving two sides

(NB. Be careful not to confuse this Treaty of Rapallo with another treaty of the same name that was signed a few months later, in April 1920, between the Soviet Union and Germany.)

↬

As a result of the Treaty of Rapallo, D'Annunzio's continued presence in Fiume seemed to serve little purpose. He did not see it that way and reacted by declaring war on Italy! As a result the existing blockade on the city was further tightened and there were skirmishes between D'Annunzio's supporters and the Italian army. Finally, the battleship, Andria Doria, was sent to bombard Fiume into submission. Although D'Annunzio swore to die in Fiume rather than surrender, on 5 January

1921, after 15 months in occupation, he finally led his legionaries out of the city.

On the one hand, the Fiume incident may be regarded as ridiculous or something akin to a comic opera. On the other, was there something more sinister about the events that suggested ill-boding omens for the future? Military aggression was received with popular acclaim and force was employed to gain political ends. Again, was it possible that D'Annunzio might have pre-empted Mussolini and himself become the Fascist dictator of Italy?

KEY ISSUE

The Fiume incident – ridiculous or a heroic act of defiance?

3 ⌐ POLITICAL PROBLEMS

Many Italians were deeply disappointed with their government's foreign policy failures They considered the failure to obtain the territories promised by the Treaty of London or to deal resolutely with D'Annunzio's occupation of Fiume to be to be signs of weakness. However, these were not the only problems that faced the government during the immediate post war period. Italy was still a poor country with large numbers of the peasantry and industrial workers living in poverty. Inflation had led to substantial price increases that were not matched by wage increases and the lira had fallen to just 20% of its pre-war value. A new American immigration law that restricted the entry of Italian immigrants to the United States further aggravated the problem of unemployment, already worsened by the return of demobilised soldiers. Burdened with war debts, with both industry and agriculture slow to recover from the war and her export trade virtually at a standstill, the Italian government seemingly had no answers to her chronic economic problems.

As the government became increasingly unpopular, peasants and workers became more militant and, some hoping to repeat the success of Lenin's Bolsheviks in Russia, caused trouble by engaging in demonstrations, strikes and riots. The demise of *transformismo* had started before the war and, with the war over, political parties with mass popular appeal appeared each with its own individual identity. However, *transformismo* still existed in the form of the Conservative-backed Liberal government of the day. Now it was under increasing pressure as public opinion polarised and Italians turned to other new political parties that offered radical alternatives.

Unable to cope with the chaos and disruption, Orlando's government finally fell in June 1919. In the elections that followed, the Socialist PSI won nearly 40% of the votes to become by far the largest party in the Chamber of Deputies. Campaigning for a programme of social reform, the Christian Democrats came second with 20% of the votes. Across the country as a whole, the PSI and DC controlled virtually the whole of northern and central Italy. The former ruling parties, the Liberals and the Conservatives (supporters of Giolitti, some Radicals and the Right Liberals), both lost heavily.

1919–1920	Francisco Nitti
1920–1921	Giovanni Giolitti
1921–1922	Ivanoe Bonomi
1922	Luigi Facta

TABLE 9
Prime Ministers 1919–22

CHART 4

Major Italian political parties

Partito Democrazia Cristiana (DC) – The Christian Democrat Party or *populari*	Established in 1919 by a Catholic priest, Luigi Sturzo, the Christian Democrat Party embraced a broad span of political views that extended from Catholics and Conservatives on the Right to moderate socialists on the Left. Generally referred to as the *populari*, it was not prepared to enter into an alliance with the old Liberals and was strongly opposed to the Communists. The party had its own trade union movement, the Italian Confederation of Workers (CIL) to rival that of the Socialists.
Partito Socialista Italiano (PSI) – Italian Socialist Party	A Socialist-type party had existed in an ill-defined form for many years. By 1920, the Italian Socialist Party had become well organised and could boast of a membership of 200,000. It was well supported in the northern industrial regions particularly in cities with a reputation for left-wing agitation such as Romagna and Turin. Nationally, it was backed by the mass circulation daily newspaper, *Avanti* and its own trade union movement, the General Confederation of Workers (CGL). The party was divided into Maximists and Minimists. The Maximists were anti-military and championed the cause of a proletarian revolution; the Minimists were more moderate and sought to achieve social reform by parliamentary means. Unwilling to enter an alliance with the Liberals, it showed little enthusiasm for going it alone in an attempt to gain power.
Partito Comunista Italiano (PCI) – Italian Communist Party	The Italian Communist Party was founded in 1921. It attracted left-wing extremists and many from the socialist PSI who were dissatisfied with the moderate policies of that party. It was to grow to become the largest Communist Party in Europe outside the Soviet Union.
Partito Republicano Italiano (PRI) – Italian Republican Party	A political party that was declining in importance. It championed the republican principles of Mazzini.
Partito futurismo – Political Futurist Party	More a movement than a political party, the Futurists were formed in 1918 by Filippo Marinetti. The Political Futurist Party aimed to bring about the 'renewal' of Italy. Members believed that Italy had a special mission in history and that the Italian people needed to be rejuvenated.
Partito Nazionale Fascista (PNF) – Fascist Party	Extreme right-wing political party founded by Benito Mussolini in 1919 (see page 73). It attracted support from all sections of Italian society from the working classes to the business/professional classes. By 1921, it had a membership of 152,000.

On 23 March 1919 at a hall in the Piazza San Sepulcro in Milan, Benito Mussolini took the first steps towards establishing a new political party. In a lengthy speech to a handful of supporters, largely war veterans and disgruntled socialists that attended the meeting, Mussolini said:

> The official Socialists want to give Italy an … imitation of the Russian experience. This all socialist thinkers are opposed to because Bolshevism, far from abolishing classes, entails a ferocious dictatorship. We are strongly opposed to all forms of dictatorship, whether of the sword or the cocked hat, of wealth or of numbers. The only dictatorship we do acknowledge is that of will and intelligence. We should quickly succeed in creating a number of *Fasci di Combattimento*, then we shall co-ordinate their activities in all centres of Italy.

Socialists (PSI)	156
Christian Democrats (DC)	101
Giolittians	91
Radicals	67
Right Liberals	23
Reformist Socialists	21
Other parties	49
(Seats contested 508)	

TABLE 10
The election of 1919

From a general viewpoint, the omens for the future success of Mussolini's new party seemed bleak. He fought the elections of 1919 on policies that were extremely left-wing, even Communist. He supported the abolition of the right of people to own private property and promised to give land to the peasants and allow workers to run their own factories. He also proposed increased taxes on the wealthy and the confiscation of all land owned by the Roman Catholic Church. Perhaps not surprisingly, his party failed to win a seat in the elections. In Milan, Mussolini, who gained just over 2% of the vote, suffered a personal humiliation at the hands of the Socialists. His jubilant opponents staged a mock funeral. The **cortège** stopped outside Mussolini's house and invited the Fascist leader to attend the funeral of his party. Their celebrations were to prove premature. Even so, it was clear that there was need for a re-think about the party's future policies.

cortège a funeral procession

Forming a long-lasting and stable government in Italy was not easy. The electoral system based on proportional representation, a system that allocated seats to parties according to their voting strength, made it difficult to form workable coalitions and no single party was large enough to form a majority government. Whilst the Christian Democrats refused to work with the Socialists, the Socialists steadfastly declined to be part of any **bourgeois** government. Consequently during the short period between July 1919 and October 1922, Italy had four different prime ministers, each of whom tried to survive on an uneasy alliance between the Liberals and the Christian Democrat Party. This meant that the country was governed by unstable and short-lived coalitions, and some even wondered if Italy was becoming ungovernable.

bourgeois representative of the middle classes

4 ↪ *BIENNO ROSSO* – 'TWO RED YEARS'

The new prime minister was Francisco Nitti (1868–1953), a former university professor and economist. In an effort to restore political stability, he tried to win the support of the Socialists for his moderate policies. Meanwhile, generated by the suffering caused by the country's severe economic problems, the unrest continued and increased in ferocity. The people were paying the price of rising inflation. The poor were affected by rising prices which lowered their living standards, whilst people who had made the effort to save saw the value of their savings fall and become near worthless. As major firms went bankrupt so unemployment soared to two million. Trade unions, now with a record membership of over two million, pressed for higher wages and strikes were commonplace. Poverty brought with it desperation and, as many turned to crime, so across the country theft and violence reached epic proportions. During 1919, as millions of workers took part in strikes, the indecisive Liberal government of the day appeared powerless to restore order in the riot-swept towns and cities.

A *Land seizures and factory occupations*

KEY ISSUE

The reasons for the land seizures and occupation of factories.

In the countryside, striking peasants refused to harvest the crops and so endangered food supplies to the towns and cities. By favouring taking all land into public ownership, the Socialists lost the support of the peasants. Even so, illegal land occupations by the peasants became commonplace. Peasant Leagues safeguarded the interests of the oppressed peasantry. Some were organised by the Socialists and others by the Catholic Christian Democrats, the *popolari*. They both carried out acts of terror – they burned down buildings, slaughtered animals and even attacked the landlords and their agents. They also seized and illegally occupied uncultivated land. This caused many of the landowners to call it a day, sell their holdings and get out whilst they could. The position was made worse when peasants who had earlier gone to the towns in search of work returned to the countryside. The Leagues acted against them and forced them to move on. With something approaching civil war taking place in the countryside, the government seemed powerless to act but instead issued decrees that gave their official approval to these illegal acts. It seemed only a matter of time before industrial workers would follow their example. During 1920, angered by the breakdown of their pay negotiations, workers in Bergamo became the first to occupy their factories. They were urged on by the extreme Left-wing syndicalists of the *Unione Sindacale Italiana*. Their action quickly spread to workers of the industrial heartland in the north that included the cities of Milan, Turin and Genoa before spreading to central and the southern Italy, to reach Rome, Florence, Naples and Palermo in Sicily. The factory occupations, which were accompanied by red flag waving parades and even music provided by workers' bands, were not sit-ins since the workers continued to produce goods. Aided by sympathetic railway workers, they were also able to market their manufactured goods. In some factories, workers' councils were set up similar to the soviets established in Russia by the Bolsheviks. The movement spread so quickly that, within three days, over 400,000 workers had occupied their factories. As the number of factories occupied grew to exceed 600 and involved over two million workers, the action assumed the

Q

During the years 1920–1, how close was Italy to revolution?

proportions of a widespread general strike. However, at a critical moment, the employers offered a 20% pay increase and this proved sufficient for the leaders of the General Confederation of Labour to call off the strike.

B *Government reaction*

After a year in office, Nitti resigned to be replaced by the veteran politician, 78-year-old Giovanni Giolitti. During his fifth period as Italian prime minister, Giolitti tried to hold his government together by avoiding decisions that might be unpopular and add to the general discontent. This explains why he was slow to remove D'Annunzio from Fiume or take any action when, in 1920, peasants in southern Italy began illegally to seize land, and workers first occupied their factories. Giolitti believed that his negative policies would allow him to survive and that eventually popular support for the Socialists and Communists would decline. Others, property owners, industrialists and those with commercial interests, did not share his view. Exasperated by his indecisiveness, they took measures to protect their land and businesses by recruiting small private armies. In 1921, Giolitti offended Roman Catholics when he proposed to tax any income received from bonds. Such income was a main source of revenue for the Church at that time. He resigned in 1921 and the King called for elections.

C *The elections of 1921*

The run up to elections of 1921 was a period of terror and confusion. During a six-week campaign, the violence in the streets reached a new intensity as black-shirted Fascist *squadristi* went on the rampage using truncheons and castor oil to humiliate, beat and even murder their opponents. With the Fascists, Socialists and Anarchists engaged in street battles, it is estimated that some three thousand were killed during these encounters. Fascist violence also extended into the provinces where Socialist councils were forcibly removed and the Peasant Leagues attacked and disbanded.

In the municipal elections of 1920, Foiana della Chiana was won by the Socialists. Early in April 1921, the Socialist mayor received a letter from the general secretary of the Fasci in Tuscany, in which the mayor and his councillors were invited to resign within a week if they did not wish to expose themselves and their families to Fascist violence. The mayor and the councillors did not obey. On 12 April more than 200 Fascists … made an 'expedition of propaganda' to the little town. They looted the town hall and the premises of the Peasants Union. On 20 April, a second 'expedition' was carried out. Twenty Fascists confiscated the red flag which the Communists usually ran up over the town hall and then proceeded to a neighbouring village on another 'propagandist trip'. On their return, they were ambushed by a group of peasants. Their lorry was received with a hail of bullets. The driver fell wounded and the car swerved into a tree … two of the Fascists were killed but the remainder managed to escape … Now began the reprisals. Five lorry-loads of Fascists left Florence early in the morning… The authorities, as usual, allowed the Fascists a free hand. The Fascists gave themselves up to ransacking and burning houses … A peasant, guilty of being the brother of a Communist, was shot … Another was forced, under threat of death, to speak against the 'violence of the Socialists' … In the night, the Fascists returned and ransacked the farmhouses, one by one, terrifying women, children and the old. The authorities, needless to say, took no action. They were engaged in rounding up the Communists who had hidden themselves in the country. Of those guilty of being involved in the ambush, four were sentenced to thirty years of imprisonment. None of the Fascists who took part in these events suffered in any way whatsoever.

From The Fascist Dictatorship in Italy *by Gaetano Salvemini, 1928*

The violence was far from one sided. Anarchists were responsible for the bombing of a Milan theatre that killed 18 people and left scores wounded. There was also a bungled attempt to assassinate Mussolini by a young Anarchist, Biagio Masi. He fled to Trieste where he was arrested. The police, military and the magistrates appeared to turn a blind eye to the Fascist outrages whilst some, clearly acting on orders, assisted the *squadristi* in their reign of terror.

In an entry in his diary on 24 November 1921, Mario Piazzesi, himself once a member of the Fascist *squadrismo*, gave his reasons for supporting the Fascists:

For some time, a new Italy had been forming, an Italy of professionals, skilled workers, peasants, the common people, all of those who had fought in the war and have patiently put up with things. But after a period of uncertainty, it is realising what it has achieved and is experiencing a feeling of pride at having shaken off a certain sense of inferiority with regard to other Europeans … The vast majority of the nation, which before was holding its breath awaiting imminent catastrophe, now feels that the Red tempest is about to be blown away. The old liberal democracy, which in its day worked for the good of the nation, has given ground on all fronts and its prestige reduced to a minimum. But most interesting changes are taking place at the top … those in authority are being drawn towards the Fascist movement. Like those who have joined the *squadrismo*, they realise that Fascism offers them the last hope that the powers and responsibilities entrusted to them will not be swept away by chaos … their motives for their shift in allegiance are honest ones. Here are the reasons why this movement made up of what are, lets face it, hotheads, is winning the support of the majority of the nation.

From Diario di Uno Squadrista *by Mario Piazzesi, 1981*

PICTURE 16

Fascist squadristi *in readiness for a 'propaganda trip'*

Mussolini recognised the opportunity offered by the political chaos. In spite of the fact that his Fascist *squadristi* were engaged in a campaign of violence against his political opponents, he presented himself as the only man likely to restore law and order and put an end to the threat posed by the Socialists and Communists. Consequently a growing number of men, many of them moderate and law abiding, turned to the Fascists to remedy the situation.

Whilst the support for the Socialists and assorted centre parties declined, the Fascist PNF won 35 seats. Apart from Mussolini who was elected a deputy for Milan, other Fascist deputies elected included Count Dino Grandi, Cesare de Veechi and Roberto Farinacci, all destined to have prominent roles in Italian politics in the future. Mussolini took his seat in the Chamber of Deputies as the leader of his party.

Socialists (PSI)	123
Christian Democrats (DC)	107
Radicals	68
Giolittians	47
Right Liberals	43
Fascists (PNF)	35
Reformist Socialists	24
Communists (PCI)	15
Other parties	73
(Seats contested 535)	

TABLE 11

The elections of 1921

The elections over, the violence continued. In Parliament, Fascist deputies seized a Socialist, known to have been a deserter during the war, and ejected him from the building. Another Socialist deputy, Giacomo Matteotti, complained that 'private justice is in operation replacing public justice'.

D *The Treaty of Pacification, 1921*

Giolitti's successor, Ivanoe Bonomi, a moderate Socialist, formed a government with the support of the Liberals and Christian Democrats. In an effort to end the continuing violence, the Church authorities called on the Fascists and Socialists to agree to a truce during Holy Week. Mussolini refused but later agreed to attend. Later Bonhomi invited political leaders to attend a meeting. This time the Fascists and the Socialists accepted the invitation but the Communists and the *popolari*, representatives of DC, refused to attend. In order to allow the everyday lives of the Italian people to return to normality, the Fascist and Socialist representatives agreed to a Treaty of Pacification and to suspend their on-going conflict. From the start some Fascists ignored the treaty and continued with their acts of terrorism whilst Grandi and Balbo, members of the party hierarchy, spoke openly against the treaty. They even hinted that D'Annunzio might be better suited to the party leadership than Mussolini! The pressure told. Mussolini accused the Socialists of breaking the terms of the treaty and then withdrew from the arrangement himself.

Bonhomi's period in office was brief and after ten months, he gave way to Luigi Facta. Facta fared no better. Deserted by the Christian Democrats, he resigned but had to be restored to office since no one was prepared to take his place! On the very day that Facta formed his new government, the Italian trade unions called for a general strike in protest at the violence used by the Fascist *squadrismo*.

E *To what extent had Italy become impossible to govern?*

The period 1919 to 1921 witnessed the gradual break-up of the old ruling Liberal alliance and a decline in the support for the largest opposition party, the Socialist PSI. By making so many concessions, the Liberals had forfeited the backing of many of its traditional supporters. A decision to requisition food supplies and sell it to the poor at more affordable prices had alienated producers and shopkeepers. Some workers resented the fact that the government allowed certain unions to operate a **closed shop** by forcing sections of industry to employ only union members. Ex-soldiers felt that they had been let down by the government and regarded their attempts to appease the Socialists as a betrayal of everything they had earlier fought for. As a result of all this, the Liberals were becoming sidelined and an increasingly irrelevant force in Italian politics. Some even wondered if they had become too conciliatory and in so doing lost the will to govern.

The PSI also faced difficulties. The extent of the industrial unrest had become a cause for great concern amongst the landowners, industrialists and the upper and middle classes. Even some Socialists wondered it events had gone too far. Seen as the main opposition to the militant Left, the Fascists gained in popularity and the membership of the party increased considerably. In addition, ex-soldiers and the military in general remembered that during the war there had been Socialists prepared to betray them by striking or attempting to sabotage the war effort. The party also faced divisions within its own ranks. Some felt that the party had for too long followed a moderate line and a third of the membership departed to join the more militant Communist PCI.

In the elections of 1921, both the Liberals and their supporters and the Socialists had lost ground. With neither the Socialists or the largely

closed shop
membership of a union a condition of employment

KEY ISSUE

Reasons for the decline in the support for the Socialists.

Catholic Christian Democratic Party (DC) prepared to form a working alliance with what remained of the Liberals, the country edged towards political breakdown. The main beneficiaries of the chaos were the Fascists, who were biding their time on the sidelines waiting for their opportunity. It had become increasingly clear that the only remedy for the situation was a period of authoritarian government. Were Italians ready to sacrifice their liberty in exchange for order, discipline and strong leadership?

5 ⤳ STRUCTURED AND ESSAY QUESTIONS

A *This section consists of questions that might be used for discussion (or written answers) as a way of expanding on the chapter and testing your understanding.*
1. To what extent were the terms of the Treaty of London (1915) fulfilled in 1919?
2. Why did the ownership of Fiume become such a contentious issue?
3. Within the Italian Socialist Party, what were the differences between 'Maximists' and 'Minimists'?
4. During the post-war period, what was the impact of rising inflation on the Italian people?
5. What were the activities the Fascist *squadristi* intended to achieve?

B *Essay questions.*
1. How successful were Italy's post-war governments in dealing with problems facing the country?
2. 'Impossible to govern.' To what extent is this a valid assessment of the condition of Italy during the period 1919–21?

6 ⤳ MAKING NOTES

Read the advice about making notes on page xix of the Preface: How to use this book, and then make your own notes based on the following headings and questions.

1. *The Peace Settlement.*
   (a) In what way did the Treaty of London (1915) infringe Woodrow Wilson's Fourteen Points?
   (b) Why did Italians consider their treatment in 1919 to represent a 'mutilated victory'?
   (c) Why did Britain and France fail to support Italy's territorial claims at the end of the war?
2. *The issue of Fiume.*
   (a) What was the basis of Italy's claim to Fiume?
   (b) What was the composition of the force that joined D'Annunzio's occupation of Fiume?

    (c) To what extent did D'Annunzio impose his own dictatorial rule on the port?

    (d) Why did he finally withdraw from Fiume in 1921?

3. *Political problems.*

    (a) In what ways did the fall in the value of the lira affect the Italian people?

    (b) Which Italian political parties might be considered (i) right-wing, (ii) centre and (iii) left-wing?

    (c) What were the aims of the Futurists?

    (d) What is meant by a system of proportional representation?

4. Bienno Rosso – *'The Red Years'.*

    (a) What steps did Italian workers take to indicate their discontent?

    (b) What were the aims of the syndicalists?

    (c) How successful were the steps taken by Giolitti to remedy the situation?

    (d) What was the reaction of the Fascists to developments in Italy at this time?

    (e) Why did an increasing number of Italians support the Fascists?

    (f) Did the Treaty of Pacification (1921) succeed in its aims?

The March on Rome (1922) – The Fascists in Power

6

INTRODUCTION

D'Annunzio's occupation and regime in Fiume might well be considered the first experiment in Fascism. What was to prove significant was the hesitation the Italian government showed in dealing with the crisis since a similar lack of resolve was to be repeated in 1922 with far more dire consequences. Whatever their shortcomings, the Liberal governments of Italy struggled to turn a struggling economy and backward society into a more advanced and progressive state. In spite of the dubious merits of *transformismo*, the country survived as a constitutional monarchy run on the Piedmontese pattern. By 1914, the Italian people enjoyed universal male suffrage and were free to elect their representatives to the Chamber of Deputies. They also enjoyed the full range of personal freedoms. This was about to be swept away by Mussolini and his Fascists.

1883	Benito Mussolini born
1902	Teacher at elementary school in Gualtieri
1903	Moved to Switzerland
	Began association with Angelina Balabanoff
	Arrest and deported back to Italy
1904	Returned to Italy to complete his military service
1911	Supported general strike in Forli
1912	Appointed editor of socialist newspaper *Avanti*
1913	Stood as a candidate but failed to win election at Forli
1914	Supported Italian neutrality in the war
	Founded his own newspaper *Popolo d'Italia* which advocated Italian entry into the war
1915	Married Rachele Guidi
	Joined the army and served in Bersaglieri Regiment
1917	Wounded and discharged
1919	Founded the Fascist Party
	D'Annunzio, who had occupied Fiume, regarded as a possible rival
	Election debacle with Fascists failing to win any seats
1920	Italian government forced D'Annunzio to withdraw from Fiume
1921	Elected to Parliament as one of 35 successful Fascist candidates
	Made to abandon support for Treaty of Pacification
	New Programme brought major policy changes
1922	The Fascist 'March on Rome'

TABLE 12
Date line showing Mussolini's early life and rise in politics

1 ⌐ BENITO MUSSOLINI

A *His childhood*

The child born to Alessandro and Rosa Mussolini on 29 July 1883 was christened Benito Andrea Amilcare. He was named Benito after the Mexican republican leader, Benito Juarez, who had earlier led a revolt against the domination of his land by the Church and the aristocracy. Benito Mussolini's birthplace was a cottage in the hamlet of Verano di Costa, outside the village of Predappio and near the town of Forli in Romagna. The cottage included a room that served as the only classroom of the village school at which his mother was the teacher. His parents presented something of a contrast. Alessandro Mussolini, the son of a poor peasant, was a staunch left-wing republican who had no formal education but had taught himself to read and worked as a part-time blacksmith. He was a man of strong character and a strict disciplinarian but he was also given to heavy drinking and womanising. His wife Rosa was the local schoolmistress and her earnings provided most of the family income. A devout Catholic, she saw to it that her children were baptised and went to church regularly. The couple had two other children – Arnaldo, a son born in 1885, and a daughter, Edvige, born three years later. At birth, there were fears that the young Benito might be dumb but he eventually learned to speak and appeared to be quite a bright child. A limited income meant that the home was sparsely furnished and the food plain – 'black bread and soup … with meat on

PICTURE 17
Alessandro Mussolini, the future Italian dictator's father

PICTURE 18
Rosa Mussolini, the future Italian dictator's mother

PICTURE 19
Benito Mussolini's birthplace at Predappio

Sundays'. Alessandro was a local Socialist councillor who regularly welcomed left-wing **malcontents** to his home and was frequently arrested for his political activities. Although he showed Benito little paternal affection, he did greatly influence his outlook and political views. He brought him up to be aware of the injustices that existed in society and to hate the oppression of the workers and their families by the upper classes and the Church. It is claimed that, as a child, Benito Mussolini was ill tempered and difficult to control, but is this a true picture?

Many stories have been told about Benito Mussolini's childhood, but how far can we believe them? Apart from Mussolini's own account, there are stories told by his Fascist admirers when he was dictator and those by his Socialist and other opponents after his downfall and death. We can possibly disregard the tales told by some of his critics of how he tore live chickens to pieces and put out their eyes; but even if we accept only the stories of his supporters, a contradictory picture emerges of little Benito. We are told that he spent many hours alone in his father's house reading books whilst his schoolmates were playing games; and we are also told that he became involved in savage fights with other boys, attacking them with knives.

From Mussolini *by Jasper Ridley, 1997*

He was first sent as a boarder to a school at Faenza run by the Salesians, a Franciscan religious order. He later recalled his experiences there with some bitterness. He was victimised because his father was a Socialist and often beaten. He particularly loathed the humiliation of being made to sit at a table set aside for those whose families could not afford the full school fees. In 1893, he led a pupil revolt against the quality of the food provided and was expelled. For a time, he had home tuition provided by his mother but was eventually sent to a more liberal establishment, the Collegio Giosue Carducci, at Forlimpopoli. The easy-going regime did not improve his behaviour and he was frequently suspended from school. Nevertheless, he completed six years of study and gained a qualification that allowed him to teach in elementary schools.

B *Adolescence and early adult years*

As a teenager, Benito Mussolini enjoyed an irascible and somewhat hot-blooded lifestyle. He had numerous casual affairs and visited brothels and, when resisted, was not above rape. Since he was ill disciplined and his behaviour often objectionable to the point of being bizarre, he made few close friends and largely kept to himself. He followed a **bohemian** life-style. He appeared unkept and found pleasure in drinking, gambling and womanising. He was known to threaten anyone who dared to criticise his way of life. In 1902, at the age of 19, he became a temporary teacher at a school in Gualtieri but his behaviour soon upset many parents who kept their children away from school. It was at this time that he first took an interest in local politics and wrote articles for left-wing newspapers and magazines.

malcontents
dissatisfied people

Q
What aspects of his youth and early years might have influenced Mussolini's character and political outlook?

bohemian
unconventional, setting aside normal standards of behaviour

PICTURE 20
Mussolini aged 14

PICTURE 21
Mussolini aged 21 living in poverty in Switzerland

PICTURE 22
Mussolini aged 29 and editor of
Avanti

C *Socialist and agitator*

In 1903, Mussolini made his way to Switzerland. The reason for his departure remains uncertain – to get away from his parents, to avoid military service or to escape from creditors are possible explanations. In Switzerland, he lived in dire poverty. He wandered the streets as a vagrant, living with other down-and-outs and occasionally found a bed in a **doss-house**. Later, in his autobiography published in 1928, he recalled those hard times:

doss-house a cheap lodging house

> From ten until eleven I stay in the public lavatory, from eleven to twelve under an old barge. The wind blows from Savoy and is cold. I return into the town and spend the rest of the night under the Grand Pont. In the morning I look at myself out of curiosity in the windows of a shop. I am unrecognizable. I meet a man from Romagna. I tell him briefly of my affairs. He laughs at me. I curse him. He puts his hand in his pocket and gives me fifty *centesimi*. I thank him. I hasten to a shop of a baker and buy a piece of bread. I feel as though I had a fortune. For twenty-six hours I had not eaten.

He was only saved from hunger by begging or an allowance sent by his mother, money that she could barely afford. In an effort to find employment, he worked in a chocolate factory, as a manual labourer on a building site, for a baker and then a wine merchant. During this time, he met Angelica Balabanoff, the Communist daughter of a wealthy landowning Ukrainian. She befriended him and encouraged him to further develop his political views by reading the works of Karl Marx and the German philosophers, Georg Hegel, Friedrich Nietzsche, and Georges Sorel, a French syndicalist. Later, after he became the dictator of Italy, she became his bitter enemy and critic. In 1903, the Swiss police arrested Mussolini as a political agitator. He was expelled and sent him back to Italy. The following year, he spent some time in France before returning to Switzerland where he again failed to find regular employment and had to live in poverty. Encouraged by Victor Emmanuel III's **amnesty** for all deserters, at the age of 21, he returned to Italy and there finally completed his military service. His mother's death later that year caused him much grief, born largely of the regret for the anguish he had caused her in his earlier years.

> **amnesty** a general pardon

PICTURE 23
Rachele Guidi who, in 1915, became Mussolini's wife

D *From Socialist and pacifist to nationalist and interventionist*

On his discharge from the army, Mussolini continued to write articles for the left-wing press and became active in local politics. His writing showed an outspoken and aggressive style and he made virulent attacks on the Church and the Italian ruling classes and *bourgeoisie*. During this time, he met and lived with Rachele Guidi, whom he married in 1915. In spite of his numerous infidelities, she remained a devoted wife and good mother to their children. His writing and speeches began to attract attention, and his arrest for supporting a general strike at Forli in 1911 made him a hero of the violent Left. Appointed editor of the Socialist newspaper, *Avanti* (Forward), he succeeded in greatly increasing the paper's circulation and won acclaim for his work. Persisting with his encouragement for violence and mass demonstrations, in the 1913 elections he stood as the Socialist candidate for Forli. He failed to get elected. When a European war broke out in 1914, Mussolini first took the view that it was a capitalist conflict with which the Italian *proletariat* should not become involved. As the war progressed, he radically changed his views and started his own newspaper, *Il Popolo d'Italia*, which he used to encourage entry into the war. He, together with Gabriele D'Annunzio and Riccotto Garibaldi, son of the great patriot, were the leading figures in the campaign to promote Italy's involvement. Mussolini also urged young men to form groups and campaign in the streets for Italian entry into the war. These groups he called *Fasci di Combattimento*. The Socialists, who expelled him from the Party, regarded his change of heart as an act of betrayal. In August 1915, Mussolini joined the army. He served in the highly regarded Bersaglieri Regiment and saw action in the trenches on the Italian front. He was promoted first to corporal and then sergeant. In 1917, he was badly wounded when a grenade thrower accidentally misfired. After a period in hospital, he was discharged. For the remainder of the war, he used his newspaper to encourage the war effort. The war over, Mussolini recognised the opportunity to further his own views

> **KEY ISSUE**
>
> *Mussolini's purpose in creating the* Fasci di Combattimento.

and political career presented by the distress and disillusionment that followed.

2 ⌐ THE THIRD FASCIST PARTY CONFERENCE, NOVEMBER 1921

At their Third Party Conference held in 1921, Mussolini formally turned his movement into a political party – the National Fascist Party. In each of the provinces, the leader of the party would be the **ras**. The *ras* was to have absolute power over Party members. He also ended his party's anti-monarchist and anti-Church stance. He told the assembled delegates:

ras formerly an Abyssinian prince but latterly the name adopted by local Fascist leaders

> I do not regret that I was once a Socialist, I have burned all my bridges with the past and feel no nostalgia. Our aim is not to introduce socialism but leave it behind … One hears it that all the masses must be won over … we do indeed wish to serve them, to educate them, but we also intend to flog them when they make mistakes. We want to raise their intellectual and moral level in order to … introduce them to the history of the nation … At the same time we are hereby warning them that when the interests of the nation are at stake … the proletariat as well as the bourgeoisie must take a back seat … I urge all of you to remain faithful to the … features of Fascism. This is our pledge: each day to love ever more deeply that adorable mother whose name is Italy.

A *The 'New Programme of the National Fascist Party'*

The Conference also received and approved a lengthy policy document the 'New Programme of the National Fascist Party'. A resumé of the main features of the programme are given in a simplified form below:

The New Programme of the National Fascist Party

Bases

Fascism has now become a political party in order to tighten its discipline and clarify its creed.

The Nation is not simply a sum of individual beings … it is the combination of all the values of the race.

The State

The State should be reduced to its main function of preserving political and judicial order.

Problems that concern the individual as a citizen of the State, and concern the State as a means of defending the supreme national interest, are the responsibility of Parliament.

The Church must not infringe the sovereignty of the State. The Church must be allowed freedom to exercise its spiritual mission.

Corporations

Corporations must be promoted for two purposes – as a means of increasing national solidarity, and as a means for increasing production. The Fascist Party intends to fight for the following principles:

- an eight-hour working day for all wage earners,
- providing workers protection against accidents, sickness and old age,
- worker representation in the management of all industries,
- management by those who are morally worthy and technically qualified, encouragement of the ownership of small farms.

Domestic policy

The Party intends to improve and dignify the level of political behaviour so that public and private morality will be of the same standard.

Foreign policy

Italy will become the upholder of Latin civilisation in the Mediterranean. It will impose firmly the authority of its law over peoples of various nationalities who have been annexed to Italy.

Financial and economic policy

Officials in public administration will bear the responsibility for any acts of negligence that cause injury to others.

Control will be exercised over the financial obligations (payment of taxes) of all citizens of the State.

Steps will be taken to protect agriculture and manufacturing from foreign competition.

Immediate objectives requiring immediate attention are:

- the balancing of the budget of the State,
- the safeguarding of taxpayers' money,
- the simplification of the system for collecting taxes,
- the ensuring that public works are really in the interests of the public.

New public works projects to include:

- completion and reorganisation of the railway system,
- electrification of the railway system,
- improvement and extension of the road system,
- improvement of port facilities.

The return to private enterprise of those industries that have been mismanaged by the State.

The ending of the monopolies held by the post and telegraph systems.

Social policy
The right to own private property guaranteed.
An end to the struggle between different classes.
Strikes in the public services to be prohibited.

Education policy
Intensify the struggle against illiteracy.
Extend compulsory education.
Schools to equip Italy's future soldiers with adequate moral and physical training.
Control of school curricula.
Financial rewards for teachers.

Justice
Improved measures for dealing with delinquency.
Penalties for breaking the law to take the form of both punishment and corrective training.

National defence
Every citizen to be obliged to do compulsory military service.

CHART 5
The New Programme of the National Fascist Party

It might fairly be claimed that much of the Fascist programme would appear in the election manifesto of any major British political party. From an Italian point of view, the programme offered something for everybody whatever their status or former party allegiance. Since so much offered prospects for a better future, it was possible to overlook its less appealing features – the supremacy of the sovereignty of the State, denial of the right to strike and compulsory military service. More importantly, nowhere does the programme guarantee the continuation of democratic government or fundamental human rights, particularly freedom of expression.

3 ⌐ THE MARCH ON ROME, 1922

TABLE 13
Date line showing the key events leading up to the March on Rome

31 July 1922	Socialists call for a general strike
	Action by *squadristi* to smash strike. Called off after one day
16 October	Plans made for a Fascist uprising
24 October	Fascist Congress in Naples
27 October	Fascists gather at three assembly points in readiness for march on Rome Fascists seize strategic buildings in some towns and cities
	Facta urged the King to introduce martial law
28 October	Victor Emmanuel agrees to declare martial law but later changes his mind
	Mussolini refuses offer of a post in a government led by Salandra
29 October	King invites Mussolini to form a government
30 October	Mussolini arrives in Rome and is appointed prime minister Fascist victory parade in Rome

A *Background*

See pages 60–1

The decision of the Socialists to call for a general strike played into Mussolini's hands. On his orders, the *squadristi* were ordered into the industrial towns and cities to cause terror and smash the strike. In Ancona, Leghorn and Genoa, the headquarters of the Socialists were burned to the ground and their presses destroyed. By the end of the first week in August, the Socialist authorities in Milan had been forcibly overthrown and the strike ended. On 24 October 1922, Mussolini addressed a large party gathering at the San Carlo opera house in Naples. In a rambling speech clearly aimed at intimidating Victor Emmanuel III and the Prime Minister, Facta, he said:

> … we are at the point when either the arrow shoots forth from the bow or the tightly drawn bowstring breaks! … Gentlemen, this problem … has to be faced as a problem of force. Every time in history that strong clashes of interests and ideas occur, it is force that ultimately decides the matter. That is why we have gathered and powerfully equipped and resolutely disciplined our legions – so that if a clash must decide the matter on the level of force, victory will be ours …

He concluded:

> And now Fascists and citizens of Naples … It is good that we have been able to come from every corner of the land to get acquainted with you and see you as you are, a courageous people who face up to life's struggle Roman-style … Long live Italy! Long live Fascism!

At the end of his speech, the Fascist delegates rose to a man to applaud and chant '*A Roma*', 'To Rome'. On 26 October, a desperate Facta reshuffled his government and offered to include a number of Fascists in his administration. Not so easily won over, Mussolini was too ambitious to accept a secondary role. He told his fellow Fascists that he did not intend to come to power 'by the servants' door'.

B *The March*

The planned Fascist *coup* involved the convergence on Rome of three columns from points outside the city. The first column under Perone Compagni was to advance from Civitavecchia on the coast, the second from Monterotondo was to be led by Ulisse Zgliori whilst the third, commanded by Giuseppe Bottai, was to move on Rome from Tivoli to the east. The furthest assembly point was only 30 kilometres from the city. Altogether an estimated 30,000 to 50,000 blackshirted Fascists were supposed to take part.

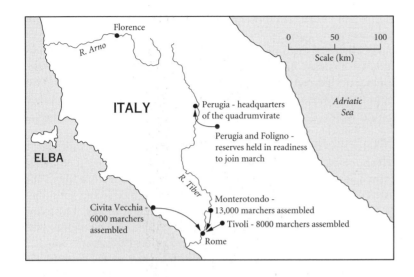

MAP 6
The March on Rome

The overall responsibility for the march was left to his lieutenants, a *Quadrumvir* or quadrumvirate consisting of Italo Balbo, Michele Bianchi, Emilo De Bono and Cesare De Vecchi. At this point, Facta found sufficient courage to urge Victor Emmanuel III to declare martial law and use the army to defend Rome against the Fascists. The King, acting on the advice of other ministers, recognised that public opinion had turned in favour of the Fascists and was uncertain of the extent to which he could rely on his 12,000 troops. Although his army commander, General Badoglio, assured him that the army could, if required, 'restore order in no time', the King dithered. During the night of 27 October, Fascists attempted to take over strategic points – post offices, railway stations and local government buildings – in towns and cities in north and central Italy. On the morning of the following day, the columns began their march on Rome. Mussolini had made his way back from Naples to the offices of his newspaper in Milan. He remained there, close to the Swiss frontier, in case things went wrong and he had to make his escape.

Sabotage of the railways meant that many Fascists failed to reach their assembly points on time or at all. Those that did were poorly armed with shotguns, farm implements and bludgeons. Heavy rain and weariness soon took their toll and as some Fascists' enthusiasm dwindled, so they dropped out. Victor Emmanuel III, who had always behaved correctly as a constitutional monarch and had shown no fondness for the Fascists, was in a difficult position. Within his own family, he was aware that his mother, ex-queen Margherita, sympathised with the Fascists, as did his cousin, the Duke of Aosta. He feared that he might be forced to abdicate in favour of the popular and personable duke. He was also aware that a number of his generals favoured the Fascists and were even involved in the march. To use those generals still loyal to him to break up the march risked open conflict and even civil

KEY ISSUE

The King's reluctance to act.

war. When he reached Rome from his country home, his first inclination was to declare martial law and defend the city. Barely two hours later, when the document authorising such action was placed before him, he changed his mind and refused to sign. In doing so, Victor Emmanuel handed what advantages he had to Mussolini. The King still hoped that Mussolini would serve in a government lead by Antonio Salandra, the former wartime prime minister, but now the Fascist leader would accept nothing other than the premiership.

Later that day, Victor Emmanuel gave way completely and made a telephone call, followed by a telegram, inviting the Fascist leader to form a government. Mussolini took an overnight train from Milan and arrived in Rome early the following morning. He received an enthusiastic reception. That afternoon, against the King's wishes, Mussolini, other leading Fascists and their supporters celebrated their victory with a march through the capital city. Even though the Fascists still only had 35 Deputies in the Chamber, the Fascist take-over of the country was well under way. At the age of 39, Benito Mussolini was the Prime Minister of Italy. Later that day, he said:

> My ancestors were peasants who tilled the earth and my father was a blacksmith who bent red-hot iron on the anvil. Sometimes when I was a boy, I helped my father in his hard and humble work, and now I have the infinitely harder task of bending souls.

Q *In what sense was the Fascist march on Rome 'a magnificent bluff'?*

In fact, Mussolini's planned march on Rome was a magnificent bluff and there is little doubt that, had the King acted resolutely, the marching columns would have been easily routed by loyal units of the Italian army. There were reasons why the King refused to act:

> Victor Emmanuel III was not the man to take the bold decisions needed. He should have insisted that the anti-Fascist forces in parliament form a coalition and called upon the army to defend the constitution. The King was not at that time a Fascist sympathiser, though some of those advising him were. But Mussolini had one ace which the King was too timid and too unimaginative to try to trump. This was the King's cousin, the Duke of Aosta, an ardent Fascist and more than likely to take the throne himself. Mussolini had hinted... that an 'unworthy King might need replacing.' What Victor Emmanuel feared most was the loss of his throne.

From Mussolini and the Rise of Italian Fascism *by R.N.L. Absalom, 1995*

VICTOR EMMANUEL III
(1869–1947)

Born in Naples in 1869, Victor Emmanuel became king following the assassination of his father, Umberto I in 1900 (see page 20). He married Princess Elena, daughter of the King of Montenegro. A shy and somewhat reclusive man, he lacked stature and Kaiser Wilhelm II was known to refer to him as 'the dwarf'. The cartoonist's delight and consequently the subject of cruel caricatures, he was also renowned for being untidy in appearance, even on public occasions. In 1915, he came out in favour of entering the European conflict and although nominally commander in chief of the Italian army, he left the conduct of war to his generals. In face of the disillusionment that followed Caporetto, he vigorously supported his country's continuation in the war. His conduct during the years after the war proved more controversial. In 1922, by refusing to back Facta, his prime minister, who called for an emergency decree and the introduction of martial law, he invited Mussolini to form a Fascist-led government. In so doing, he largely contributed to the collapse of Italian democracy. During the years of Mussolini's Fascist dictatorship, he was king in name only. His relationship with *Il Duce* was never easy. Even so, he happily accepted the titles that came with Italy's overseas conquests – Emperor of Ethiopia (1936) and King of Albania (1939). He was also widely criticised for signing the Fascist race laws which came into effect in 1938 (see page 138). When in 1943, during the Second World War, the Fascist Grand Council voted against continued support for Mussolini, he dismissed the dictator and placed him under arrest. When German troops occupied Rome after the Italian surrender to the Allies, Victor Emmanuel fled to Brindisi in the south. In 1944, he was forced to abdicate in favour of his son, Umberto II. For some years he lived in exile in Egypt and died in Alexandria in 1947 at the age of 78.

PICTURE 24
Victor Emmanuel III
(1869–1947)

As the historian B.R. Rowlands has written, in a matter of 24 hours, 'a group of murderers and bullies had taken over the government of Italy.' Mussolini had seized his opportunity and the myth of a Fascist revolution was born.

4 ∾ WHO SUPPORTED THE FASCISTS?

A *The appeal of Fascism*

By 1922, Fascism had gained a dubious type of respectability by dropping its republicanism and anti-clericalism, or so it appeared to various sections of the Italian people. The reasons for this were various. The majority of people who supported the Fascists simply hoped for better

PICTURE 25

The Fascist leaders, Balbo, de Bono, Mussolini, de Vecchi and Bianchi, lead the victory parade in Rome

times – the restoration of stable government based on strong leadership, enforced law and order, social reform and an improvement in the country's economic condition and their own family's living standards. There were those who thought that Fascism would bring an end to the years of inept Liberal government and would bring a new glorious age in Italian history which would witness a national revival and the restoration of the country's international prestige. Some saw Fascism as a means of frustrating the further spread of Marxist-inspired Bolshevism and godless Communism. The popularity of Fascism was also aided by the excellent use of propaganda and the charisma and stirring oratory of Mussolini himself. On the other hand, fear of the *squadrismo* also played a part.

B *Support for Fascism*

Those who supported the Fascists came from all sections of Italian society. The central pillar of support came from long-standing Fascist fanatics who had marched as Blackshirts or fought in the streets as *squadristi*. For the most part, the remainder of those who supported the Fascists did so not out of conviction but because it suited their interests to do so. These included:

squadristi armed irregulars who acted as terrorists and were used to intimidate those opposed to Fascism

See page 61

- The landowners, industrialists, bankers and others with business and commercial interests thought that the Liberals had already made too many concessions to the Left and feared that, in view of the unrest in both industrial and rural areas, the country was ripe for revolution.
- The upper and middle classes felt likewise as did sections of the working classes who thought that Socialist militancy had gone too far. The so-called *petit bourgeoisie* – the professional men, civil servants, skilled artisans and traders and shopkeepers – thought they would be more likely to prosper under the Fascists than they had under the former Liberal governments.

- The peasantry too saw the Socialist threat to take over their lands as a good reason to support the Fascists.
- The Roman Catholic Church, whilst having no great liking of Fascism, thought the party the most likely to oppose Marxist atheism.
- The nationalists together with the military and ex-soldiers who had fought in the First World War saw the Fascists as the most likely to appreciate and reward their efforts and seek to redress the terms of the 'mutilated victory' that followed.
- Once the Fascists abandoned their republicanism in 1922, many monarchists also lent their support to Mussolini.
- The ranks of the Fascist also included idealistic students as well as young hooligans and social misfits who thrived on street violence and intimidation.
- Undoubtedly, some supported the Fascists for reasons of fear – fear of the *squadristi*.

5 ⌐ FASCISM – THE DIFFICULTIES OF DEFINITION

Firstly, there is the question of spelling. References to the Italian experience require a spelling in the upper case with a capital 'F' – Fascism, Fascist. However, if it is a general reference to fascism as a political creed, then the spelling should be in the lower case with a small 'f' – fascism or fascist. The origin of the word is said to derive from *fasces*, a bundle of rods with an axe projecting which, in the days of Ancient Rome, was carried by a lector who walked ahead of a chief magistrate. This was to become the symbol of the Italian Fascist movement. The definition of fascism that appears in the Chambers dictionary reads, 'A form of authoritarian government in Italy from 1922–1943 characterised by extreme nationalism, militarism, anti-communism and restrictions on individual freedom (also without capital if referring to the political theories generally). The Oxford and other dictionaries are less specific, 'An authoritarian or totalitarian political system characterised by aggressive nationalism and the absolute sovereignty of the state over individual rights and interests.' As you might expect, Russian dictionaries of the Stalinist period saw things differently, 'The most reactionary and openly terroristic form of the dictatorship of finance capitalism established by the imperialistic bourgeoisie to break the resistance of the working class and all progressive elements in society.'

A *Some definitions of fascism by Fascists*

In a lecture entitled *Che cosa e il fascismo?* (What is fascism?) given in 1925 by Giovanni Gentile, a leading political theorist, scholar and so-called 'Philosopher of Fascism', who was later appointed by Mussolini to be his Minister of Education, he said:

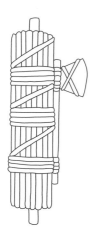

DIAGRAM 2
Fasces emblem

Fascism is a party and a political doctrine … But Fascism … is above all a total conception of life. It is impossible to be a Fascist in politics and not in school, not in one's family and office … Thus Fascism embodies what may be called its own characteristic, namely taking life seriously. Life is toil, effort, sacrifice and hard work; a life in which we know perfectly well there is neither matter nor time for amusement …

The historian Denis Mack Smith in commenting on fascism said, 'But what was it? What did fascists believe in, if anything. The word fascism is an Italian word and anyone wanting to know about it must go the original, because it was Mussolini's invention.' When Mussolini was once asked to define fascism, he defensively replied, Fascism is too subtle a body of ideas to be understood by laymen and foreigners.' Nevertheless, he did write an essay on the doctrine of fascism. In it, he wrote:

… the Fascist system of life stresses the importance of the State and recognises the individual only in so far as his interests coincide with those of the State … Fascism stands for liberty and for the only liberty worth having, the liberty of the State and of the individual within the State. The Fascist conception of the State is all embracing; outside of it no human or spiritual values may exist, much less have any value. Thus understood, Fascism is totalitarian …

The problem is that Mussolini was always changing his mind and much of what he wrote or said was contradictory. This raises the point, did the creator of Fascism even have a clear view of what it was all about?

B *Other interpretations of fascism*

A leading authority on Mussolini and Italian Fascist ideology, Denis Mack Smith, has commented:

From a lecture given by Denis Mack Smith that later appeared in Modern History Review, *1990*

Fascism, he [Mussolini] sometimes said was not a doctrine, but a technique; it was a means to get power. Oddly enough, the basic question whether fascism was something of the left or of the right is still sometimes in doubt, because it had elements of both … It was revolutionary, but could also sometimes claim to be conservative. It was Monarchist but also Republican, at different times. It was Catholic but also anti-clerical; it claimed to be socialist, but could also be strongly capitalist whenever it suited the *Duce* to be so. [*Duce* (leader) was a title later assumed by Mussolini.]

There were no consistent ideas in fascism. I think that Mussolini had no sincere beliefs at all, or at least none that he did not contradict at some stage in his life. He only believed in himself, his own power and success. Fascism to him was a technique for winning power.

Another leading authority, the historian Roger Griffin, has defined fascism as:

> ...a modern political ideology that seeks to regenerate the social, economic and cultural life of a country by basing it on a heightened sense of national belonging and ethnic identity. Fascism rejects liberal ideas such as freedom and individual rights, and often presses for the destruction of elections, legislatures, and other elements of democracy. Despite the idealistic goals of fascism, attempts to build fascist societies have led to wars and persecutions that caused millions of deaths. As a result, fascism is strongly associated with right-wing fanaticism, racism, totalitarianism, and violence.

The view of fascism by the historian, Stuart Woolf, is:

> A dictatorial system of government, with popular appeal and substructure, which served to establish, strengthen or maintain a substantially capitalist economy against the real or imagined threat of a socialist take-over, invasion or revolution.

From The Nature of Fascism
by Stuart Woolf, 1968

So where do these views leave us? Although the various theories of fascism may be confusing and often contradictory, there are features that remain reasonably constant. As we shall see as we progress through this book, Italian Fascism was based on a one-party dictatorship. It was militaristic and nationalistic and demanded the obedience and conformity of the Italian people. It insisted on the supremacy of the State and was intolerant of civil and human rights. Perhaps there is more truth than the author intended in the humorous comments made to highlight the essential differences between political systems:

Capitalism	'You have two cows. You sell one and buy a bull.'
Communism	'You have two cows. The government takes them both and gives you some milk.'
Nazism	'You have two cows. The government takes them both and shoots you.'
Socialism	'You have two cows. The government takes one and gives it to your neighbour.'
and Fascism	'You have two cows. The government takes them both and sells you the milk.'

6 ᵔ STRUCTURED AND ESSAY QUESTIONS

A *This section consists of questions that might be used for discussion (or written answers) as a way of expanding on the chapter and testing your understanding.*

1. In what ways might Alessandro Mussolini have influenced the views of his son?
2. To what extent might Mussolini's early lifestyle be described as bohemian?
3. Why did Mussolini change from being a socialist and pacifist to a nationalist and interventionist?
4. Who were the *ras* and what part did they play in the organisation of the Fascist Party?
5. Did the New Programme of the Fascist Party consider the welfare of the people?
6. Why did Emmanuel III refuse to act against the Fascists in 1922?
7. Of the definitions of fascism given on pages xx, which do you consider to be the most accurate?

B *Essay questions.*

1. 'A consequence of years of feeble government.' To what extent is this a satisfactory explanation of Mussolini's rise to power in 1922?
2. Was political instability in post-war Italy the main reasons for the success of Mussolini's Fascists in 1922?

7 ᵔ DOCUMENTARY EXERCISE ON THE FASCIST MARCH ON ROME

The first rumours that Mussolini's Fascists had begun their insurrection spread about midnight on Friday. Everywhere they mobilised and requested local mayors to transfer their powers to the Fascisti. The railway stations, post and telegraph offices and other public buildings were occupied particularly in the towns of Central Italy so that communications with Rome could be cut and the capital thus isolated. So far, it appears that there were no conflicts and that the revolutionary movement was carried out without bloodshed. Almost everywhere, the officers of the army have treated the Fascisti with great friendliness. The text of a Fascist proclamation is as follows:

'Fascisti! Italians! The time for determined battle has come. Four years ago the National Army launched the final offensive which brought victory. Today the army of Blackshirts seizes again the mutilated victory, and going directly to Rome, carries it back to the glories of the Capitol … The martial law of Fascism now becomes a fact … Following upon an order of the *Duce*, military, political and administrative powers are assumed by a secret Quadrumvirate of action with dictatorial powers. The army, the safeguard of the nation, must not take part in this struggle ... Fascism, furthermore, does not march against the police, but against the political class both cowardly and imbecile, which in four long years has not been able to give a government to the nation ... Fascists of all Italy! We must and shall win! Long live Italy! Long live Fascism!'.

SOURCE
From a report in The Times,
30 October 1922

1. *What is meant by*
   (a) 'the martial law of Fascism'? (5 marks)
   (b) 'a political class both cowardly and imbecile'? (5 marks)
2. *To judge from the source, how well planned was Mussolini's march on Rome? (8 marks)*
3. *How valuable is the source to an understanding of the events in Italy in 1922? (12 marks)*

8 ⤳ MAKING NOTES

Read the advice section about making notes on page xix of the Preface: How to use this book. Now use the chart below to indicate if the groups shown supported or opposed Mussolini's Fascists and give the reasons:

Group	Did they support or oppose the Fascists?	Reasons
Catholic Church		
Military		
Landowners and industrialists		
Peasantry		
Socialists and Communists		
Liberals		
Monarchists		
Republicans		

7

The Fascist Consolidation of Power 1922–6

INTRODUCTION

When in 1933 Adolf Hitler was appointed Chancellor of Germany, he took office with the backing of 34% of the members of the Reichstag. Earlier in the elections of June 1932, the Nazis had secured 196 of the 584 seats and just 33% of the popular vote. It was far from an overall majority, yet within the following 20 months Hitler was able to eliminate all opposition to become the *führer* dictator of his country. Eleven years earlier, when Benito Mussolini was appointed prime minister of Italy, his power base was less than 7% of the Chamber of Deputies. To establish a Fascist dictatorship, he would clearly have to be far more circumspect than Hitler and to achieve his aims he would need to employ both stealth and terror. He would also need to proceed slowly and cautiously. Apart from broad definitions of the aims of fascism, Mussolini had few detailed policies of his own. However, he was absolutely sure of the correctness of his view regarding the relationship of the State and its citizens. This was best illustrated in the popular Fascist slogan of the time: 'Everything within the State, nothing against the State, nothing outside the State'. In other words, in all matters the position of the State was one of unquestioned supremacy. Beyond the aim of establishing a totalitarian state, he wanted employers and employees to work harmoniously in the interests of the State. He also wanted Italy to achieve *autarky*, self-sufficiency in food and essential raw materials. In its foreign policy, his aim was to show greater resolve and aggression and seek national glory. The problem was that neither

autarky see pages 156–9

1922 Mussolini voted emergency powers
Fascist Grand Council established
1923 Acerbo Law passed
1924 First elections under new system gave Fascists an overwhelming majority
Matteotti's speech to the Chamber
Murder of Matteotti
Aventine Secession
1925 Mussolini's speech to the Chamber
Law on the Power of the Head of Government passed
Vidoni Palace Pact
Secret societies abolished
Press Laws passed

TABLE 14
Date line showing key events in establishing Mussolini's Fascist dictatorship

Mussolini nor any of his Fascist colleagues had any previous experience of government.

1 ✍ PLANS TO MANIPULATE THE ELECTORAL SYSTEM

On coming to power, Mussolini first headed a coalition government. His cabinet was made up of four Fascists, two *Popolari*, three Nationalists, two Liberals, two Social democrats and one non-party member. Mussolini took three Cabinet positions himself. He was President of the Council as well as in charge of both domestic and foreign affairs. The other Fascist ministers in the Cabinet included Aldo Oviglio (Justice), Alberto di Stefani (Finance) and Giovanni Giuriati who was responsible for the Liberated Provinces (provinces gained by Italy after the First World War). A new position was also created for Emilio De Bono, that of the Director-General of Public Safety. This appointment was a veiled threat to the Party's opponents since the old general and veteran Fascist had already earned himself something of a reputation for his leadership of the Fascist *squadristi*. Otherwise, Mussolini appeared to be conciliatory. Although very much in control, he felt a need to show moderation and create a good image both at home and abroad. Consequently he took no immediate steps against the other political parties and even restored their offices and presses that had previously been occupied or suppressed. As a gesture of goodwill to the Church, he abandoned his anti-Catholic stance and ordered the restoration of the teaching of religious education in schools and colleges. He also banned obscene publications and declared swearing in public and the sale of contraceptives to be crimes. He next sought a vote of confidence and an agreement from the Italian parliament to grant him emergency powers for a year. In a speech made to the Chamber of Deputies on 16 November 1922, he said:

> Gentlemen, what I am doing now in this hall is a mark of respect towards you for which I ask no special recognition. For many years, too many, government crises were made and solved by the Chamber by means of tortuous manoeuvres and scheming, so much that a crisis was regularly called an attack and a ministry was represented as a tottering stagecoach ... I am here to defend and enforce in the highest degree the revolution of the blackshirts, injecting them intimately into the history of the nation as a force of development, progress and stability ... I told myself that the best wisdom is the wisdom that does not abandon one after the victory. With three thousand youths fully armed, fully determined and ready to act on any command of mine, I could have chastised all those who have defamed and tried to harm fascism ... I could have kicked out Parliament and constructed a government exclusively of Fascists but I did not want to, at least not for the present ...

> I have formed a coalition government, not with the intention of having a parliamentary majority, which I can now do very well without, but in order to call to the aid of a gasping nation as many as are willing to save the nation itself over and above all smoke of parties … I believe that I also interpret the thought of the assembly and certainly the majority of the Italian people in expressing warm devotion to the Sovereign, who refused to listen to the useless reactionaries and … avoided civil war.
>
> Before attaining this post I was asked on all sides for a programme. Alas it is not programmes that are wanting in Italy, it is the men and the willingness to apply the programmes. All the problems of Italian life have been solved on paper, but the will has been lacking to translate them into fact. The government today represents this firm and decisive will … We demand full powers because we want to assume full responsibility … I do not intend to exclude voluntary co-operation which we shall accept cordially whether it comes from deputies, senators or competent private citizens.

platitudes empty or unimportant remarks

Mussolini's speech contained both **platitudes** and concessions as well as implied threats.

Giolitti was certainly impressed with what he heard and commented, 'The country needs strong government that looks beyond living from day to day … I wholly approve of the speech made by the Prime Minister'. As a result, when the vote of confidence was held, the Italian parliament agreed by 306 to 116 votes to grant Mussolini emergency Powers for a year. Those who voted in favour included five previous prime ministers – Giolitti, Salandra, Orlando, Bonhomi and Facta. In the Senate only 26 senators voted against. In effect, this amounted to Mussolini being granted dictatorial powers. During the same period, his brother, Arnaldo, was appointed editor of the Party newspaper, *Il Popolo d'Italia*. Fascists previously imprisoned for their murderous conduct were pardoned and it is claimed that student activists who had been detained or wounded received their degrees without taking an examination. In December 1922, he created the Fascist Grand Council.

KEY ISSUE

The extent of the powers of the Fascist Grand Council.

A *The Fascist Grand Council*

This Council was to be the main policy-making body and the highest authority in the Fascist Party. This group of high-ranking Fascists was to act as the link between the Party and the government. It was to discuss and approve government policy and then place its proposals first before the Cabinet and then parliament. In this way, the task of introducing new government policy was taken from parliament and given to a group that represented the interests of the Fascist Party. Mussolini nominated the 22 members of the Council and they met once a month.

In January 1923, the *squadristi* gained some respectability when it became a paid, full time militia – the Voluntary Fascist Militia for

National Security. Its members took an oath of loyalty to Mussolini and not the King. As the process of turning Italy into a totalitarian state continued, the Fascist leader needed to change the electoral system so that it would be to the advantage of his Party.

B *The Acerbo Law, 1923*

Promoted by a Fascist under-secretary, Giacomo Acerbo, a law was passed which allowed proportional representation to remain but otherwise abolished the old electoral system. The country was to be divided into 15 large constituencies. In each constituency, parties would be expected to submit a list of candidates. It was further agreed that in future elections, any party gaining 25% or more of the votes would automatically be allocated two-thirds of the seats in the Chamber of Deputies. The remainder of the seats would be divided between the other parties. Acerbo's proposals were opposed by the Socialists, Communists and Liberal Democrats but with the militiamen in close attendance, the majority conceded and the measure was passed by 223 votes to 123. Once in effect, the Chamber of Deputies was dissolved and elections set for April 1924. It would be the first election to be fought under the new rules.

> **KEY ISSUE**
>
> *The purpose of the Acerbo Law.*

Parliamentary issues and the future of the opposition parties were not the only problems that concerned Mussolini. He also had to keep an eye on the activities of the troublesome *ras* in the provinces. Some, particularly Roberto Faranacci, the *ras* of Cremona, who looked for more positive action and decisive move to the right in politics, were becoming restless. In many provincial towns, the previously freely elected councils were forcibly removed and replaced by Fascist administrations.

C *The elections of 1924*

In February 1923, Mussolini brought about the merger of the Fascist and Nationalist Parties. This was simply a tactical move, a marriage of convenience, intended to ensure a Fascist electoral victory. In any case, the opposition parties were hopelessly divided and were either unable or unwilling to form a common front. The elections of April 1924 were contested in an atmosphere of unmatched intimidation and violence. The Fascist militia arrested thousands of their opponents and many were beaten and some killed including one Socialist candidate. The people were subjected to a massive propaganda campaign whilst the opposition press was carefully watched and its access to the media limited. Corruption was everywhere and with the militia in attendance at the polling booths, much pressure was exerted on the electorate to make the right decision! Afterwards ballot boxes were lost and there were many obvious discrepancies in the counting so that, in some constituencies, the elections were blatantly rigged.

With so much pressure exerted on the electorate, the outcome of the election was never really in doubt as erstwhile political opponents found it prudent, and certainly safer, to change their views and support Mussolini. As it was, 66% of the people voted for the Fascists and their Nationalist allies to give them 374 of the 535 seats in the Chamber.

TABLE 15
Election of 1924

Government		Opposition	
Fascists	274	*Populari*	39
Other supporters		Socialists	24
Nationalists etc.	100	Communists	19
		Various others	79
	374 seats		**161 seats**

The election was a resounding victory for the Fascists and their supporters. With 65% of the votes and the opposition reduced to a bunch of quarreling and ineffectual bunglers, many wondered if all the earlier commotion about the Acerbo Law had been necessary. However there were a few still brave enough to voice their concern about Mussolini's tactics. One of the most outspoken in his criticism was Giacomo Matteotti, the 39-year-old rising star of the Socialist Party.

2 ↩ THE MATTEOTTI CRISIS

A *Matteotti's speech to the Chamber of Deputies*

On 30 May 1924, a tense Chamber listened as Giacomo Matteotti, in a two-hour speech, listed the abuses practiced by the Fascists during the election campaign. He then demanded that the elections be declared invalid. As tempers rose, deputies stood to gesticulate and shout abuse at the speaker. There were shouts of 'We will teach you respect with a shot in the back' and 'Go to Russia.' Matteotti responded – 'You may kill me but you will never kill my ideas. The workers will bless my corpse ... Long live Socialism.' Some deputies could take no more and walked out. At the end of his speech, Matteotti turned to his friends and said, 'Now you can start drafting my funeral oration.' Throughout, a stony-faced Mussolini sat in silence but was later known to comment 'that man should no longer be in circulation.' Five days later, Matteotti resumed his attack on the Fascists but this time Mussolini stood to reply. He accused the Socialist deputy of presenting a one-sided argument and pointed out that numerous Fascists had also been killed and wounded during the election campaign. He ended with a threat, 'In Russia, you would have been shot. There is still time.'

GIACOMO MATTEOTTI
(1885–1924)

Born in 1885, Giacomo Matteotti was the son of a wealthy landowner from the Fratta Polestine in the Rivigo region of Italy. At the age of 14, his brother introduced him to socialism. During his university years when he was a law student, he became actively involved in socialist activities. His brand of socialism was of a moderate, non-militant variety. In 1924, he was appointed secretary of the Unitary Socialist Party. Opposed to Italian involvement in the First World War, he nevertheless served as a noncombatant but was rejected for officer training because of his attitude. A pacifist, he was considered defeatist and unreliable. His gifted and spirited oratory earned him the nickname 'the Tempest'. An outspoken intellectual, he was not popular with all sections of his party. He published a book, *The Fascists Exposed*, that brought to public attention the grim reality of their barbaric methods. In the introduction, he wrote, 'The statistical and historical date … that never as in the last year, during which Fascism has been in power, has the law been so thrust aside in favour of arbitrary action, the State so subjugated by a faction, or the nation so split up into two classes, the dominating and the subject class'. During the election campaign of 1924, he was one of the Socialist candidates attacked by the *squadristi* now operating under the name Voluntary Fascist Militia. After the election, he was one of the few prepared to speak out against the irregularities and the activities of the Fascist thugs. His murder in 1924 led to a crisis that threatened Mussolini's Fascist government.

PICTURE 26
*Giacomo Matteotti
(1885–1924)*

B *The murder of Matteotti*

On the morning of 10 July, five men seized Matteotti as he left his apartment in the Lungo Tevere Arnaldo da Brescia. He was bundled into a waiting Lancia car. As he struggled to escape, he was stabbed repeatedly. The intention of the gang leader, Amerigo Dumini, was to drive some distance to Tuscany and bury him in a location where he would not easily be found. However, members of the gang panicked and, after driving around for some hours, his body was placed in a shallow grave a short distance from the centre of the city. As a search was mounted, Matteotti's wife visited Mussolini and demanded to know what had become of her husband. On 12 July, Mussolini addressing Parliament said:

I believe that the Chamber is concerned with what has happened to Deputy Matteotti, who disappeared suddenly on Tuesday afternoon at a time and in circumstances that are uncertain but can support the view that a crime has been committed, can only arouse the indignation and the grief of the government and Parliament.

The following day, a number of deputies from the opposition parties withdrew from Parliament in what became known as the Aventine Secession.

C *The Aventine Succession*

Q

What did the Aventines hope to achieve?

The Aventines, as they were known, were copying the action taken in 500 BC when the plebs, a less privileged section of the people of Ancient Rome, withdrew to the nearby Aventine Hill in protest at the dominance of the patricians, the Roman aristocracy. In so doing, they hoped to gain a say in government. In July 1924, the Aventines arranged to meet away from the Chamber of Deputies and watch events from a distance. Their aim was to pressurise Mussolini so that he would take action to deal with the perpetrators of the crime. A few even considered calling for a general strike and proclaiming themselves the legal government of Italy. The majority rejected this idea. In reality, they were playing into the hands of Mussolini since their absence from the Chamber made his position even stronger.

On 16 August, Matteotti's mutilated and naked body was discovered in a shallow grave on wasteland 20 kilometres outside Rome. Mussolini immediately claimed that he knew nothing of the killing. Three inquiries were subsequently held, the latest in 1947, and no positive evidence came to light to prove that he had ordered the slaying of the deputy. On the other hand, his innocence remains far from certain and many would say highly unlikely. However there was a great deal of evidence to implicate other leading members of the Fascist Party. Amerigo Dumini was a known gangster who was given to boasting of the number of murders and assassinations he had committed. The other members of the gang – Augusto Malacria, Amieto Poveromo, Giuseppe Viola and Albini Volpi – all ex-members of the *squadristi* but considered lesser fry in the criminal world. They all belonged to a group of murderous assassins that took its name from Lenin's infamous secret police in Bolshevik Russia, the *Cheka*. There were witnesses to the abduction of Matteotti, and the ownership of the car, still with blood-stained seats, was traced to Filippo Filippelli, the editor of the Fascist newspaper *Corriere Italiano* and an associate of Mussolini. There was evidence too of the involvement of Cesare Rossi, a senator, and of Filippo Marinelli, a member of the Fascist Grand Council.

Mussolini's first reaction was to express his horror at the atrocity and convey his condolences to Matteotti's wife and her two young sons. He strongly denied that the murder was a Fascist conspiracy and undertook to provide the deputy's family with a pension. He also promised to hunt down the killers. In the Chamber, he said, 'If there is anyone in this room who more than all the rest, has the right to be angered, it is I. Only one of my enemies could commit this crime that fills us with horror and stirs us to cries of anger.'

Dumini was arrested at the railway station attempting to leave Rome. Filippelli, Rossi and Marinelli were also taken into custody. Under cross-examination, Dumini confessed to the killing of Matteotti whilst the other three admitted their involvement in the crime. The extenuating circumstances, so they claimed, was the fact that they were sure that Mussolini wanted to eliminate the Socialist deputy. The men held responsible for Matteotti's murder were finally brought to trial in March 1926. Dumini, Poveromo and Volpi were found guilty but since it was claimed that they had acted under provocation, since Matteotti had resisted their attempt to kidnap him, they were treated leniently. They were all sentenced to six years' imprisonment but released after two years. Malacria and Viola were found not guilty. In court, Roberto Farinacci acted as the defence council for Marinelli and Rossi, who had planned the murder, and Filippelli, who had provided the car. The case dragged on for a year until finally all were found not guilty and released from custody. Afterwards, Marinelli resumed his position in the Fascist Grand Council. In January 1944, at a time when Marinelli was himself awaiting execution, he stated that Mussolini had not known of the plan to murder Matteotti and that it had been arranged without his leader's knowledge.

See page 211

D *The repercussions*

From Mussolini's viewpoint, Matteotti's murder was a major blunder. The majority of the Fascists in the Chamber refuted all the claims made against their Party whilst the King, Victor Emmanuel III, realising that his own position was now dependent on Mussolini's patronage, refused to even read the documentary evidence relating to the case. Across the country, there was a widespread belief that Mussolini was responsible for, or at very least had prior knowledge of, Matteotti's murder. There was public outcry followed by a wave of popular protest with anti-Fascist demonstrations in the streets. Many ex-servicemen and even some Fascists expressed their concern with a few going as far as to tear

PICTURE 27
A cartoon that appeared in the Italian newspaper Becco Giallo

KEY ISSUE

How close was Mussolini to being overthrown?

up their party membership cards. Former ex-prime ministers such as Orlando and Giolitti, who still had some influence with the masses, began to reconsider their support of Mussolini. The Fascist leader's position was certainly under threat and he seemed uncertain how to react. A visitor described him as '*red eyed and unshaven*' and living in fear of an imminent *coup*. At this stage, there is some reason to believe that had the opposition made a determined attempt to get rid of Mussolini, they would have had the support of most Italians. There is no evidence to suggest they even considered such a move and even if they did, they dithered for too long and so the opportunity was lost.

However, Mussolini was not without support. Within the Chamber, the bulk of the Fascists remained loyal to him and he also had support from other more unexpected quarters.

The London *Times* condemned the murder of Matteotti … but hastened to add that it would be very wrong for the opposition in Italy to try to use the incident to bring down Mussolini's government… *The Times* was confident that Mussolini would handle the situation 'in only the right way' … The *Daily Mail* hailed Mussolini as 'the Saviour of Italy' and declared: 'We in England have confidence in Signor Mussolini; so have the Italians. Ramsay MacDonald (the British Prime Minister) unwittingly helped Mussolini … [by agreeing] the treaty ceding Jubaland to Italy. The agreement was initialled at the Foreign Office in London on 9th June 1924, the day before Matteotti was murdered. The news of this diplomatic success came just at the right time to help Mussolini during the furore about the murder. The Ethiopian prince Ras Tafari, who later became the Emperor Haile Selassie … also unwittingly helped Mussolini. On 18th June Ras Tafari arrived in Rome on a state visit. Even the Soviet ambassador, Yurenev, came to Mussolini's aid. The day before Matteotti was murdered, he had sent Mussolini an invitation to attend a banquet at the embassy … At the height of the uproar over the murder, the Italian Communists and Socialists asked Yurenev to withdraw the invitation. He refused to do so.

From Mussolini
by Jasper Ridley, 1997

In order to appease his critics, Mussolini first made some concessions. De Bono, the chief of police, was sacked and the Prime Minister handed over his own responsibilities for domestic affairs to Luigi Federzoni. With the Fascist regime under threat there were extremist elements in his own party, particularly the *ras*, who urged Mussolini to take more positive measures. Even though on 27 December, the newspaper, *Il Mondo*, presented further damning evidence against Mussolini when it published a confession made by Cesare Rossi that clearly implicated him, it was already evident that he was going to survive the storm. The truth was that as long as the threat of Communism existed, those with vested interests – the industrialists, the upper and middle classes, the army and the Church – supported Mussolini simply because their fear of Bolshevism was greater than their fear of Fascism.

On 3 January 1925, Mussolini finally went on the offensive and turned on his accusers. In a speech to the Chamber of Deputies, he said:

> The speech I am about to make may not be … a parliamentary speech. I tell you here, in the presence of this assembly, and before the whole Italian people, that I alone assume the moral and historical responsibility for everything that has occurred … If Fascism has been only a business of castor oil and club, and not a proud passion of the best of Italian youth, the blame is on me. If Fascism has been a criminal plot, if violence has resulted from a certain historic, political and moral atmosphere, the responsibility is mine, because I have deliberately created this atmosphere … Now the time for faint heartedness is passed … the Aventine sedition has born consequences … a revival of Communism, but Fascism, at once a party and a government, is at the height of its power, and so the moment comes to say enough … Gentlemen of the Aventine, you have deluded yourselves …

He ended his speech with a promise and a threat:

> Italy wants peace and quiet, work and calm. I will give these things with love if possible, and with force if necessary … You may be sure that within the next forty-eight hours everything will be clarified.

Mussolini's speech was a decisive moment, a **watershed** in the history of Fascist rule in Italy. It signalled the start of a process that would turn Italy into a **totalitarian** state.

watershed an important time, a turning point

totalitarian a form of government that controls every aspect of its citizens's lives and allows no opposition

3 ～ STEPS TOWARDS A FASCIST TOTALITARIAN STATE

The years 1925 and 1926 were to witness the wholesale erosion of democratic government and the elimination of the personal liberties of the Italian people. It was also a period during which there were four attempts on Mussolini's life.

See page 98

A *The opposition parties*

For the best part of two years Mussolini had tolerated the existence of opposition parties and, on coming to power in 1922, had even included their representatives in his coalition government. This was sham democracy since the Fascists began to pass laws by decree without reference to Parliament. After the Matteotti affair, the *squadristi*, now masquerading as militia, were put in a state of readiness to deal with any further trouble caused by the opposition parties. In February 1925, Roberto Farinacci, amongst the most radical and ruthless in the hierarchy, was appointed secretary of the Fascist Party. At the Party Congress in June, it was decided to ignore the opposition and disregard their protests. The summer months of 1925 were a period of renewed and unrestricted Fascist violence against their political opponents. Leaders of the opposition parties were beaten, killed or forced into exile. The violence gradually subsided after a call for greater discipline 'in the name of our beloved *Duce* and of deputy Farinacci.' The remaining months of 1925 saw the removal of the last semblance of democratic government in Italy. In December, parliamentary government ended with the passing of the Law on the Power of the Head of Government. Mussolini now took the title Head of Government and was only accountable to the King. All new laws had to be first submitted to him and he had the sole responsibility for introducing new legislation. He now officially had the power to **rule by decree**.

In the same month, the United Socialist Party, Matteotti's former party, was banned and shortly afterwards the ban was extended to all opposition parties said to be 'obstructive rather than constructive and politically educational'. Anyone found guilty of offending the honour or prestige of the Head of Government became liable to a five-year prison sentence; anyone involved in anti-Fascist activity became liable to lose his or her Italian citizenship. With ministerial responsibility and parliamentary control a thing of the past, Italy was now effectively run by Mussolini and, when he cared to consult it, the Fascist Grand Council.

> **rule by decree** pass laws without consulting parliament

B *Local government*

Since they had already forcibly removed opposition parties from office in many areas, local government affairs were already largely in the hands of the Fascists. This situation was finally confirmed in 1926 when nominated Fascist officials replaced any remaining elected local leaders. Elected mayors were removed and their places taken by **podesta**. In addition, the local Party secretary now had to be involved in any planning or decision making.

> **podesta** A Fascist appointed local government official intended to replace the elected mayors.

C *Trade unions*

Socialist and Catholic trade unions had been allowed to continue but they were kept under close scrutiny and their activities limited. Once the Fascists set up their own unions or syndicates, the existing workers' organisations were banned. Fascist syndicates were intended to represent the interests of both employers and workers. By the Vidoni Palace Pact of 1925, both sides agreed to be represented solely by Fascist syndicates. This agreement, the Law of Corporations, which was passed in 1926, also abolished the right of workers to strike and employers to lock-out their workers. The ultimate aim was to group the whole of the nation's industries into nine confederations.

See pages 151–6

D *Other associations*

Other associations, both political and otherwise, were placed under surveillance. Whenever it could be easily accomplished, their funds were confiscated and their premises closed. In November 1925, a law was passed that prohibited secret societies. The main target of these measures was Freemasonry. Fascists were not allowed to be Freemasons and in the end they were declared illegal and their lodges disbanded.

E *The press*

Until 1925, Mussolini had tolerated some limited freedom of the press but only the boldest of newspaper owners allowed their editors to be critical of the Fascists. Cartoons and articles in popular satirical magazines that caused the authorities embarrassment were still allowed to be published. To start with, the Fascist authorities attempted to buy out independent newspapers and then appoint pro-Fascist editors to manage them. This all finally came to an end in 1925 when independent newspapers were closed and many of their editors arrested. Afterwards, Federzini rigorously enforced the Press Laws and all views expressed had to be pro-Fascist. The censorship of the Italian press was complete.

PICTURE 28

Cartoon by Giuseppe Scalarina illustrating the means used by the Fascists to gain power. 'The flower of Fascism' shows how the petals of the flower, the support given by banks, big business and agriculture, hide the reality of Fascist violence, the clubs in the centre

PICTURE 29

Cartoon by Giuseppe Scalarina illustrating the means used by the Fascists to gain power. The methods used by the person in control of local government, are shown as a club and castor oil

4 ⌐ ATTEMPTS TO ASSASSINATE *IL DUCE*

In spite of what appeared to be overwhelming support for Mussolini and his regime, the period 1924 to 1926 witnessed no less than four attempts on his life. The first came in November 1924 when a Socialist deputy, Tito Zaniboni, made plans to shoot him when he appeared on the balcony of the Foreign Office in Rome. He foolishly boasted of his intentions to friends, who informed the police. Zaniboni was arrested a few minutes before Mussolini appeared and was subsequently sentenced to 30 years' imprisonment.

An eccentric member of the Anglo-Irish aristocracy, the Honourable Violet Gibson, made a second attempt on his life in April 1926. The sister of Lord Ashbourne fired a shot at Mussolini as he went to his car after opening an international medical congress in Rome. The bullet grazed his nose. Afterwards the Italian secret police, the OVRA, could find no connection between the woman and any political group. Accepting that she was mentally unstable, she was released and deported. In September of the same year, Gino Lucetti, a stonemason and self-confessed anarchist, threw a bomb at Mussolini's car. Whilst he escaped unhurt, several onlookers were wounded. Sentenced to 30 years in prison, he was released in 1943 only to be killed during an Allied air raid. In October 1926, 16-year-old Anteo Zamboni, acting entirely on his own initiative, decided to assassinate Mussolini during his visit to Bologna. Wearing the uniform of a member of a Fascist youth movement in order to get close to his intended victim, he fired as his car passed by but missed. Zamboni was seized and lynched by the outraged crowd who stabbed him repeatedly before literally tearing him limb from limb. Later his arms and legs were carried around the city and put on display by local Fascists. No witnesses came forward to identify the boy as the would-be assassin and it has been claimed that Zamboni was no more than an innocent bystander. Some have suggested that the youth was an unfortunate pawn in a plot to stir up anxiety about public safety. It certainly provided the Fascists with another excuse to take steps to set up a dictatorship? The attempts on Mussolini's life led to the passing of a law on public safety. A tribunal was set up to deal with those thought to be a threat to society and a risk to the state.

5 ⌁ IMPORTANT FIGURES IN THE FASCIST LEADERSHIP

ITALO BALBO (1896–1940)

From Farrara, Balbo was one of the more flamboyant members of the Quadrumvirate at the time of the March on Rome in 1922. A member of the Fascist Grand Council and a general in the Fascist militia, he served Mussolini as Italy's first Minister of Aviation. He was largely responsible for the development of aviation in Italy and led mass flights, the most notable being from Rome to Rio de Janeiro and Chicago. He was not greatly liked by Mussolini who suspected his loyalty. In 1938, he annoyed his leader by criticising Italy's alliance with Germany. Appointed governor-general of Libya in 1933, he worked hard to win Islamic support for Fascism. In 1940, he was killed when his aircraft was shot down accidentally by Italian anti-aircraft fire when flying over Tobruk in Libya.

PICTURE 30
Italo Balbo (1896–1940)

MICHELE BIANCHI (1882–1930)

Early on, Bianchi was one of Mussolini's closest supporters. A member of the Quadrumvirate, he was often at odds with Grandi and de Vecchi. In turn, he served as Secretary of the Fascist Party, Under-Secretary of the Interior and Minister of Public Works. His early death in 1930, robbed Mussolini of one of his most reliable friends and close associates.

PICTURE 31
Michele Bianchi (1882–1930)

DINO GRANDI (1895–1988)

A Bologna-born lawyer, Grandi was a member of the Fascist Quadrumvirate at the time of the March on Rome in 1922. A member of the Fascist Grand Council, he was appointed Mussolini's foreign minister (1929–32) and then served as Italian ambassador in London (1932–9). Afterwards he was Minister of Justice. In 1943, he led the revolt against Mussolini and was one of those who demanded his resignation. To escape arrest, he fled to Portugal. Sentenced to death in his absence, he lived as an exile in Brazil until he returned to Italy in 1971.

PICTURE 32
Dino Grandi (1895–1988)

PICTURE 33
Roberto Farinacci (1892–1945)

ROBERTO FARINACCI
(1892–1945)

Born in Isernia, Farinacci was the most extreme member of the Fascist hierarchy, who was disliked by Mussolini and most other members of the Grand Council. He became Party secretary in 1935 and Minister of State three years later. He also edited the Party newspaper, *Regime Fascista*. A racialist with strong anti-Semitic views, he was pro-German and established a close relationship with Adolf Hitler. He was amongst those who encouraged Italy's entry into the war on Germany's side in 1940. He was largely responsible for the eventual persecution of Italian Jews. Captured and tried by Italian partisans in 1945, he was shot.

PICTURE 34
Rodolfo Graziani (1882–1955)

RODOLFO GRAZIANI
(1882–1955)

From Filettino and with the additional title the Marquess of Neghelli, Graziani was a career soldier. He served in the First World War and, in 1935, was appointed governor of Somaliland. Later, between 1936 and 1937, he was the ruthless Viceroy of Ethiopia. During the Second World War, he commanded the Italian armies in Tripoli but failed in his effort to invade Egypt and resigned. In 1943, he was appointed Minister of Defence and led what remained of the Italian armed resistance to the Allied invasion of his country. Captured by his own countrymen, he was put on trial for war crimes. He was sentenced to a term of imprisonment but, since he was in his mid-70s, he was granted an early release. (See also page 182).

6 ⌐ STRUCTURED AND ESSAY QUESTIONS

A *This section consists of questions that might be used for discussion (or written answers) as a way of expanding on the chapter and testing your understanding.*

1. What is meant by *autarky*?
2. Why did Mussolini abandon his anti-Catholic stance and look for better relations with the Church?
3. For what reasons did Mussolini ask the Italian parliament to grant him emergency powers for a year in 1922?
4. What powers did the Fascist Grand Council possess?

5. To what extent might the Acerbo Law (1923) be considered undemocratic?

6. What evidence is there to suggest that Mussolini was involved in the murder of Matteotti?

B Essay questions.

1. To what extent had Mussolini been successful in eliminating all opposition to Fascist rule by 1926?

2. 'Made possible mainly through the use of terror.' How valid is this assessment of the means by which the Fascists consolidated their power in Italy during the period 1922–6?

7 ∾ DOCUMENTARY EXERCISE ON THE MURDER OF MATTEOTTI

Study the sources below and then answer the questions which follow:

SOURCE A
From a speech made by Mussolini to the Italian Chamber of Deputies in November 1922

All the problems of Italian life, all of them I say, have been solved on paper; but the will has been lacking to translate them into fact. The government today represents the firm and decisive will ... we demand full powers because we want to assume full responsibility...

SOURCE B
From the plan for electoral reform put forward by Giacomo Acerbo in November 1922

Two thirds of the seats in Parliament to be allocated to the party which receives 25% of the votes in a general election; the remaining third to be divided amongst the opposition parties.

SOURCE C
An extract from Matteotti's book, The Fascists Exposed, *1922*

This book shows that never, during the year the Fascists have been in power, has the law been so set aside, the State controlled by a group, or the nation split into two classes, the ruling and the oppressed classes.

SOURCE D
From a speech made by Mussolini to the Chamber of Deputies on 13 June 1924.

If there is anyone in this room who more than all the rest has the right to be moved and angered, it is I. Only one of my enemies ... could commit this crime [the murder of Matteotti] that fills us with horror and stirs us to cries of anger.

SOURCE E
From a speech made by Mussolini to the Chamber of Deputies on 3 January 1925.

I tell you here, in the presence of this assembly and before the whole Italian people, that I alone assume the moral and historical responsibility for everything that has occurred ... Italy wants peace and quiet, work and calm. I will give these things with love, if possible, and with force if necessary.

> **Q**
>
> **1.** *What do sources A and B reveal about Fascist plans for the future government of Italy? (5 marks)*
> **2.** *Comment on the reliability of Source C. (5 marks)*
> **3.** *Compare Sources D and E. To what extent do they reveal a change in the attitude of Mussolini? (5 marks)*
> **4.** *To what extent does Source C support Source E in suggesting that Italy was in need of strong government? (5 marks)*
> **5.** *How full an understanding do the sources provide of the background to Matteotti crisis? (10 marks)*

8 ↪ MAKING NOTES

Read the advice section about making notes on page xix of the Preface: How to use this book, and then make your own notes based on the following headings and questions.

1. *Plans to manipulate the electoral system.*
    (a) Steps taken by Mussolini to appease the Church.
    (b) What are militia?
    (c) The type of people appointed to the Fascist Grand Council.
    (d) The reasons for the Acerbo Law of 1923.
    (e) What conclusions can you draw from the result of the 1924 elections?
2. *The Matteotti crisis.*
    (a) The reasons why Matteotti's speech to the Chamber of Deputies on 30 May 1924 infuriated the Fascists?
    (b) The aim of those involved in the Aventine Succession.
    (c) From the evidence available in 1926, was it possible to identify those responsible for the murder of Matteotti?
    (d) The overseas reaction to Matteotti's murder.
3. *Steps towards a Fascist totalitarian state.*
    (a) The steps taken by Mussolini to eliminate:
        (i)   the opposition parties
        (ii)   local government opposition
        (iii) trade unions
        (iv)   associations such as Freemasonry
        (v)   the freedom of the press.

Mussolini and The Early Years of His Fascist Dictatorship

8

INTRODUCTION

In 1940, United Artists made a film, *The Great Dictator*, that was a satire based on the life of Adolf Hitler. In the film, Charlie Chaplin played the part of the character that was supposedly the German dictator, whilst Jack Oakie played Benito Mussolini. In his caricature of *Il Duce*, Oakie portrayed him as a mock-heroic, jabbering buffoon, easily led and always in awe of his ally. For his part, Oakie was nominated for an Academy Award, but just how accurate was his portrayal?

1 ⌐ BENITO MUSSOLINI – THE MAN AND THE MYTH

A *The man*

i) *His character and life-style*
As *Il Duce* the Fascist leader of Italy, Benito Mussolini was by no means a wholly loathsome character. He was exceptionally vain and lacked a sense of humour. Nevertheless, he could be charming and good humoured and always made a point of trying to impress visitors. Mussolini always lacked social graces and his table man-

PICTURES 35 (LEFT) AND 36 (RIGHT)
The two faces of Benito Mussolini: respectable politician and rabble-rousing orator

ners left a lot to be desired, but these improved. In appearance, he was on the short side being barely 1.67 metres tall, of stocky build and with a rapidly receding hairline. He was extremely conscious of his appearance and physical condition. His style of dress was very conservative – usually a plain suit and tie – and he sometimes wore a shirt with a butterfly collar and spats on his shoes. Later, he took to always appearing in uniform. He took regular exercise and his diet consisted mainly of health foods and fruit juices. He very rarely consumed alcohol and eventually gave up drinking coffee. During his period in the army, Mussolini had been a heavy smoker but he gave up the habit. In the mid 1920s, he suffered stomach cramps and gastric ulcers and was so ill that he had to retire briefly from public life. It was rumoured that his illness was at least in part the consequence of years suffering from venereal disease. He was in bed by 10 pm each evening with an order not to be disturbed. He usually rose early and began work at 8 am. During the afternoon, he often rested but seldom enjoyed a full siesta. There were times when his day was filled with a round of meetings, conferences and receptions. Mussolini was a private man who was not keen on being exposed to the glare of public life but preferred to live quietly with his wife and children at their home, the Villa Torlonia, in the outskirts of Rome. There he was looked after by his bossy cook and housekeeper, Cesire Carrocci, and served by his butler-cum-servant, Quinto Navarra. He liked to spend his weekends in the country away from the affairs of state. He was quite a well-read man who had learned to speak French fluently and English reasonably well. He was little concerned with the trappings of high office. When he travelled, he went either by chauffeur-driven car or special train. He had held a pilot's licence since 1921, which meant that when he flew, he often piloted the aircraft himself.

ii) *His family*

If anything, his wife, Rachele, was even more reclusive. They were first married in 1915 at a civil ceremony but in 1925, much against her wishes, they repeated their marriage vows at a religious ceremony. She disliked city life in Rome and did not enjoy the company of her husband's political friends. Until 1925, she lived with her children in Milan but moved to Carpena in Romagna before finally joining her husband in Rome in 1929. In spite of Mussolini's many infidelities, their marriage survived and she still regarded her husband with affection. The family lived comfortably on his moderate primate minister's salary and the **royalties** he received from his speeches and writing that earned millions of lire. The Mussolinis had five children. The eldest child, Edda, was born in 1910, five years before her parents married. She was to become her father's favourite. Unfairly described as 'fat and unshapely', she was certainly intelligent and vivacious. Amongst her early suitors was a Jewish boy but her father objected to the marriage. She finally married Count Galeazzo Ciano, the son of an

royalties payments made to authors for every book sold

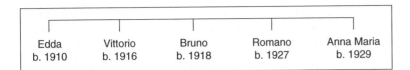

Edda	Vittorio	Bruno	Romano	Anna Maria
b. 1910	b. 1916	b. 1918	b. 1927	b. 1929

CHART 6
The Mussolini children

admiral and a loyal Fascist. Their marriage was the social event of 1930. With her husband appointed Italian envoy to China, the newly weds moved to Shanghai and it was there that their first child, Mussolini's first grandchild, was born a year later. In 1936, Ciano was appointed Foreign Secretary. In 1943, during the course of the Second World War, he was one of those who voted for his father-in-law's removal. Arrested during a visit to Germany, he was charged with high treason and shot. Edda never forgave her father for agreeing to her husband's execution. Vittorio, born in 1916, was destined to become a film producer. He worked on propaganda films but never gained any great success. He served in the armed forces during the war and afterwards made his way to Argentina. Bruno, born two years after his brother, became a pilot in the Italian airforce and took part in the invasion of Abyssinia in 1936. He was killed in 1941 when test-flying a bomber. His aircraft crashed near Pisa. In some ways, their youngest son, Romano, might well be considered the most successful of the Mussolini offspring. He became a fine jazz pianist and during his career toured Europe and the United States. During an early visit to Nazi Germany he angered his hosts by playing boogie-woogie which they considered to be American and decadent. Later, he played with many of the American jazz greats and won much critical acclaim. He married Anna Scicolone, the sister of the actress Sophia Loren. (Their daughter, Alessandra Mussolini, became a model and acted in erotic films before being elected a right-wing deputy to the Italian Parliament in 1992.) A second daughter, Anna Maria, was born to the Mussolinis in 1929. Her parents were distraught when she was stricken with poliomyelitis. She later married but had no children. Mussolini insisted that his children received no special privileges and they were all educated at state schools.

See page 211

iii)   *His friends and associates*
Mussolini, who once boasted that he had made no friends in his life, was a very private man who disliked entertaining. Amongst the few people whose company he enjoyed were Ezio Garibaldi, grandson of the patriot, Emil Ludwig, the German author, and his own brother, Arnaldo. Garibaldi kept him in touch with the real feelings of the Italian people since, unlike his many flatterers, he could trust him to tell the truth whilst Ludwig exercised his mind by engaging him in philosophical discussions. Mussolini was very close to his brother who helped him to write his autobiography and advised him on the content of his speeches. Many of those he entertained found him sophisticated and charming. Amongst the British guests he received were Sir Oswald Mosley, the leader of

PICTURE 37

Benito Mussolini, his wife Rachele and their five children

the British League of Fascists, Sir Austen and Lady Chamberlain, the British Foreign Secretary and his wife, and Clementine Churchill, wife of the future wartime prime minister. In letters to her husband, Clementine Churchill described Mussolini as 'very dignified' and 'one of the most wonderful men in the world.'

iv) *Mussolini – womaniser and seducer*

During his lifetime Mussolini was involved in many affairs and had numerous mistresses. He once bragged that the aristocratic and university-educated Angelica Balbanoff had been his mistress. An older woman and his intellectual superior, his claim might well have been a boast intended to impress others. In 1909, he had a short-lived affair with Fernanda Facchinelli who worked at the trade union headquarters. She died shortly after they met but he later helped her ageing mother financially. His affair with the well-educated and unconventional convert to Islam, Leda Rafanelli, lasted for most of 1913. Ida Dalser, daughter of a Sardinian innkeeper, was beautiful but neurotic and there is documentary evidence that he married her. However, in 1915, the same year as Mussolini married Rachele Guidi, Ida gave birth to a boy, Benito Albino. Mussolini never denied that he was the father of the child and paid the mother maintenance. Once in power, Leda began to pester him claiming that she was his legal wife. In 1926, she was arrested, certified insane and sent to a mental home where she died in 1937. It is uncertain what became of the son. One story is that he spoke too freely about his parentage and was also sent to an institution, where he died in 1942 aged 26. Another version is

PICTURE 38
*Claretta Petacci who first had a
crush on Mussolini when she
was a schoolgirl*

that he served with honour in the Italian navy and was killed in
action in 1940. Mussolini also had an affair with a Jewish woman,
Margherita Sarfatti. An art critic working for *Avanti*, their association lasted until the passing of new race laws put her at risk. He
saw to it that she went safely to the United States. He next met the
girl who is generally regarded as the true love of his life, Claretta
Petacci. A former schoolgirl fan and 29 years his junior, she was
the daughter of a respected Vatican physician. Separated from her
husband, who was discretely posted to Japan as an air attaché,
their relationship lasted until she chose to die with him in 1945.

See page 216

B *The myth*

i) *Mussolini and the 'cult of personality'*
There was another side to Benito Mussolini, a more dominating,
robust and threatening side that was not always apparent when he
was in the company of family and friends. This was the image that
he, his propagandists and those responsible for his public relations
sought to create – a cult of personality, 'the cult of *Il Duce*'. Backed
by the popular slogan 'Mussolini is always right', he was presented
to the Italian people as their saviour. He was the infallible leader
and world statesman who had saved them from Communism and
was about to restore their national prestige and take steps to bring
about their economic recovery. When Mussolini said 'The crowd
does not have to know, it must believe, it must submit to being
shaped', he indicated his appreciation of the value of public
opinion. More important, he knew how to manipulate it!

Benito Mussolini – multi-talented superman?

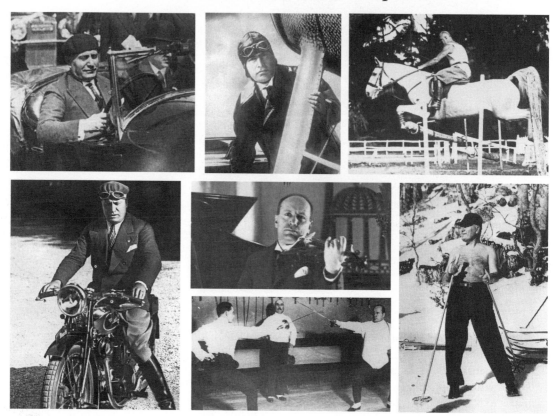

PICTURE 39 *Photographs of* Il Duce *were intended to prove to the Italian people that Mussolini was not like other men. Top left clockwise – Mussolini the daredevil driver, fearless aviator, skilled horseman, master skier, swashbuckling swordsman, expert biker and virtuoso on the violin (centre)*

ii)   *Mussolini – 'Artist in Propaganda'*

It was Mussolini's obsession to ensure that Fascism permeated through all aspects of Italian life and the everyday lives of its citizens. It was to be reflected in business, industry, education, the judiciary, the armed services, art and culture, sport and, if possible, even religion. Everywhere posters and slogans were used to promote his image and the ideals of Fascism. They ranged from the simple declaration 'Mussolini is God' to the instruction 'Believe! Obey! Fight!' to the more profound 'Better one day as a lion than a hundred years as a sheep'. Each day newspapers and magazines carried pictures of *Il Duce* and they also appeared on walls and public buildings. Newspaper editors were under instruction to expand and embroider the achievements of Fascism and play down or not mention at all its failures. Obituaries were no longer published since Mussolini disliked references to death and in 1933 there was no call to celebrate their leader's fiftieth birthday. Out to prove that he was not like other men, Fascist propaganda promoted Mussolini as a superman-type figure – an energetic, virile and assertive man of action. Pictures were circulated of him stripped to the waist driving a tractor or helping to harvest crops or in poses that illustrated his many skills as a horseman, wrestler, swimmer, racing car driver, pilot, violinist, writer and poet. Abroad this attracted much ridicule although ironically, he was accomplished in most of these skills, though not to the degree he claimed.

> In this construction of a *Duce*, sport, with its combination of masculinity and modernity, was an instant theme. Once sport had seemed 'made in England', a commentator noticed, but now the *Duce* himself the complete sportsman ... On a typical day, readers were assured, he would rise at seven, take a cold bath, scoff a glass of milk and then proceed to an hour's riding, leaping on to his horse like 'a born cowboy'. That exercise over, he might proceed to fence. He preferred the most manly and brutal weapon, the sabre, and, with his teeth set in grim determination, typically fought 'with a style that was totally personal' ... Similarly he was a devoted swimmer, and had just told an American journalist that he yearned also to have the time to practise football, tennis and even golf. No wonder the first issue in 1928 of the journal *Lo Sport Fascista* saluted the '*Duce*, aviator, fencer, rider, first sportsman of Italy'.

From Mussolini *by R.J.B. Bosworth, 2002*

iii) *Mussolini the master orator*
In public, Mussolini's personal dynamism and magnetism were most apparent in his spellbinding oratory. He was not just a ranting rabble-rouser, he was a skilled motivator. His speeches were vigorous and delivered **staccato** style. He always began quietly and downbeat but as he progressed he became increasingly agitated, his eyes rolled, he used his hands to make wild gesticulations and his voice rose to a **crescendo**. Then he would pause and stand akimbo with hands on hips and chin jutting forward to give his ecstatic crowd time to applaud. Later, he would watch his performance on film and study its affect on his audience. He always preferred to appear stern faced and, in order to maintain this image, he invariably refused to smile for photographers. Instead he maintained a facial expression that was half scowl and half pout. Always seemingly oozing with self-confidence, he once said, 'I would often like to be wrong, but it never happens.'

> **staccato** spoken rapidly in short sentences

> **crescendo** voice gradually increasing in volume

iv) *Mussolini the public figure*
Mussolini also liked to appear in public with celebrities. In 1933, he was frequently seen with Primo Carnera, nicknamed the 'Ambling Alp', who had won the world heavy-weight boxing title. Carnera was quickly dropped when a year later he lost his title to the American, Max Baer. Later Carnera expressed anti-Fascist

sympathies and spent the war years in a labour camp. Similarly *Il Duce* was seen in the company of the world famous conductor, Arturo Toscanini, until the maestro protested against new racial laws and left to make his home in the United States. Mussolini had better luck with the tenor, Beniamo Gigli, whom he referred to as 'the people's singer of Italy', and the eminent inventor, Guglielmo Marconi, who joined the Party in 1923 and later became a member of the Fascist Grand Council.

Mussolini was also given to gross exaggeration and this was particularly evident in his statements regarding Italy's military preparedness. He claimed that in a short time he could mobilise 'eight million bayonets' and manufacture sufficient aircraft 'to blot out the sky'. He boasted to his generals about armies that they well knew didn't exist. Balabanoff, an earlier friend who grew to despise him, said that Mussolini only had two aims – to become famous and to gain revenge on society. The view of many historians is that Mussolini's bombast, flamboyance and self-promotion were nothing more than a façade – a cover for a man who was basically very insecure. The American historian, T. Koon, is of the view that 'Mussolini's greatest talent, perhaps his only genuine talent, was his ability to manufacture myths and slogans that captured the popular imagination'. The problem was that as the myth grew, Mussolini became so divorced from reality that he came to believe it himself. He seemed to reach a point where he couldn't distinguish between what was true and false and what was relevant and superfluous. He spent more time on propaganda and self-promotion than he did making decisions and formulating policy. From a national point of view, the sheer weight of propaganda so engulfed the Italian people that it was inevitable that some, maybe many, maybe most, succumbed to it. If the election results of 1929 are accepted as accurate, then 8,506,576 Italians voted for the Fascists and a paltry 136,198 against. The result was an avalanche by any standards but was it a true reflection of the views of the people?

2 ↩ *IL DUCE*, THE PARTY AND PARLIAMENT

KEY ISSUE

Mussolini moves towards a one-man dictatorship.

As we have seen, during the years 1924, 1925 and 1926 Mussolini took steps to ensure that the Fascist Party was dominant in Italian politics. In April 1924, the first general election held under the Acerbo Law gave the Fascists an overwhelming majority in Parliament. Stirred into further action by the crisis over Matteotti that threatened to topple him, press censorship was introduced. In January 1925, Mussolini declared his intention of establishing a Fascist dictatorship. Then came a series of measures that prohibited non-Fascist trade unions (Vidoni Pact) and, in December, banned opposition parties. Finally, in January 1926, Mussolini assumed the right to rule by decree – to pass legislation on his own say so and without the approval of Parliament. However, the supremacy of the Fascist Party was not his main priority. His over-riding aim was to concentrate all power in his own hands and create what was to be in effect a one-man dictatorship. To achieve this, he needed to first be assured of his undisputed leadership of the Party, then to control Parliament and its associate institutions, and to establish his authority over institutions such as local government, the civil service, the judiciary and the armed services and reduce the status of the king, Victor Emmanuel III, to an irrelevance.

A *Winning control of the Party*

To exercise total control over the Fascist Party would need a subtle strategy. Whilst local Party leaders, the *ras*, paid him lip service and accepted his leadership, they were not always prepared to go along with and implement his policy decisions. The *ras* represented the more radical views in the Party and the capitalist industrialists and landowners feared their intentions. Mussolini's position was strengthened when he turned the rabble and cornerstone of the authority of the *ras*, the

ras see page 73

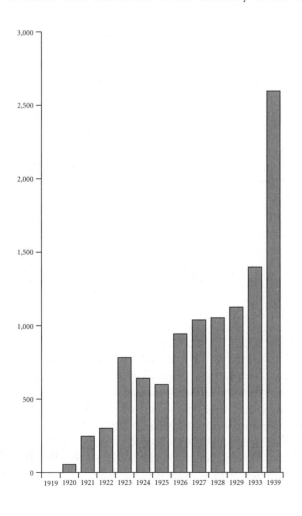

1919	3,000
1920	55,000
1921	249,000
1922	300,000
1923	783,000
1924	642,000
1925	600,000
1926	940,000
1927	1,035,000
1928	1,051,000
1929	1,124,000
1933	1,400,000
1939	2,600,000

TABLE 16
*Membership of the Italian
Fascist Party (PNF)*

DIAGRAM 3
*Membership of the Italian
Fascist Party (PNF)*

1925–26	Roberto Farinacci
1926–30	Augusto Turati
1930–31	Giovanni Giurati
1931–39	Achille Starace

TABLE 17
Secretaries of the Fascist Party 1925–39

KEY ISSUE

The need to remove possible rivals.

elites the most influential and privileged groups

squadristri, into a more disciplined militia under his control. The earlier establishment of the Fascist Grand Council as the main policy-making body was also to his advantage. Since he appointed its members, he exercised full control over the Council. At the Party Conference in 1925, Mussolini felt sufficiently secure to demand that his deputies cease their in-fighting and internal wrangling and unite under his leadership. During this period he purged the Party of dissidents and any whose loyalty was suspect so that by the end of 1928, he was firmly in control of the Party. Even so, differences of opinion based on self-interest still existed within the Party between the socialist, nationalist and conservative elements. To ensure that these differences never posed a threat, Mussolini skillfully played one off against the other. Open expressions of these differences became increasingly muted and finally lapsed altogether. In the end, the Fascist Party surrendered to Mussolini with surprising ease. In order to secure his position even further, *Il Duce* saw to it that the most important post in the Party, that of Party Secretary, was held by someone of undisputed loyalty.

He also cunningly promoted to senior positions within the Party men who presented no threat to him. Such appointees were by nature yes-men, totally dedicated to him and, in some instances, prepared to show a willingness to offer patronage and accept bribes. In return for their loyalty, they held steady if not over-demanding positions for which they received more than generous salaries. The few men of charisma and with any drive and ambition, such as Italo Balbo and Dino Grandi, were given relatively insignificant postings abroad to get them out of the way – Balbo was appointed governor-general of Libya and Grandi sent to London as the Italian ambassador.

B *Exercising control over Parliament*

Measures had already been taken that effectively robbed Parliament of all its influence. With no power to discuss policy or debate and amend legislation, it was reduced to a sham institution without any meaningful function. With the opposition parties banned and changes in the electoral system ensuring the continuation of Fascist rule indefinitely, Parliament merely rubber stamped decisions already agreed by Mussolini. In fact, they had no need to meet at all since policy decisions were invariably accepted *en bloc* by a chorus of approval without even the formality of a vote.

C *Controlling other institutions*

In order to avoid damaging confrontations with other institutions that largely represented the Italian **elites** such as local government, the civil service, the judiciary and the armed services, Mussolini adopted a policy of infiltration and encroachment – he sought to gain control by stealth. In some instances this did not prove too difficult since upper and middle class bureaucrats already favourably disposed to him dominated certain institutions. First, he saw to it that people likely to be difficult were removed and replaced by men appointed by the Party. This had already happened in local government when, in 1926, men nominated by the Party replaced the remaining elected representatives and mayors were deposed in favour of *podestas* appointed from Rome.

Career officials not averse to Mussolini's style of government already largely staffed the civil service. They soon learned that membership of the Fascist Party enhanced their promotion prospects and, by 1935, it was a condition of service that civil servants were Party members. The number of civil servants was increased to become part of what the historian Mark Robson has described as a 'bloated bureaucracy offering secure undemanding jobs to Fascist supporters'.

In the judiciary, judges, barristers and solicitors who were opposed to or were not sufficiently enthusiastic about Fascism were declared undesirable and purged. Whilst the old judicial system was largely retained, there were occasions when Mussolini directly intervened in cases to decide verdicts and punishments. Malcontents were liable to be taken before a special tribunal or subject to arrest and imprisonment without trial.

See page 115

Although the army's declared loyalty was to the King, gaining control of the armed services presented no problem. This was because the military and Mussolini generally shared the same ambitions – the expansion of the forces, the increased production and development of more modern weapons and a more vigorous foreign policy aimed at gaining further overseas possessions. The army gave up its traditional salute in favour of the Fascist-style Roman raised arm salute and agreed to have Fascist-type insignia on their uniforms.

The overall affect of the Fascist domination of the major national institutions was to bring about major changes in the make up of the Party. The influx of technocrats and white-collar workers meant that their representation in the Party increased substantially whilst the membership of workers and peasants, once over 30% of the total, fell dramatically. This was because further electoral changes introduced in 1928 had limited the vote to men over 21 who were members of syndicates and those who paid substantial sums in taxes. Consequently, with sections of the working class disenfranchised, the electorate fell from 10 to 3 million. Another affect was to increase even more the delay and confusion in the administration and to make the offer of bribes a way of life. Too often promotion depended on having the right contacts and the wherewithal to offer a *bustarella*, the name Italians gave to the brown envelope that contained the bribe. They also spoke of men gaining office in that way as being *sottogoverno* – a lower or unworthy government.

See page 87

3 ⌐ MUSSOLINI AND KING VICTOR EMMANUEL III

To a degree, Victor Emmanuel III was responsible for Mussolini's rise to power and his survival in office. In 1922, he had refused to call on the army to disperse the Fascist march on Rome and instead offered

See pages 90–2

Mussolini the premiership; in 1924 at the time of the Matteotti crisis, he had declined to be part of any move to replace the Fascist leader. Later, he did nothing to prevent Mussolini infringing the Italian Constitution which, on his accession to the throne, he had sworn to uphold. He also bestowed upon Mussolini and other leading Fascists medals and decorations he might have withheld. Both men shared the title Field Marshal of the Empire.

A *Relations between the King and his Prime Minister*

Although in public both put on pretence of friendship, in reality relations between the two men were always tense. The King appreciated that he needed Mussolini's support to retain his throne whilst Mussolini, who could have easily removed Victor Emmanuel, hesitated to do so in case he offended many on the Right – conservatives, monarchists and the military. Twice weekly, the Prime Minister went through the ritual of conferring with the King, and the monarch dutifully signed new decrees placed before him. There were some occasions when they disagreed. Victor Emmanuel did not favour the inclusion of the Fascist emblem on the national flag or agree with Mussolini's decision to increase the powers of the Fascist Grand Council. They seldom appeared together in public and when they did so, Mussolini delighted in taking steps to exploit their difference in height. There was no love lost between the two men. In private, Victor Emmanuel expressed the view that his prime minister was 'vulgar and offensive' whilst Mussolini had a range of crude nicknames for his king. Yet it was probably for fear of offending Mussolini that the King declined to attend the funeral of the former five times prime minister and devoted suckling monarchist, Giovanni Giolitti, when he died in 1928. By 1930, the King had abdicated his responsibilities, though not his position, and the Italian monarchy had become an irrelevance. Later, in 1943, Victor Emmanuel did order Mussolini's arrest but by this time the Second World War was going badly for the Axis powers and Italy was clearly on the losing side. In 1946, the King abdicated and spent the remainder of his life living as an exile in Egypt. In the same year, a referendum rejected the monarchy and Italy became a republic.

See page 210

See page 226

4 ～ OPPOSITION AND REPRESSION

With so much popular support for Mussolini and his Fascists, it is questionable if many Italians saw the need let alone had the courage to oppose their regime. Yet there were opposition groups, though they were of little consequence.

KEY ISSUE

The effectiveness of the Italian opposition to the Fascist regime.

A *Opposition*

Some Communists formed underground cells and published and circulated their own clandestine newspaper, *Unita*, Unity, and distributed anti-Fascist leaflets. The movement was to grow but in the 1920s attracted less than 7,000 active members. Another opposition group was *Giustizia e Liberta*, Justice and Liberty. It was led by Carlo Roselli who, in 1929, escaped from prison and made his way to France. His aim was to bring about an alliance between Italian Socialists and Liberals. From Paris, he made the world's press aware of the atrocities being carried out by Mussolini's regime whilst, in Italy, Roselli's supporters circulated anti-Fascist literature. During the Spanish Civil War (1936–9), he supported the Republicans and fought with the International Brigade. During this time, he famously used the slogan 'Today Spain; tomorrow Italy'. In 1937, he returned to France to recuperate from wounds received in Spain. There, Roselli and his brother were murdered on the French Riviera by a group of French Fascists, the *Cagoulards*. Subsequent investigations proved that Count Ciano had played a part in organising Roselli's assassination.

B *Repression*

In Italy, opponents of Mussolini had long faced the terror of the Fascist gangs, the *squadristi*. It has been estimated that by 1926, the *squadristi* had murdered 2,000 victims and wounded or maimed thousands more. As a more legitimate way of ensuring law and order, Mussolini greatly increased the number of civilian police, the *polizia*, and turned the *squadristri* into an official militia, the *Milizia Voluntaria Per La Sicurezza Nationale*, MSVN, a force of some 50,000 men. Its purpose was to act as an auxiliary police force and help the regular police to maintain law and order. Its organisation was deliberately styled on the Roman army with units known as legions and ranks that included centurions. The leader of the militia was Arturo Bocchini (1880–1940), an unusual choice for such a role since he was known to have a gigantean appetite for both food and women and a reputation for accepting bribes and treating police funds as his own. However, it was the attempted assassination of Mussolini by Anteo Zamboni in 1926 that finally 'took the brakes off state repression'. In 1926, a Law for the Defence of the State led to the establishment of a secret police force, the *Organizzazione Vigilanza Repressione Antifascismo*, the OVRA, and set up a special tribunal, the *Tribuna Speciale Per La Difesa Dello Stato*. The new law was the work of Luigi Federzoni (1878–1967) of the Ministry of the Interior and the Minister of Justice, Alfredo Rocco (1875–1935). Amongst those identified by the new law as being a danger to public safety were:

See page 98

> Those who have committed or have shown any intention of committing any act intended to disturb the national, social or economic regulations of the State … or to impede the carrying out of the functions of the State in such a manner as to injure in any way the national interests either at home or abroad.

Such people became liable to:

> A sentence of compulsory domicile that will last no less than one and no more than five years, and will be carried out either in a colony or commune of the kingdom other than the normal residence of the person who has been sentenced.

OVRA agents were granted powers to arrest and hold suspects if necessary without trial, carry out searches, tap telephones and intercept mail. They also committed acts of violence although members of the general public not suspected of being politically active and hostile to Fascism were usually left alone. The real purpose of OVRA was to impress on Italians the need to conform and the risks involved in doing otherwise. The tribunal sat in judgement of people thought to be a danger to the state. During the period 1927 to 1943, it met on 720 occasions to consider 13,547 cases. Of these, 5,155 were found guilty but only 49 sentenced to death. Of these, only 31 were actually carried out. Others received prison sentences of varying length. Other forms of punishment included being held under house detention or subject to *confino*. *Confino* meant being banished to what amounted to a penal colony on Lipari, Lampedusa, Tremiti, Ponza, Venotene and other islands off the coast where conditions were far from severe:

From Mussolini *by Jasper Ridley, 1997.*

> The victims of the *confino* … were not worked to death like the inmates of Stalin's labour camps, or subjected to the calculated cruelties of Hitler's concentration camps … Mussolini's internees were lodged in cottages of their own choice on the prison islands. They were obliged to attend roll-call twice a day, but otherwise could move at will on the island and do what they wished. They were paid five lire a day, which was later increased to ten lire, which they could spend in buying what they fancied from the shops on the islands. Their families at home were paid two lire a day and one lira a day for each child. The internees could be granted leave of absence for a few days for compassionate reasons, though some of them took advantage of their leave to escape, in breach of their promise to return to confinement. Several of them escaped to France, and Paris became the main centre for Italian anti-Fascist refugees.

Fascist repression and intimidation was also extended to societies both legal and illegal that were considered a threat to the state. Although it was known that Giuseppe Garibaldi, Victor Emmanuel II and other eminent Italians had been members, steps were taken against Italian Freemasons. To start with, Party members were not allowed to be Freemasons but this turned to open violence when the homes of Freemasons as well as their lodges were burned down. Finally Freemasonry itself was abolished. To their credit, the Fascists finally turned on the illegal criminal brotherhood, the *Mafia*. Following Mussolini's instructions, Cesare Mori (1883–1942) set out to crush the *Mafia* network in Sicily and elsewhere in Italy. During the period 1925–8, thousands of *Mafiosi* were arrested, their leaders brought to trial and their activities brought to an end. Abroad, the foreign press praised Mussolini for his removal of this notorious criminal element in Italian society. The Fascists also took steps to 'Italianise' the German, French

Q

Why were the Fascists opposed to Freemasonry?

CHART 7
Mussolini's fascist regime – its strengths and weaknesses

Strengths	Weaknesses
The popular appeal of Mussolini's policies that promised to bring political stability, economic prosperity and the restoration of national prestige.	Lack of clear-cut policies led to scepticism. In the long run, evidence of failure, inefficiency and corruption turned to disillusionment.
Mussolini was able to play on the fear of the advance of Communism. This ensured that he had the continued support of the industrialists, landowners and the elites of the upper and middle classes.	For a time Mussolini's leadership was under threat from the *ras* and the more ambitious members of the Fascist hierarchy.
Mussolini's personal charisma. The successful promotion of his personality cult – an infallible, superman figure. He was also a fine orator and had the ability to manufacture popular slogans.	From the start, there were those who saw Mussolini's self promotion as a super-human cult figure as nothing more than crude posturing. Some thought his antics absurd.
The Fascist regime was a one-man dictatorship in which Mussolini controlled the Party (PNF), the Grand Council and Parliament. The opposition parties and the trade unions had been eliminated.	Hostile public opinion could still be aroused as was evident following the murder of Matteotti. Although resistance movements such as the Communists and *Giustizia e Liberta* were ineffective they could develop into something more substantial. It should also be remembered that both the Monarchy and the Church still retained a degree of independence.
Imposed censorship made it difficult for opposed points of view to be heard.	The Fascist regime's attempt to censor the media was far from effective. It tried but failed to prevent details of Pope Pius' encyclical of 1931 becoming known (see page 124).
Public fear of the Fascist militia (MVSN) and OVRA.	The activities of the MVSN and OVRA were seldom over brutal and failed to intimidate the majority of the Italian people.
The passing of the Lateran Treaty in 1929 further increased Mussolini's prestige and won the regime the support of many Roman Catholics.	The truce in the conflict between the Church and State brought about by the Lateran Treaty was soon broken over disagreements about Catholic Action and later, the treatment of Italian Jews.
The indoctrination of the young went some way towards ensuring the future continued support for Fascism.	Many parents as well as the Roman Catholic Church opposed the indoctrination of Italy's young people.

See page 139

and Slav racial minorities living in their border regions. However, it was not until 1938, and at Hitler's instigation, that Mussolini finally turned on Italian Jews.

As we have seen, during the years after 1922, Mussolini's Fascist regime continued to retain the support of the majority of the Italian people. For as long as the realisation of Mussolini's promises of a better and more secure future seemed likely, they were willing to back him and countenance his methods. However, once his achievements failed to match his rhetoric, things began to go badly wrong.

5 ⌐ STRUCTURED AND ESSAY QUESTIONS

A *This section consists of questions that might be used for discussion (or written answers) as a way of expanding on the chapter and testing your understanding.*

1. Do you agree that 'Mussolini was by no means a wholly loathsome character'?
2. What is meant by 'a cult of personality'?
3. What methods were used to promote the image of Mussolini?
4. Why did Mussolini seek the power to rule by decree?
5. To what extent did Mussolini control the Fascist Grand Council?
6. What was the significance of *bustarella*?
7. To what extent might the relationship between Mussolini and Victor Emmanuel III be described as cordial?
8. Who were mainly subject to the punishment known as *confino*?
9. Did the Fascist authorities successfully curb the activities of the *Mafia*?

B *Essay questions.*

1. 'His greatest gift was his ability to manufacture myths and slogans.' To what extent do you agree with this view of Mussolini?
2. Was the opposition to Fascist rule in Italy of any real significance?
3. To what extent had Italy become a totalitarian state by 1930?

6 ⌐ MAKING NOTES

Read the advice section about making notes on page xix of the Preface: How to use this book, and then make your own notes based on the following headings and questions.

1. *Benito Mussolini – the man and the myth.*
   (a) Mussolini – his character and personality
            – his lifestyle and daily routine
            – as a husband and father.

(b) The methods used by Fascist propagandists to develop Mussolini's 'cult of personality'.

(c) To what extent did Mussolini contribute to the popularity of the Fascist Party?

2. *Il Duce, the Party and parliament.*

   (a) What was the significance of the Vidoni Pact?

   (b) Mussolini's strategy to retain control of the Party.

   (c) The reasons for the increase in the membership of the Fascist Party during the late 1920s and 1930s.

   (d) The social make-up of the membership of the Party.

3. *Mussolini and King Victor Emmanuel III.*

   (a) The nature of the relationship between the King and his prime minister.

   (b) To what extent would it would it be true to say that 'there was no love lost between the two men'?

4. *Opposition and repression.*

   (a) Evidence of opposition to the Fascist regime in Italy.

   (b) Means used by the Fascists to repress opposition.

   (c) The importance of OVRA.

   (d) Fascist measures against   (i) Freemasonry

   (ii) the *Mafia.*

9

Fascist Italy – Domestic Policy 1922–1939

INTRODUCTION

During this period, the Fascists set about implementing policies that would complete the transformation of Italy into a one-party totalitarian state or, as the Fascist philosopher, Emilio Gentile put it, a situation in which there would be 'no individual or groups outside the State'. At the same time, Mussolini had to ensure that his regime remained popular and continued to have the support of the masses. As we shall see, efforts were made to finally end the rift with the Catholic Church, to use the education system and youth organisations to indoctrinate the young, to dictate the role of women in Fascist society and to ensure that Fascism entered into every aspect of Italian social and cultural life. It was also a time during which Mussolini went back on his word and, in order to impress Hitler, agreed to introduce anti-Semitic policies. To what extent were Mussolini and his Fascists successful in their attempt to convert the masses and then retain their confidence? Was this a time when the myth of Mussolini and the frailty of Fascist policies were cruelly exposed?

1 ⌐ THE FASCIST STATE AND THE ROMAN CATHOLIC CHURCH

See page 5

The problem created in 1870 when Pope Pius IX refused to recognise the new Kingdom of Italy still had to be resolved. Although, at least on

1909	Futurist movement founded
1923	*Opera Nazionale Dopolavoro* established
1924	Nationwide radio broadcasting started
1925	Women able to vote in local elections
1926	Start of the Battle for Births
1928	*Balilla* established
1929	Lateran Treaty and Concordat agreed
1931	Pope Pius XI's encyclical *Non Abiamo Bisogno* published
	Teachers to take oath of loyalty to regime
1933	Employment of women regulated by quota system
1937	Teachers to belong to Fascist Association
	Ministro Della Cultura Popolare (Minculpop) set up
1938	*Ministro Degli Sceinziati Razzisti* (Manifesto of Racial Scientists) published
	Fascist Decalogue published
	Fascist Race Law introduced
	Pius XI criticised Fascist anti-Semitism
1939	Bottai's Fascist School Charter

TABLE 18

Date line showing domestic policy in Fascist Italy

the face of it, the Fascist regime and the Roman Catholic Church appeared to co-exist harmoniously, there was a need to reach a formal agreement on the status of the Papacy within Italy. It was well known that Mussolini had earlier been an opponent of Roman Catholicism. He had poured scorn on the Church's rites and teachings and had written a pamphlet, *God Does Not Exist*, and a novel, *The Cardinal's Mistress*, which had caused offence to many Catholics. More recently, Fascist extremists had attacked Catholic churches and other religious buildings and interrupted religious processions. Although the Fascist leader was not a religious man and had once professed atheism, he fully appreciated the importance of the Catholic faith to the vast majority of Italians and realised that any open conflict with the Church might be damaging. It was in the interests of both sides to heal the rift between the State and the Church. From Mussolini's point of view, it would add further to his prestige both at home and abroad; from the Church's viewpoint, it would help to restore their influence on the every day lives of the Italian people. Consequently Mussolini took measures to appease the Papal authorities so that instead of being considered 'an enemy of true faith', he would appear to be more acceptable.

A *Steps towards reconciliation*

In 1923, during his maiden speech to the Chamber, Mussolini made favourable references to the Church. Mussolini's decision to outlaw Freemasonry had pleased the Catholic authorities, as did the reintroduction of a wide range of measures that appeared to support Catholic teaching. Catholic ritual was restored to public ceremonies as well as the crucifix in school and the law courts. Religious instruction again appeared in the syllabus of state schools and Milan's Catholic university was given official recognition. State allowances to Catholic priests were increased and they were exempt from taxation. Protection was given to religious processions. Now as a champion of family values and guardian of public morals, Mussolini saw to it that the laws relating to divorce were tightened, penalties were introduced for adultery, contraception frowned upon and abortion made almost impossible. *Il Duce's* new morality extended even further – gambling and heavy drinking were to be discouraged, swearing in public made an offence and infection by syphilis classified as a crime. For Italian women, the wearing of short skirts and excessive make-up were discouraged and dancing, now deemed to be 'immortal and improper', strictly regulated. As a further gesture, in 1925, Mussolini and his wife, Rachele, went through a religious ceremony in Milan ten years after the initial civil ceremony and had their three children baptised. For their part, some Catholic priests spoke favourably about Fascism in their sermons and agreed to bless Fascist regalia and banners. However, the position remained far from settled since there was no way in which the Fascist government would agree to restore former lands, the Papal States, or Papal influence in temporal matters in Italy. There also remained those in the Church and the Fascist Party who remained bitterly opposed to any form of agreement with the other. Both sides would clearly need to show a willingness to compromise.

With Cardinal Pietro Gasparri representing the Papacy and Francisco Pacelli, the brother of Eugenio Pacelli, the cleric destined to be the next Pope, involved from time to time, negotiations began in an atmosphere of suspicion and distrust on both sides. Progress was slow and was to extend over three years of hard bargaining. On 11 February 1929, the Lateran Treaty was finally signed but even then under duress. Mussolini had made it clear that if no agreement was reached he would unloose a campaign of violence against Catholic organisations.

B *The Lateran Treaty of 1929*

The final agreement consisted of two documents, a treaty and a Concordat.

i)   *The treaty*. The treaty, which covered the territorial and financial arrangements, was largely political in content. In Part I, Papal sovereignty was recognised over 44 hectares of land in the centre of Rome around St Peter's, the Vatican City. It was to have its own diplomatic corps, army, police and courts, radio station, newspaper and postal services. In return, the Pope recognised the Kingdom of Italy under the rule of the House of Savoy with Rome as its capital city. Part II of the treaty covered the financial arrangements. In return for giving up its claim over Italian territory, the former Papal States, the Church was to receive 750 million lire in money and a further 1,000 million lire in government bonds.

ii) *The Concordat*. The Concordat was intended to regulate the relations between the Church and the State. Under its terms, Roman Catholicism was recognised as the established or the State Church of Italy although the State maintained the right to veto Church appointments and Catholic clergy agreed not to belong to any political party. Civil marriage became no longer necessary and divorce was not possible without the sanction of the Church. Religious teaching became compulsory in all state primary and secondary schools.

iii) *Who got the best deal – the Church or the Fascist State?*
     Some Fascists thought that Mussolini had got the worst of the deal. They felt that he had gone too far and given away more than was necessary. However, across the country as a whole, delighted Italians gave thanks to Mussolini, the man who, so they claimed, had 'given back God to Italy and Italy to God'. In a speech made a month later to the government, Mussolini said:

I think it is far from absurd to maintain that only in a regime based on this Concordat can the logical, normal, healthy separation between Church and State become a reality, thus delimiting the tasks and functions of each. Each has its own rights, its own duties, its own authority, its own sphere of competence. Only on this assumption can the two collaborate on certain issues on the basis of their own sovereignty. The peace between the Quirinal (Italian government) and the Vatican is an event of supreme importance, not only for Italy, but for the world. For Italians it is enough to remember that on 11th February 1929 the Kingdom of Italy, ruled over by the House of Savoy and with Rome as the capital of the Italian State, was finally and solemnly recognised by the Supreme Pontiff.

To what extent had Mussolini actually got his way? The Fascist leader thought that he had won the blessing of the Catholic Church at minimal cost to the Fascist State. He did not consider the Lateran Treaty to be an agreement between equals but an alliance that left the Catholic Church subordinate to him. He was also determined to confine the influence of the Church to religious matters. He certainly did not envisage any Church involvement in Italian politics or a situation in which he would tolerate any Papal criticisms of Fascist policies. Consequently, old differences soon re-emerged and these became only too evident; on his first to the Vatican after the treaty, Mussolini made a point of declining to kiss the Pope's hand. More serious was the crisis that developed over Catholic Action.

C *Catholic Action*

Catholic Action had originally been set up in 1865. A lay organisation, it consisted of several sections one of which was responsible for the organisation and management of Catholic youth groups. With the abolition of Catholic trade unions and the Catholic Boy Scout movement, it was the only remaining body actively engaged in caring for the

PICTURE 40
Roman Catholic priests parading in Rome appear to indicate their endorsement of Fascism

interests of Catholics. Though Article 43 of the Concordat recognised its independence, Mussolini felt that its activities encroached on those of Fascist youth movements and decided to eliminate it. Catholic Action was subject to hostile attacks in the press and there were attacks on the premises and members of the organisation. Pope Pius XI was not easily brow-beaten. In 1931, he responded with the encyclical *'Non Abiamo Bisogno'* – 'We Have No Need'. In his circular letter to his bishops he wrote:

> We have protested against the campaign of false and unjust accusations which preceeded the disbanding of the associations of young people and of the university students affiliated with Catholic Action. It is wrong for the Fascists to monopolise completely the young from the tenderest years up to manhood and womanhood, and all for the exclusive advantage of a party, of a regime based on ideology which clearly resolves itself into a true and real pagan worship of the state … The idea of a state which makes young generations belong entirely to it … cannot be reconciled by a Catholic with the Catholic doctrine and the Catholic practice …

Publication of the encyclical was banned in Italy but the influential American Cardinal, Francis Spellman, saw to it that copies reached France and it was consequently published in the Papal newspaper *L'Osservatore Romano*. Smuggled out of the Vatican, the Fascist authorities failed to confiscate copies so that the content of the encyclical was widely read by the Italian public. The outcome was a compromise agreement by which Catholic bishops agreed not to appoint officers to Catholic Action that belonged to 'groups adverse to the regime' and the Action's juvenile members would not become involved in sporting activities. In future, it had to concentrate on educational and other recreational activities. In other words, Catholic Action could no longer engage in activites that brought it into direct competition with Fascist youth organisations. Afterwards there was a period of relative accord between the Church and Fascist regime that ended when Mussolini began a campaign against Italy's Jews.

See pages 138–40

2 ᕦ INDOCTRINATION – THE FASCIST EDUCATION SYSTEM AND YOUTH MOVEMENTS

KEY ISSUE

The need to indoctrinate the young.

As was the case in Nazi Germany and Stalinist Russia, the indoctrination of the young was essential in order to guarantee continued support for the Party and ensure a firm foundation for Mussolini's Fascist regime. Across Italy, education was provided by state schools and a range of independent schools of which the majority were Catholic. The aim of the Fascist education system was not merely to produce loyal, unquestioning citizens but also to mould the characters of children and so create, both mentally and physically, the perfect 'new Italian men and women'. However, the old problem of illiteracy persisted and much needed to be done before Italy could produce young men and women with the skills needed to lead the country forward into an advanced technological age.

The first Fascist Minister of Education was Giovanni Gentile (1875–1944). A university professor, educationalist and the so-called 'philosopher of Fascism', Mussolini gave him the task of laying down the guidelines for the future development of education at all levels. He was also to oversee the publication of the *Enciclopedia Italiana*, a work of scholarship not unlike our own *Encyclopedia Britannica*. Gentile allowed considerable freedom of thought as he sought to improve educational standards at all levels. Part of his plan was to provide facilities for the most able children to attain standards of excellence and more suitable and relevant education for those less gifted. His policies were not well received by all Fascists and his influence diminished as Mussolini and the government became more involved in framing future education policy.

A *The curriculum*

Gentile's successors followed very different principles and school curriculum was frequently revised to accommodate their changing views. In all schools, the cult of Mussolini was emphasised. A portrait of the Fascist leader was hung in all classrooms alongside that of Victor Emmanuel III whilst wall posters illustrated Fascist achievements and attitudes. Teachers had to emphasise Mussolini's genius and superman qualities and each day began and ended with the chanting of Fascist slogans such as '*Mussolini ha sempre ragione*' – 'Mussolini is always right'. Textbooks had to conform to the Fascist view and this meant that many had to be rewritten and some banned. In 1928, one government-authorised textbook was introduced into junior schools, the *libro unico*. It covered all subjects. Much teaching concentrated on Italian history and literature. Children were taught that Italy was 'the true cradle of European civilisation' and exaggerated claims were made about Italian achievements. History teaching concentrated largely on – the greatness of Roman Empire, the Italian Renaissance, the *Risorgimento* and, of course, Mussolini and the saga of the Fascist rise to power. History textbooks that lacked adequate patriotic content were considered unsuitable and replaced with books that showed less concern for the truth. For an example, with regard to the First World War classes were told, 'It was Italy's entry that decided the outcome of the war … It was Italy that won the war at the Battle of Vittorio Veneto.'

Schools, which were all single sex, also placed great emphasis on physical fitness and out-door activities. In accordance with Mussolini's apparent revised views on religion and the terms of the Lateran Treaty, religious instruction was introduced into all schools and the crucifix returned to the classroom. Fascist indoctrination took many forms and

See page 122

was often subtle. Children were taught to read and write by using books full of Fascist cartoons and quotations from Mussolini speeches. Even at an early age, youngsters were instructed in the need for unquestioning obedience and to this end they chanted *Credere! Obbedire! Combattere!* – 'Believe! Obey! Fight! Mussolini also reminded children, 'The eyes of the *Duce* are on every one of you ... A child who even while refusing to obey an order, asks 'why?' is like a bayonet made of milk. You must obey because you must.'

In 1938, the authorities published a Fascist Decalogue that amounted to a distorted version of the biblical Ten Commandments. Used in secondary schools and colleges, it read:

1. Remember that those who fell for the revolution and for the empire march at the head of your columns.
2. Your comrade is your brother. He lives with you, thinks with you, and is at your side in battle.
3. Service to Italy can be given at all times, in all places and by every means. It can be paid with toil and also with blood.
4. The enemy of Fascism is your enemy. Show him no mercy.
5. Discipline is the sunshine of armies. It prepares and illuminates the victory.
6. He who advances to attack with determination has victory already in his grasp.
7. Conscious and complete obedience is the virtue of the soldier.
8. There do not exist important and unimportant things. There is only duty.
9. The Fascist revolution has depended in the past and still depends on the bayonets of its soldiers.
10. Mussolini is always right.

In 1939, Giueseppe Bottai (1895–1959) put forward a Fascist School Charter that was intended to replace the old system, which he considered to be too bourgeois, with one more responsive to the needs of less able, non-academic pupils. Its aim, he claimed, was to promote 'the eternal value of the Italian race and its civilisation.' The main tasks of the new schools were twofold. They were 'to provide cultural and professional orientation so that men capable of facing the actual problems of scientific research and production may be trained according to reason and needs' and 'strengthen children and young people on the path of the traditional religion and destiny in Italy'. Italian schools were to be classified as elementary, intermediate and superior. Pre-school *Scoula Materna* or nursery schools were provided for children aged four to six. There followed a period at elementary schools until the age of 14, then five years at an intermediate school before proceeding to lyceums and institutes. Promotion from one stage to the next was by examination and the State provided all textbooks and other materials. In 1943, Bottai, the education reformer, quarrelled with Mussolini. Using the name André Bataille, he escaped from Italy to join the French Foreign Legion and fight against the Germans.

B *Teachers*

From the outset, those in the teaching profession who could not be reconciled to Fascism were dismissed. In 1931, teachers were made to take an oath of loyalty:

> I swear to be loyal to the King, to his successors, to the Fascist regime, to observe loyally the Constitution and the other laws of the State, to exercise the profession of teacher and to carry out all academic duties with the aim of training upright and hardworking citizens who are devoted to the fatherland and to the Fascist regime. I swear that I neither belong to nor shall belong to associations or parties whose activities do not harmonise with the duties of my profession.

The vast majority of teachers took the oath and some of those who hesitated were urged to do so on the grounds that it was only an unimportant formality. In the same year, all teachers' associations were merged into a Fascist Association and two years later, all teachers had to be members of the Fascist Party and were expected to wear Fascist uniforms on special occasions. In 1937, membership of the Association also became compulsory.

It is difficult to assess the extent to which the Fascist attempt to use the education system to indoctrinate the young was successful. It had obstacles to overcome – the Church, unconvinced teachers and parents who objected to having their offspring brain-washed. However, there were also positive aspects. The school leaving age was raised, the illiteracy rate fell and government expenditure on education more than doubled.

C *The universities*

There was less need for the Fascists to be concerned about influencing university education. By this time, students would have already passed through the state system of elementary and secondary education and been subjected to some twelve years of Fascist indoctrination. With some students, it would certainly have worked but others would have resisted the propaganda. In any case, with intelligent and more mature students the battle for their minds would already have been won or lost. Nevertheless, university students were expected to join the *Gioventi Universitaria Fascista*, the University Fascist Youth. The majority did so because of the immediate benefits of membership – the use of sports facilities, half price admission to places of entertainment and part exemption from future military service – and future benefits – enhanced career prospects. At universities, the real struggle was to bring the academic staff – the professors and lecturers – into line. Unlike schoolteachers, those who lacked enthusiasm for Fascism could not be so easily be sacked and replaced. Many were reluctant to both join the Party and take the oath of allegiance and had to be coaxed by being told they were nothing more than formalities. Even so, out of 1,250 only 11 refused and some went further and agreed to wear black shirts on special occasions such as graduation day. Again, there were positive aspects. During the Fascist period, the number of students at Italian universities increased from 54,000 in 1921 to 165,000 in 1942 and they came from more diverse backgrounds than had previously been the case.

D *Fascist youth movements*

The indoctrination of Italian children was not confined to the classroom but continued afterwards, in the evenings and at weekends, by membership of one of several youth organisations that made up the *Opera Nazionale Balilla*, ONB or just simply the *Balilla*. The movement took its name from Giovan Battista Perasso, a young hero who was nicknamed Balilla, who had played a part in the uprising against the Austrians in Genoa in 1756.

Type of unit	Details of membership
Figli della Lupa (Children of the She-Wolf)	Boys and girls aged 6–8
Balilla	Boys aged 8–14
Avanguardisti	Boys aged 15–18
Piccole Italiane	Girls aged 8–12
Giovani Italiane	Girls aged 13–18

CHART 8
The Opera Nazionale Balilla *(ONB)*

KEY ISSUE

The appeal of membership of Balilla *to young Italians.*

See pages 123–4

In addition to ensuring the continued influence of Fascist propaganda, the various sections of the *Balilla* youth movement provided a wide range of activities for its members. Sports, physical exercise and keep-fit classes were encouraged as was attendance at weekend rallies and summer camps. Much attention was also given to the militaristic aspects of the movement and uniformed members were expected to take part in drill and parades. Girls were encouraged to take part in more feminine pursuits and received domestic training in cookery and childcare to prepare them for motherhood. Amongst both boys and girls there were some whose enthusiasm waned and attendance lapsed. Moreover, the *Balilla* had to contend with the counter attractions provided by other youth organisations, particularly those of the Catholic Church.

Not surprisingly, the Fascist youth organisations adopted the motto 'Believe! Obey! Fight!' and members had to swear an oath of loyalty:

> In the name of God and Italy, I swear to follow the orders of the *Duce* and to serve the cause of the Fascist revolution with all my might and, if necessary, with my blood.

They also had to learn by heart the *Balilla* Creed which was a crude adaptation of the Apostles' Creed:

> I believe in Rome the Eternal, the mother of my country, and in Italy her eldest Daughter, who was born of the virginal bosom by the grace of God; who suffered through the barbarian invasions, was crucified and buried; who descended to the grave and was raised from the dead in the nineteenth century, who ascended into Heaven in her glory in 1918 and 1922, who is seated on the right hand of her mother Rome; who for this reason shall come to judge the living and the dead. I believe in the genius of Mussolini. In our Holy Father Fascism, in the communion of its martyrs, in the conversion of Italians, and the resurrection of the Empire.

Members of the *Balilla* wore black shirts, the *camica nera*, blue scarves, black tasseled caps and grey short trousers. The *Avangardisti* were provided with uniforms that resembled those worn by adult Blackshirts. They were also provided with miniature rifles and bayonets. At their evening and weekend meetings, members joined together to sing the popular Fascist hymn – the *Giovinezza*, or Youth.

Hail, O people of heroes,	The poets and the craftsmen,
Hail, O immortal fatherland,	The gentry and the peasants,
Thy children are reborn,	With the pride of Italians,
With faith in the ideal.	Swear loyalty to Mussolini.
	There is no poor district
Within the Italian boundary,	Which does not send its tale,
Italians have been re-fashioned,	Which does not unfurl its banners
Re-fashioned by Mussolini,	Of Fascism the redeemer.
For the war tomorrow,	
For the joy of labour, Youth!	Youth!
For the peace and the laurel,	Springtime of loveliness,
For the shaming of all those	In the bitterness of life,
Who their country deny.	Your song rings out, and away.

Lictor youth who ran in front of a magistrate carrying a *fasces* – a symbol of his authority

See page 136

Initially, the leader of the Fascist youth movement was Renato Ricci. In 1937, he quarrelled with the Party secretary, the loathsome Achille Starace who plotted his removal. Afterwards, the ONB became part of the Party controlled *Gioventu Italiana Del Littorio*, GIL or Young Fascists of the **Lictor**. Once the rival Catholic youth movement was banned and membership of GIL made compulsory, the membership climbed to over 8.5 million.

PICTURE 41
A gathering of young gun-waving members of the Balilla. *In the centre, the youth leader gives the Fascist salute*

It is impossible to calculate the extent of the success of the various movements in winning over the minds of Italian youth. To start with, many joined to take advantage of the benefits of membership rather than out of political conviction. Once membership became compulsory, joining became an automatic and meaningless gesture. Some became **blasé** and joined the increasing number of absentees who failed to attend meetings. It should be noted that when Mussolini was overthrown in 1943, the movement immediately disintegrated leaving behind little or no legacy of the fanatical enthusiasm and patriotic fervour of its heyday.

blasé fed up or indifferent

3 ⌐ THE ROLE OF WOMEN IN FASCIST ITALY

So far in our study of Fascist Italy, women have received little mention. Those referred to have been largely members of Mussolini's family – his mother, Rosa, his wife, Rachele, and his daughters Edda and Anna Maria – and a string of his mistresses. The fact was that Fascist Italy was a male-dominated state in which women had a very defined role. It was one of those areas in which the Fascist regime and the Roman Catholic Church were in agreement. Mussolini did not mince words:

> Child bearing is woman's natural and fundamental role in life.
>
> Women should be exemplary wives and mothers, guardians of the hearth, and subject to the legitimate authority of their husbands.

In *How Fascism Ruled Women*, the Italian historian Victoria De Grazia states, 'Women's duty was maternity, their primary function was to procreate and manage the family functions'.

A *The employment of women*

Fascist Italy was a man's world with the role of women being largely limited to child bearing and the domestic duties involved in running the home. Consequently, there seemed little point in extending their education and although women were not banned from a college or university education, they were certainly not encouraged. For those that gained an advanced qualification, job opportunities were few and promotion to the most prestigious positions virtually unheard of. Of course, women were still employed in their traditional work as teachers and nurses, they could take up work provided by the invention of the typewriter and telephone and more menial employment as waitresses and cleaners. Women were also employed in factory work although, in some industries, this was soon to be subject to limitation by a **quota system**. In the countryside, the employment of women on the land, particularly at times of planting and harvesting, was essential to the rural economy. However, whatever employment they followed did not excuse them from their child-bearing role.

quota system a system that allocates a fixed share

B *The appearance of women*

The Fascists were prudish regarding the appearance and activities of their womenfolk. The ideal was that a woman should be amply built and matronly but then in a country where the staple diet is pasta and pizza and, according to *Il Duce*, a family of 12 was said to be ideal, that would inevitably be the norm anyway! Rachele Mussolini certainly conformed to the Fascist ideal but not her daughter, Edda, or her husband's mistress Claretta Petacci. Women were also encouraged to wear simple, plain clothes and to avoid short skirts and trousers, revealing dresses, high-heeled shoes and cosmetics. Since Italy was a country where widowhood, irrespective of age, brought with it the necessity to wear black, the overall appearance of Italian women would have been drab in the extreme. Women were also discouraged from appearing in public on their own and from attending parties that involved excessive drinking and dancing.

See page 107

It should also be remembered that the wives and daughters of the elites often disregarded the Fascist concept of the ideal woman and continued to buy their clothes from Paris fashion houses and freely use

Yet though the National Committee for Cleaning Up Fashion might campaign against the 'horrid vice' of indecent and scandalous dress, millions of Italians went to the cinemas where they could catch glimpses of American actresses' breasts, and thousands of women performed scantily dressed in athletic parades. Fascists had a confused attitude to female sport; it could promote health, vigour, discipline and national pride, but it also might distract women from their main job of child production, and encourage lesbianism, and female liberation. Mussolini feared female involvement in sports (riding, skiing, cycling) because it was believed that they caused infertility!

From Fascist Italy *by John Hite and Chris Hinton, 1998*

French perfumes. It is also perhaps ironic that this period witnessed the birth of two women destined to be amongst Italy's most celebrated beauties – the film stars Gina Lollobrigida (born in 1927) and Sophia Loren (born in 1934)!

Women were largely excluded from politics. By 1919, the franchise had been extended to all adult males but when the vote was finally extended to women in 1925 it was only for use in local government elections. There were a number of women only sections to the Fascist Party but they had little influence and their role was played down. The best known of these was the *Fasci Femminili* that later became divided into the *Sezione Massaie* for peasant women and the *Sezione Operaie e Lavoranti a Domicilio* or SOLD for working class women. Women could also take part in the activities of the *Opera Nazionale per la Maternita* that was set up to help housewives and mothers in need. In 1927, Mussolini launched the Battle for Births.

C *The Battle for Births*

KEY ISSUE

The need to increase the birth rate.

Mussolini was concerned by the continuing decline of the birth rate in Italy. He was convinced that, in order to supply the manpower needs of the army, and govern and populate its overseas empire, it was necessary for the country to have an increasing and predominantly young and vibrant population. It was therefore essential for Italy that the birth rate be substantially increased.

In 1927, Mussolini launched a 'Battle for Births'. Its aim was to increase the current population of Italy which was then some 40 million to 60 million by 1950. In order to achieve this, he put forward a policy that included generous recognition for those who married and contributed to the growth in population and penalties for those who remained single. He went as far as to suggest that 12 children per family was the ideal optimum. The 'Battle' was backed by a propaganda campaign that urged women to produce children for *Il Duce*. Loans were offered to couples when they married and part of the loan was cancelled with every child born. The slate was wiped clean with the birth of a sixth child! Each year in the Palazzo Venezia, Mussolini himself presented financial rewards and medals to the mothers of the largest families.

The other side of the coin imposed higher levels of personal taxation on bachelors as a punishment for their 'unjustified **celibacy**'. Employment was made more readily available for married men and in some occupations, the promotion of bachelors was blocked. In 1933, a quota system was introduced which limited the employment of women in the public sector to 10% of the total workforce. This was later extended to large and medium firms in the private sector but was not applied to women employed in low paid, menial occupations. In December 1934, an article in *The Times* read:

celibacy an unmarried state, abstention from sex

> Again this year, Christmas Eve in Italy was the feast of mothers who had given the largest number of children … Signor Mussolini personally distributed prizes to ninety-three mothers, one from each of the provinces, chosen from women who have the greatest number of children. In Milan and other centres, there were similar ceremonies; prizes in money and goods were presented to the poor mothers and diplomas to the rich ones … The population problem is one that Signor Mussolini has most at heart … The decline in births in Italy leads to the conclusion that in the event of mobilisation there would be a shortage of 600,000 soldiers. The Fascist revolution will do its best to fill this gap. You must get married and have children, a lot of children. There are inducements – the citizens who have at least six children are exempt from all taxation, and there are penalties … The bachelor is hit by a special tax which is highest for those aged between thirty-five and fifty. That is not all. He is also handicapped in his career. A married man is always preferred to a bachelor. In articles in *Popolo d'Italia*, the *Duce* denounced cities where the birth rate is falling. The articles do not need to be signed to know that they come from his pen. Nowadays when a man takes a bride, he receives the so-called nuptial policy issued by the National Insurance Institute, by which, when he becomes the father of six, he will be entitled to half the money due and will make no further payments on the other half. Once married, he is entitled to help with special payments, the first of which is the cost of the honeymoon railway journey. To Rome, of course.

Much of the concept of the Battle for Births coincided with Catholic doctrine – its teaching on divorce and opposition to abortion and contraception – and was supported by the Church. Yet, in spite of the system of rewards and penalties, there was no significant increase in the number of marriages and the birth rate marginally declined!

Even his plan to reduce the number of women in the workforce failed. By 1936, it was only 3% less than it had been in 1921. In addition, the number of female students entering higher education increased

PICTURE 42
A Fascist family that appears to have fulfilled Mussolini's wishes!

	Number of births per thousand of the population		Number of deaths per thousand of the population		Total population (millions)	
TABLE 19 *Birth and death rates 1900–50*	1900	33	1900	23.8	1920	37
Source: International Historical	1920	32.3	1920	19.0	1927	40
Statistics, Europe 1750–1988 *by*	1930	26.7	1930	14.1	1940	45
B.R. Mitchell, 1992	1940	23.5	1940	13.6	1950	47.5

infant mortality rate
the number of babies
that die during the first
year of their lives per
thousand births

significantly. The Fascist authorities blamed their failure on a lack of
patriotism and the vanity and pleasure seeking of Italy's young women.
In fairness, there were some beneficial aspects. The additional care for
mothers and their children provided after 1925 by the *Opera Nazionale
Per La Maternita Ed Infanzia* (ONMI) contributed to a considerable fall
in the number of still births and the overall **infant mortality rate**.

4 ⮌ FASCIST INTRUSION INTO THE EVERYDAY LIVES OF THE ITALIAN PEOPLE

To what extent did the Fascist regime interfere in the lives of ordinary Italians? As we have seen, it banned them from belonging to other political parties and trade unions, it subjected them to a torrent of propaganda in an attempt to win their support for Fascism, and it censored the press, radio, films and theatrical productions to prevent them being influenced by contrary views. It also used the educational and youth services to indoctrinate their children, it hindered women's opportunities to benefit from higher education and limited their job opportunities and it urged young people to marry early and raise large families. It made young men liable for compulsory military service and tried to impose styles of dress and a code of conduct on young women. People also had to withstand the uniform wearing, drum beating and slogan chanting that was part of the pomp and **razzmatazz** of Fascist pageantry. Apart from those employed by state organisations and other occupations such as teaching, membership of the Party was not compulsory. Nevertheless, the advantages of membership were such that a great many found it **expedient** to join. Among those who did their utmost to impose Fascist standards on the people was the Party Secretary, Achille Starace (1889–1945).

razzmatazz dazzling show

expedient advisable or in their best interests

Starace was responsible for orchestrating public occasions and went out of his way to impress, particularly if Mussolini was to make an appearance. He was the prime mover in the campaign to get people to greet each other with the raised arm Fascist salute and to conclude their private letters with *Viva Il Duce*. He was also excessively keen on the wearing of uniforms and went as far to suggest that people should stand and salute at the mere mention of Mussolini's name. In 1932, he did his utmost to make a visit to the exhibition staged in Rome to mark the tenth anniversary of the Fascist revolution compulsory. Generally speaking, upper class Italians and the elites were less affected by Fascist intervention in their way of life than others. They still carried on with their social round, high life and foreign holidays much as they had always done.

However, not all Fascist intrusion was undesirable. Ordinary Italians benefitted from some improvement in their standing of living and the range of welfare measures introduced. Although earlier Liberal governments had first introduced many of these measures, further improvements were made in the provision of sickness and unemployment benefits and a limited range of family allowances made available. ONMI provided welfare for mothers and their children. Special payments were also made to help poor families during the winter months. Overall, whilst these measures may have been useful, they fell far short of the provision of a 'welfare state' and were undertaken more for political motives than genuine social concern. More impressive was the regime's attempt to provide the people with improved leisure facilities through the *Opera Nazionale Dopolavoro* (ONP).

PICTURE 43
Achille Starace (1889–1945)

ACHILLE STARACE (1889–1945)

Achille Starace was born at Gallipoli in southern Italy in 1889. His father was a wine merchant and the family was quite well off. He qualified as an accountant and served in the First World War with distinction. In the 1920s, he became an active member of the Fascist movement and quickly earned promotion. Described by Denis Mack Smith as 'unintelligent, humourless, utterly obedient and an unctuous flatterer', Starace was a thoroughly unpleasant man and Mussolini was aware of his police record and involvement in vice, drugs, rape and embezzlement. He was, says Mack Smith, 'just the man for Mussolini'. *Il Duce* and Starace schemed to get rid of the Party secretary, the reliable and honest Augusto Turati. They pulled no punches in their attempt to ruin his reputation by accusing him of sado-masochism, incest and paedophilia. They were successful and in 1931, Starace replaced him as Party secretary. He had two aims – to further promote Mussolini's cult of personality (see page 107) and to introduce Fascist uniformity into the every day life of the people. He was, says Richard Bosworth, to be 'responsible for the choreography of the regime'. To achieve both these ends Starace worked strenuously and to the absolute limit. It was his view that 'one man and one man alone must be allowed to dominate the news everyday'. He organised parades and rallies, made the wearing of uniform near compulsory – even by teachers and civil servants – and insisted on the Roman salute. He is also credited with coining the slogan '*Credere, Obbediere, Combattere*' (Believe, Obey, Fight) popularly used by Mussolini. Behind the scenes, he schemed, manipulated and purged the Party of those he disliked and thought undesirable. His loyalty to Mussolini was absolute and he barely deserved his leader's estimate that 'he was a cretin but an obedient one'. In 1939, he favoured Italy's immediate entry into the war on Germany's side but by this time, his star was on the wane. In the same year the much younger Ettore Muti replaced him as Party secretary. He retired to Milan where he is said to have 'faded into a pathetic old man'. However, he was not forgotten and when the war ended he was arrested and publicly executed by Italian partisans.

A *The Opera Nazionale Dopolavoro*

The *Opera Nazionale Dopolavoro*, or simply *Dopolavoro*, the National Institution for Leisure Activities, was a further attempt by Achille Starace to influence the masses and win them over to Fascism, this time by regulating their free time. Founded in 1923, it provided a wide range of leisure activities – recreational, sporting, educational and cultural – at subsidised prices, and was available to all sections of Italian society. According to articles relating to its foundation, it was:

(a) To provide healthy and profitable leisure time activity for the workers by means of instructions that develop their physical, intellectual and moral qualities;

(b) To promote the development of these institutions by providing them with the necessary support ...;

(c) To co-ordinate all such associations and equip them for propaganda purposes and other common aims and interests;

(d) To publicise the advantages of these institutions, and to making provisions for improving the quality of life of the working classes;

(e) To award certificates of merit to those members who have proved themselves to be particularly deserving, or who have shown noteworthy proficiency and activity in promoting the aims and objects of the organisation.

Quoted in File on Fascism *by D. Mansel Jones, 1990*

In a speech made in 1934, Starace claimed that the aims of *Dolopavoro* were:

To loosen their (the Italian people) muscles in joyful and simple sporting contests, to familiarise them once more with the glorious and charming traditions of their people, whether expressed in colourful costume, the harmony of song or a religious procession ... To teach them and enthuse them with the love of music, song, dance, painting, sculpture, poetry, all the arts in which Italy has always led the way ...

Quoted in Fascism *edited by Roger Griffin, 1995*

Dopolavoro covered a wide spectrum of activities including:

- the provision of libraries both permanent and mobile
- making films available for public showing
- providing radio sets
- making travel arrangements – organising trips, excursions and longer holidays
- sponsoring travelling theatre groups
- sponsoring brass bands and orchestral concerts
- the provision of stadia and gymnasia and the arrangement of sporting activities and fixtures
- arranging summer camps
- the provision of *Dopolavoro* clubhouses to cater for the needs of local communities.

It was also concerned with the welfare of workers and distributed food and clothing to poor communities. It became extremely popular and in 1927 control of *Dopolavoro* passed from the Ministry of National Economy to the Fascist Party. Its activities were financed partly by membership subscription and partly by a subsidy paid by employers and the State. By 1939, its membership had grown to over 4 million. It provided 8,625 libraries and 1,350 theatres and sponsored 3,324 brass bands and 2,208 dramatic societies. Art exhibitions were held in the various regions and well known orchestras and opera companies toured the country. Nevertheless, the facilities provided by *Dopolavoro* were more readily available to those living in urban areas than those in remote villages. Even so, each village soon came to have its own *Dopolavoro*-provided community centre with bar and billiard table. Such centres often challenged and sometimes even replaced the local Catholic church as the centre of community life. Free holidays were provided for children in the Fascist youth movement. During lengthy visits to the countryside, the coast or the mountains, they stayed at centres run by the *Donne Fasciste* organisation and received thorough medical examinations.

Some historians regard *Dopolavoro* as one of the few real successes of Mussolini's Fascist regime largely because it concentrated on providing relaxation and entertainment rather than political indoctrination. Others see it as nothing more than an a more subtle means of political indoctrination and an attempt to compensate for the meagre wages and poor living conditions of the working classes, particularly the peasantry.

5 ⌐ RACISM AND ANTI-SEMITISM

At the start, Italy's Fascist regime did not appear to be racialist or anti-Semitic. In fact, Mussolini had shown contempt for and ridiculed Hitler's virulent anti-Semitism. In an interview in 1932, he said:

> Anti-Semitism does not exist in Italy. Italians of Jewish birth have shown themselves good citizens and they fought bravely in the war. Many of them occupy leading positions in the universities, the army and the banks.

Later, in a speech, he made clear that if indeed he was racist then it was nothing more than a form of Italian nationalism:

> ... I love those of my own race, those that speak my language, that share my customs, that share with me the same history ... I have been involved with racism since 1922, but a racism of my own. The health, the conservation of the race, its betterment, the struggle against tuberculosis, providing mass sport, sending children to camps – that was racism as I understood it. But there was also a moral racism ... the pride of belonging to this race born between the snows of the Alps and the fire of Etna ... The elevation of Italian prestige, of the genius of our civilisation ...

assimilated to become like or absorbed into

In Italy, the 57,000 Jews represented less than 15% of the total population. They had long been **assimilated** into the national way of life and contributed to the country's prosperity and progress. Some 10,000 were members of the Fascist Party and two, Aldo Finzi and Guido Jung, held positions in the government.

A *Mussolini's switch to anti-Semitic policies*

Before he turned upon the Jews, Mussolini had shown racialist tendencies in his colonial policies, particularly at the time of the Italian invasion of Abyssinia in 1935. He claimed that Italians were 'Aryans of a Mediterranean type' and stressed the superiority of his country's culture and racial superiority over African tribalism. He recognised a need, even a duty, to impose Italian civilisation on the native populations of Libya and Abyssinia. *Il Duce*'s anti-Semitism first became apparent in 1936 when he showed signs of a willingness to discriminate against the Jews. It was following Italy's alliance with Hitler's Nazi Germany that his campaign against the Jews intensified. Mussolini may have been influenced by a desire to match or even exceed Hitler's anti-Semitic policies and he was certainly aware that a common policy against the Jews would further cement the alliance between the two countries. Hitler had also succeeded in convincing him that international Jewry was in league with the Bolsheviks to achieve world domination. He was also under pressure to adopt an anti-Semitic stance by racialists within the Party, particularly Roberto Farinacci. Farinacci, a **vociferous** supporter of anti-Jewish measures, was also a staunch supporter of an Italian alliance with Germany. He and those who were like-minded claimed that too many Jews had 'wormed their way into strategic positions in Italian life'. In his diaries, Mussolini's son-in-law, Count Ciano, recalled how in 1937, *Il Duce* was critical of the United States referring to it as 'a country of niggers and Jews'. He also claimed that by the end of the century 'the acid of Jewish corrosion' would destroy many European countries. Other considerations that influenced Mussolini were the facts that at the time of the Abyssinian conflict, foreign Jews had been active in the campaign to impose sanctions on Italy and that the Jewish brothers Carlo and Nello Rosselli, Italian socialists now living in exile, had been successfully recruiting Italians to fight for the Republicans in the Spanish Civil War.

In 1938, the regime published the *Manifesto Degli Scienziati Razzisti*, the Manifesto of Racial Scientists. The manifesto, which first appeared in the magazine *Giornale d'Italia*, was claimed to be the work of a group of scholars from Italy's most prestigious universities. In fact, Mussolini was the main contributor to the series of ten points set out like commandments that might have been taken directly from the pages of Hitler's ***Mein Kampf***. These included:

> The people of present-day Italy are of Aryan origin and their civilisation is Aryan.

> … the majority of our present 44 million Italians are descendants of families that have been inhabiting Italy for a millennium.

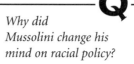

Why did Mussolini change his mind on racial policy?

See pages 187–8

vociferous outspoken in a loud voice

See pages 181 and 183

See page 187

Mein Kampf a book written by Hitler in which he outlined his political views

A pure 'Italian race' is already in existence ... This ancient purity of blood is the Italian nation's greatest title of nobility.

It is time for Italians to proclaim themselves to be racists ... Italians should recognise that European characteristics are essentially different from all non-European races.

The Jews do not belong to the Italian race ... The Jews represent the only people that have never been assimilated in Italy, and this is because they are made up of non-European racial elements ...

The purely European physical and psychological characteristics of the Italians must not be altered in any way. Marriage is admissible only within the context of the European races ...

The publication of the Manifesto was soon followed by an anti-Semitic press campaign with blatantly racial articles appearing in *La Vita Italiana* and *La Difesa Della Razza*. The Fascist intellectual, Giuseppe Bottai, openly expressed the view that 'racism should be displayed to resist Jews.' Pope Pius XI, who had earlier congratulated Mussolini for refusing to copy Hitler's anti-Semitic policies, did not shrink from criticising Fascist racial policy. He was amongst the first to attack Mussolini's change of heart when he said '... it is not possible for a Christian to take part in anti-Semitism'. Unfortunately he died in 1939 and his successor, Pope Pius XII, was far less outspoken and made no public condemnation of the treatment of the Jews in Italy or elsewhere in Europe. Another critic was Balbo who resented German influence in Italian affairs but this did not deter the Fascist regime from increasing the pressure on Italian Jews. Up to 1936, an estimated 3,000 German Jews had sought refuge in Italy. Now the immigration of Jews from overseas was banned and Jews were no longer allowed to teach in schools and universities. Finally, in November 1938, came the Race Law that introduced measures intended to 'protect the Italian race'. In content they were similar to the Nuremberg Laws introduced by the Nazis in Germany in 1935.

See pages 219–20

B *Il Diritto Razzista – The Race Law: 'Provisions for the Defence of the Italian Race'*

The new Race Law:

- banned marriages between 'Italian citizens of the Aryan race' and people belonging to other races;
- defined a Jew as a person born of parents who were both Jews, even if they did not practise the Jewish faith, and a person born to parents only one of which was a Jew;
- ordered that the names of all Jews had to be listed on public registers;
- stated that Italian citizens of the Jewish race may not:
  – join the armed services

- act as a guardian or custodian of a minor or disabled person who was not a Jew
- be proprietors of firms that employ more than 100
- be people or have contracts with the defence industry
- be owners of land valued at more than 5,000 lire
- be the owners of buildings which have a tax value of more than 20,000 lire;
● ordered that Jews must not employ Italians as servants.

The majority of Italians did not take easily to the new anti-Semitic legislation and consequently the authorities found it difficult to apply the laws rigorously. Mussolini saw to it that his former Jewish mistress, Margherita Sarfatti, managed to escape abroad and later even admitted that his own sons took steps to protect their Jewish friends in the family home! Mussolini's racialism and the fact that he appeared to be toadying to Hitler offended many Italians. Some turned against Fascism and it became a contributory factor to *Il Duce*'s final overthrow. They took steps to provide Jews with secure places of refuge and hindered their transportation to Nazi extermination camps in Poland. In 1942, Heinrich Himmler, head of the German SS who supervised the concentration camps, went to Rome to encourage Mussolini to deport Italian Jews to camps in Poland. He said that they would be humanely treated. Consequently Mussolini agreed that Italian Jews would be interned but not deported. Afterwards Himmler accused him of weakness and 'sentimental humanitarianism'.

Of Italian anti-Semitism, the Australian historian, Richard Bosworth, has written:

> **KEY ISSUE**
>
> *The reaction of the Italian people to the Race Law.*

After the anti-Semitic legislation of 1938 and some follow-up in 1939, the pace of official persecution in Italy slowed. Moreover, on race as on so many other issues, the official line adopted in 'legal Italy' was not always followed in 'real Italy'; whatever the case may have been among Germans. The Italians showed few signs of being the 'willing executioners' of Jews. To absolve Mussolini from any responsibility for the Holocaust as some Fascist nostalgics have done is absurd. To understand him as a philosophically convinced anti-Semite or any form of racist is equally implausible. As Farinacci had the gumption to reveal, Fascist racism was more opportunist and short-term than fanatical. It was as hollow as were many other aspects of Mussolini's administration.

From Mussolini *by R.J.B. Bosworth, 2002*

One means of measuring the extent to which Fascist race laws were applied is to compare the survival rate of Italian Jews with those in other countries across Europe that experienced the worst of the Holocaust.

TABLE 20
The Holocaust

	Jewish population (September 1939)	Number of Jews that survived	Percentage of Jews that survived
Poland	3,300,000	500,000	15%
Czechoslovakia	315,000	55,000	18%
Germany	210,000	40,000	19%
Greece	75,000	15,000	20%
Yugoslavia	75,000	20,000	27%
Soviet Union (German occupied)	2,100,000	600,000	28%
Austria	60,000	20,000	33%
Italy	**57,000**	**42,000**	**74%**

6 ⌐ ART AND CULTURE IN MUSSOLINI'S ITALY

KEY ISSUE

Was there such a thing as Fascist culture?

Together with the Greeks, Italians can fairly claim that their early civilisations were the nursery of European culture. During the centuries that followed, Italians remained predominant in the arts so that details of their illustrious painters, sculptors, composers and writers fill pages in any encyclopedia. Reflecting on the Mussolini years, in 1972, the Italian political philosopher, Norberto Bobbio, wrote, 'Fascist culture never really existed in Italy'. Does this mean that during the period 1922 to 1944, Italy became a cultural backwater? Limited freedom of expression and the toleration of only officially approved attitudes are features of all totalitarian regimes. Yet in this respect, Fascist Italy was at least marginally different from Nazi Germany and Communist Russia in that the authorities did permit writers, artists and film makers to enjoy some freedom of expression. Again, whilst many artists, writers and intellectuals chose to flee the oppressive regimes of Hitler and Stalin, in Italy a goodly number chose to remain. This was because the regime showed them a degree of tolerance as long as they did not use their opinions to stir public unrest.

Whilst it may be true that artistic and cultural activity may have declined under Fascism, it certainly did not disappear. The last opera of Giacomo Puccini (1858–1924), *Turandot*, was first performed in Milan in 1926, whilst the works of Pietro Mascagni (1863–1945), particularly the *Cavalleria Rusticana*, were popular worldwide. Although the 'world's greatest tenor', Enrico Caruso, died in 1921 others, such as Beniamino Gigli (1890–1957), achieved equal fame. Alfredo Cocozza, better know as Mario Lanza (1921–59), became a star of Hollywood musicals whilst even the present-day popular tenor, Luciano Pavarotti (born 1935), spent his childhood living under Fascist rule. A leading novelist of the period was Grazia Deledda (1875–1936). She together with the short story writer, Luigi Pirandello (1867–1936), were awarded the **Nobel Prize** for Literature in 1927 and 1934.

In 1935, the doctor, painter and writer Carlo Levi (1902–75) was forced to live in exile in a backward village in southern Italy because of his opposition to the Italian invasion of Abyssinia. He later described

Nobel Prize a series of prizes awarded annually for work in science, medicine, literature etc. Alfred Nobel was the inventor of dynamite

CARLO LEVI (1902–75)

Carlo Levi was born of Jewish parents in Turin in 1902. He studied medicine and qualified as a doctor. During his student days, he first came into contact with socialism and became an active member of the PSI. He was an opponent of Fascism and, in 1930, formed a resistance movement, the *Giustizia e Liberta*. An accomplished writer and artist, his outspoken criticism of the Italian invasion of Abyssinia in 1935 led to his arrest. The following year he was exiled to the village of Gaglaino in the southern province of Lucania. The village was in a desolate, malarial region where the local peasants, ignored and neglected by the Fascist regime, lived in dire poverty. Levi worked as a doctor amongst the oppressed villagers who became his friends. After his release, he left Italy and went to live in France. Being a Jew, during the years of the Second World War, he had to hide in order to avoid deportation and, for a time, lived in one room. It was during this time that he wrote *Cristo Si E Fermato A Eboli*, Christ Stopped at Eboli, in which he described his time in the village of Gagliano. As a doctor, he had witnessed the suffering of the people at first hand, as an artist, he was aware of the desolation of their land. The title of the book is derived from the fact that in Levi's view, Christ never reached the village but stopped short at the nearby village of Eboli. His book became an international bestseller. On his return to Italy, he worked as a journalist and again became involved in politics. In 1963, he was elected to the Italian Senate and he died in 1975.

PICTURE 44
Carlo Levi (1902–75)

his experiences in his bestselling *Cristo Si E Fermato A Eboli* (Christ Stopped at Emboli). Ignazio Silone (1900–78), former editor of the socialist newspaper *Il Lavoratore*, fled Italy to win fame as an outstanding novelist based in Switzerland. Some of those out to achieve fame were quick to apply for membership of the Fascist Party. Puccini went as far as to personally congratulate Mussolini when he first came to power in 1922. As we have seen, the *Opera Nazionale Dopolavoro*, contributed significantly to popularising Italian culture as did the *Ministreo Della Cultura Popolare*, or *Minculpop*, which was made responsible for cultural affairs after 1937.

A *Italian Futurism*

In 1909, Filippo Marinetti (1876–1944), a poet and writer, founded the Italian Futurist movement. His ideas, first made known in a manifesto published in 1909, *Manifeste du Futurisme*, influenced literature and then spread to other branches of the arts. He claimed that his manifesto was a clarion call to those who been 'wearing second-hand clothes for too long'. Futurism represented an extreme reaction against what Marinetti regarded as the sentimentalism and romanticism of the bourgeoisie. By comparison, Futurism was seen as 'a celebration of the machine age, glorifying war and favouring the growth of Fascism'. Unlike those who retained a fondness for the old and classical, Futurism favoured the advance of modern technology and exalted in such aspects of contemporary life as speed, noise, pollution and the growth of towns and cities. Neither did Marinetti hide his hatred of learning and academics. In 1914, he wrote:

From Futurismo e Fascismo *by Filippo Marinetti, 1914*

> The war will sweep from power all her foes: diplomats, professors, philosophers, archaeologists, critics, cultural obsession, Greek, Latin, history, senilism, museums, libraries, the tourist industry. The war will promote gymnastics, sport, practical schools of agriculture, business and industry. The war will rejuvenate Italy, will enrich her with men of action, will force her to live no longer in the past, off ruins and the mild climate, but off her own national forces.

Further Futurist manifestos, written by Marinetti's followers, were published covering architecture, music, painting and sculpture. Attempts were made to make Futurism relevant to aspects of everyday life such as clothing, food and human relationships. It was as if Futurists were trying to re-invent life and create 'a new race in the form of machine-extended man'. With regard to literature, Futurist writing was to contain no adjectives, adverbs or punctuation and **phonetic spelling** was considered acceptable.

phonetic spelling spelt according to the way it sounds

Futurist art, which was to be a forerunner of cubism and modernism, was to portray movement and be 'forged out of the beauty of speed and the glorification of war'. In 1911, Marinetti published a book, *Le Futurisme*, and arranged an exhibition of the work of Italian Futurist painters. The views of the Futurists were strongly opposed by the world art establishment. In architecture, Futurists rejected flamboyant, ornamental styles in favour of that which was plain and functional. The Fascist regime chose to sit on the fence and neither condemned it nor proclaimed it as official Fascist art that had to be adopted nationally. *Il Duce* tactfully offered his support to both sides. He was in a difficult position – dare he claim that Futurist architecture was superior to the classical architecture of ancient Rome and such heritage cities as Florence? In spite of his professed hatred of **academia**, in 1929, Filippo Marinetti accepted membership of the Italian Royal Academy!

academia the world of learning

B *The cinema*

One aspect of Italian culture that advanced significantly during the Fascist period was the cinema. Stalin once said, 'Film is the strongest art' by which he meant that film-making was a great vehicle for conveying propaganda. Mussolini exploited this to the full. In many short newsreel-type films, Fascist ideology was extolled and the image of Mussolini promoted to the full. The Italian film industry also produced a string of melodramas and comedies for general consumption but they were not of a high quality. The *L'Unione Cinematografica Educativa* acted as a board of film censors to ensure that there was a link between the plot of each film and Fascist politics. In 1933, a law was passed that made it illegal to dub Italian films into a foreign language and conversely, all foreign films had to be dubbed into Italian. In 1934, the *Diresione Generale Per La Cinema* was set up to award prizes to films that best extolled the virtues of Fascism. It modified rather than banned films thought to be unacceptable. The following year, the *Ente Nazionale Industrie Cinemato Grafiche* became the most important body in the film industry with the responsibility for regulating the use of foreign films in Italian cinemas. Cinema-going was exceptionally popular amongst Italians. By 1927, the takings of cinema box offices accounted for 50% of the income from all forms of entertainment. This rose to 70% in 1936 and 83% in 1941. The shame was that it became necessary to limit the income gained from showing foreign films, mainly American, that accounted for 87% of the total! Mussolini's son, Vittorio, was involved in the film industry and the 1930s and 40s also saw the emergence of many who were to become the most illustrious of Italy's film directors and producers. These included Roberto Rossellini, who made propaganda films for the Italian navy, Vittorio de Sica (born 1901), Carlo Ponti (born 1910) later to become famous producing the film *Doctor Zhivago*, Frederico Fellini (born 1920) and Franco Zeffirelli (born 1923). *Daro Un Milione*, Mario Camerini's film of 1935, is still considered one of the best thousand films of all times whilst *Il Signor Max* (Mr Max) (1937) and *Quattro Passi fra le Nuvole* (Four Steps in the Clouds) (1943) were also highly rated.

See page 105

It is also interesting to note that this was a time when emigration to the United Sates increased and many Italians made their reputations as restaurateurs and in the catering trade generally. Many too found fame in Hollywood but not as refugees from Fascist tyranny but second generation sons of families that had left their homeland earlier in search of better opportunities for themselves and their children. Amongst the most celebrated was Radolpho Di Valentina D'Antonguolla (1895–1926) who emigrated to the United States to become the screen idol, Rudolph Valentino. Others included the popular singers Pierino Como (1912–2001) whose family emigrated from Palena, Dino Crocetti who achieved fame as Dean Martin, Francis Sinatra (1915–98) whose father was Sicilian and mother a Genoan, and Antonio Beneditto who was born in 1926 and achieved fame as Tony Bennett. Anunzio Mantovani (1905–80), the famous orchestra leader, was the son of the principal violinist at La Scala, Milan.

Radio broadcasting, which began in 1924, also developed rapidly during this period. The Fascist authorities followed the example of the BBC and granted a monopoly in broadcasting to one company, the *Unione Radiofonica Italiana* or URI, later, in 1927, to become the EIAR. Radios known as *Radiobalilla*, were produced in large numbers but because of the needs of autarchy, they were made cheaply and proved

KEY ISSUE

To what extent did the Fascist regime control the media?

unreliable. Whilst *Dopolavoro* helped to make radios widely available, those in isolated areas could only hear broadcasts on loudspeakers set up in public squares, schools, factories and public meeting places. By 1942, there were an estimated two millions Italians who regularly listened to the radio. Much against the regime's wishes, the availability of radio sets allowed Italians to listen to foreign radio stations. Whilst the Socialist press was banned, other newspapers were allowed to publish but rigidly censored. In the end, the ownership of the majority of the newspapers passed to men sympathetic to Fascism. The Vatican radio was also a good source of information for Italians as was its newspaper, *Osservatore Romano*.

7 ↶ STRUCTURED AND ESSAY QUESTIONS

A *This section consists of questions that might be used for discussion (or written answers) as a way of expanding on the chapter and testing your understanding.*

1. In signing the Lateran Treaty (1929) what concessions did Mussolini make to the Church?
2. Why were the activities of Catholic Action of concern to the Fascists?
3. 'No more than joining the Boy Scouts.' To what extent do you agree with this estimate of the commitment of young Italians joining the *Balilla*?
4. Why was the publication of the encyclical, '*Non Abiamo Bisogni*' banned in Italy?
5. What did Mussolini mean when he said, 'women should be the guardians of the hearth'?
6. Would it be fair to say that Achille Starace was a totally despicable person?
7. How strictly were Mussolini's Race Laws applied in Fascist Italy?
8. What did Himmler mean when he accused Mussolini of 'sentimental humanitarianism'?

B *Essay questions.*

1. How important was the support of the Catholic Church to the maintenance of the Fascist regime in Italy?
2. 'One of the few real successes of Mussolini's Fascist regime.' How valid is this assessment of *Dolopavoro*?
3. To what extent did the Fascist regime succeed in their attempts to influence the everyday lives of the Italian people?

8 ⌇ DOCUMENTARY EXERCISE ON THE NATURE OF THE FASCIST EDUCATION SYSTEM

Study the sources below and then answer the questions which follow:

Article I.	The *Balilla* is intended to provide moral and physical training for the young, in order to make them worthy of the new standard of Italian life ...
Article XXX.	The *Balilla* Institution shall also train the conscience and minds of these boys, since they are destined to become the Fascist men of the future, from whose ranks national leaders will be selected.

SOURCE A
Regulations governing the aims of the Balilla *Institution, 1926.*

**SOURCE B
(PICTURE 45)**
An illustration from an Italian primary school textbook of 1929

The regime intends to prepare spiritually, all the youth of Italy ... for this purpose it has created the *Balilla*. The young – more than anyone else – must know how to obey, to acquire the right, or rather, the duty of commanding; more than the rest, they must know how to dare; more than others they must despise indifference, or what is worse, comfort.

SOURCE C
From an Order of the Day to Fascist Youth Organisations, 1930.

Thy children are reborn
With faith in the ideal.
Within the Italian boundary
Italians have been refashioned,

Refashioned by Mussolini,
For the war of tomorrow
For the joy of labour
For the peace and the laurel.

SOURCE D
Part of the Giovinezza, *the hymn of Fascist youth*

SOURCE E

From a speech made by Mussolini in 1930

The eyes of the *Duce* are on every one of you … A child who, even while not refusing to obey, asks 'why?' is like a bayonet made of milk … You must obey because you must.

SOURCE F

Part of the oath taken by Italian teachers, 1931

I swear to be loyal to the King, to his loyal successors, to the Fascist regime … to exercise the profession of teacher and to carry out all academic duties with the aim of training upright and hardworking citizens who are devoted to the fatherland and the Fascist regime …

1. *What do Sources C and E reveal about the Fascist emphasis on obedience? (5 marks)*
2. *Comment on the reliability of Sources B and D. (5 marks)*
3. *Compare Sources A and C. How far do they reveal the same ideals about the training of Italian youth? (5 marks)*
4. *To what extent do sources A, D and F emphasise the need for loyalty to the Fascist state? (5 marks)*
5. *How full and understanding do the sources provide of the part played by indoctrination and propaganda in the education and training of the youth of Italy? (10 marks)*

9 ↜ MAKING NOTES

Read the advice section about making notes on page xix of the Preface: How to use this book. Much of this chapter has dealt with the extent to which Italy's Fascist regime tried to become involved in aspects of the lives of the people. Complete the chart below by indicating the extent to which this intrusion took place.

Aspect of the lives of the people.	Extent of Fascist involvement
Religious worship	
The schooling of children	
Out of school activities	
Women and family life	
Leisure and sporting activities	
Matters of race	
Matters of culture	

The Italian Economy 1922–40

10

INTRODUCTION

Although he pretended to be an expert on the subject, neither Mussolini nor any of the Fascist hierarchy were economists. Consequently, when the Fascist leader made known his plans for the Italian economy they were, at best, promises based on broad generalisations that contained little substance. When he introduced the New Programme of the National Fascist Party at the Third Fascist Congress in 1921, he stated his intention was the 'Preparation of an organic plan for public works to conform to the nation's new economic, technical and military needs.' In 1923, Mussolini told the Senate, 'My ambition is this: to make the people of Italy strong, prosperous and free.' He also made an oblique reference to the connection between the economy and the need to impose a Fascist dictatorship on the people when he said, 'There is freedom in times of prosperity which is not the freedom to be allowed in times of poverty.'

See pages 73–4

From the start, the Fascist regime inherited many problems and to these were soon to be added others of their own creation. There were still those associated with Italian involvement in the First World War – unemployment, financial difficulties and shortages. In addition, Italy's industrial development was proceeding at a slower pace than the other major European powers whilst, in the south, the problems of a technically backward and poverty stricken peasantry remained. The country also had a rapidly growing population.

Mussolini's twin aims were to make Italy more self-sufficient and develop the economy along lines that would allow it, in the long run, to achieve its full military potential and engage in a war of colonial conquest.

Total population (millions)		Major towns and cities (thousands)		
1911	35.4		1900	1950
1931	40.3	Rome	463	1,652
1951	46.7	Genoa	235	648
		Milan	493	1,260
		Naples	564	1,011
		Palermo	228	491
		Turin	336	711

TABLE 21
Italy's population
Source: European Historical Statistics, 1750–1970, B.R. Mitchell, 1975

SOME TERMS COMMONLY USED IN ECONOMICS

In considering economic developments in Fascist Italy, it is necessary to use a range of words and phrases commonly used in economics. To assist your studies, the meanings of the words and phrases used are given below and appear in bold-type in the text:

autarky economic self sufficiency

balance of payments the relationship between a country's payments to all other countries for goods and services received from them (mainly imports) and the payments received from other countries for the goods and services sent to them (mainly exports). It is clearly best to have a favourable balance – to export more than is imported

cartels the coming together of firms to gain the advantages of monopoly (see below)

deflation a situation in which prices and wages fall and chase one another in a downward spiral

direct and indirect taxes direct taxes are those imposed directly on what a person earns, like income tax; indirect taxes are imposed on what a person spends, like VAT and duties on petrol, alcohol and tobacco

extensive farming a situation in which previously unused land is brought into cultivation. It is land on the edge of profitability

gold standard the situation that exists when a nation's currency can be measured against a fixed amount of gold

inflation a situation in which prices and wages rise and chase one another in an upward spiral

intensive farming a situation in which the same land is repeatedly cultivated to increase the yield per hectare

laissez-faire the view that State interference in industry and commerce should he kept to a minimum

lock out a situation when employers refuse to allow employees into their place of work. It is most often used to enforce a cut in pay or change in working conditions or in retaliation for strike action

monopoly in the strictest sense, a monopoly exists when one producer controls the total output of a product. This seldom happens because of the availability of substitutes

public spending spending on that part of the economy run by the State

protection/protectionism the imposition of duties (see tariffs) on imported goods in order to make them more expensive and so give home producers an advantage over their foreign competitors

real wages wages expressed in terms of the quantity of goods and services they will buy. It is usually compared with money wages, the actual amount of money received. Remember at a time of inflation, it is possible for money wages to increase and for real wages to fall simultaneously

recession a period during which there is a decline in business activity. At such times, the demand for goods and services falls, production is cut and unemployment increases

subsidies a payment made by the State to producers to cover part of the costs of production and thereby reduce the price of the product to the public

tariffs duties placed on imported goods to make them more expensive so that consumers will buy home-produced products (see protection).

1 ⟿ TOWARDS A CORPORATE STATE

During the period 1922–5, Italy in common with most other European countries was enjoying an economic upturn. Mussolini appointed the university economist and scholar, Alberto de Stefani ((1879–1969), as his Finance Minister. Determined to balance the nation's budget, Stefani followed traditional liberal *laissez-faire* policies. He reduced taxation, cut public spending, removed regulations and trade restrictions and limited government intervention in the economy. Whilst he encouraged investment, he was against **protectionism** and paying **subsidies** and wanted businesses to compete with one another on an equal footing. His policies, which appeared to be working, pleased many industrialists and bankers, though not all. The point was that whatever was good for the economy was not necessarily good for the Fascist regime if it did not coincide with Mussolini's plans for the future. In order to create a Fascist totalitarian state, the economy would have to be run along very different lines. There were policy disagreements and in 1925, Stefani was dismissed and replaced by the industrialist and banker, Count Giuseppe Volpi. Italy now entered on a new and very different phase in her economic development. It was a phase that was intended to bring the country's economy within the overall framework of a Fascist totalitarian state.

1891	Papal encyclical *De Rerum Novarum*
1923	Palazzo Chigi Pact
1925	Dismissal of de Stefani
	Vidoni Palace Pact
	Start of the Battle for Grain
1926	Syndicalist Law
	Law abolished the right to strike
1927	Labour Charter
	Start of the Battle for the lira
1929	Wall Street Crash
1930	National Council of Corporations established
1933	*Institu Per La Ricosstruzione Industriale* set up

TABLE 22
Date line showing Italy's move towards a Corporate State

A *The concept of a Corporate State and the doctrine of corporatism*

The idea of a Corporate State was based on many different and often unrelated strands of political and economic thinking. These included the old traditions of the medieval Catholic guilds in which men and their masters co-operated. This means of eliminating class conflict and offering a Catholic alternative to Socialism had been expounded in Pope Leo XIII's encyclical of 1891, *De Rerum Novarum*, which dealt with the condition of the working classes. Then there were the views of the French philosopher Georges Sorel whose syndicalist ideas aimed at securing worker-controlled industries. These ideas were later taken up by Edmondo Rossoni who wanted to prepare Italians for 'the life of

See page 23

tomorrow' that would create a new social order which would last for centuries to come. The Fascist theorist, Giuseppe Bottai, destined to be the first Minister of Corporations, supported the corporate philosophy based on these ideas. However, within the Fascist movement there were differences of opinion. Michele Bianchi and Edmondo Rossoni regarded corporatism as a way of winning the popular support of the working classes; others, particularly Roberto Farinacci, saw it as a means of bringing the workers directly under the control of the Party. Whatever, the basic aim of corporatism was to achieve the political and economic integration of Italy under Fascist leadership. To this end, Mussolini decided to set up syndicates of workers and employers organised and co-ordinated by the government. Each syndicate was to represent a particular trade, industry or profession. It was the Fascist leader's hope that his plan would eliminate strike action, bring about industrial peace and bring to an end class warfare. D'Annunzio had adopted these ideas during his occupation of Fiume, 1919–20. Hand in hand with the introduction of syndicates there was to be a programme of public works financed by deficit spending. The long-term intention was to create a sound economy capable of supporting Mussolini's plans for military aggression and his colonial ambitions.

B *The structure of the Corporate State*

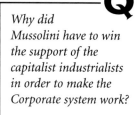

Why did Mussolini have to win the support of the capitalist industrialists in order to make the Corporate system work?

The Corporate State was to be based on a complex network of syndicates – organisations run by employers and workers at local, provincial and national level. At the top and controlling the network was the National Council of Corporations. In reality, the key policy decisions were to be made by state agencies presided over by the Minister of Corporations. In order to make the system work, Mussolini had to win over the support of the capitalist industrialists and bring the trade unions into line so that they were under Fascist control.

In 1923, the Palazzo Chigi Pact was agreed between the *Confidustria*, the employers' Confederation of Industry, and the Confederation of Fascist Corporations that represented the workers. The Pact was a declaration of intent:

> ... both labourers and industrialists can avoid the damages and losses caused by work interruptions if harmony between the various elements of production assures the continuity and tranquility of industrial development ... a permanent Commission, consisting of five members for each side, will be appointed to supervise the fulfillment of the above mentioned principles both at the seat of government and in the outlying regions, and to co-ordinate the major bodies of the two Confederations so that syndical activity will proceed in accordance with the directives set forth by the Head of Government.

This was followed in 1925 by the Vidoni Palace Pact. By this agreement the *Confidustria* agreed to deal only with Rossoni's Fascist trade unions. This as good as deprived the rival Socialist and Catholic trade unions of their negotiating powers and made them obsolete. In future, industrial bargaining would be carried out, on the one side, by negotiators chosen by the employers and, on the other, by officials of the Fascist Labour Corporations. Clearly this was much to the advantage of the employers since it denied the workers representation by freely elected shop stewards who, in the past, had proved **truculent** and determined in their defence of working class interests.

In 1926, a new law prohibited strikes and lockouts. However, this created a problem.

The International Labour Organisation, an agency of the League of Nations, was pledged to respecting the right of 'freedom of association'. Mussolini got around this by allowing employers and employees who did not wish to join the Fascist Corporations to form their own unions. He then used the *squadristi* to hound them out of existence. By the Syndicalist Law of that year, 16 syndicates comprising of employers and workers were set up covering every industry and profession. These included agriculture, commerce, maritime and air transport, road and inland waterway transport, banking and intellectual learning. Members paid their dues to their syndicate and took orders from their Fascist-appointed officials. The controlling body was the Ministry of Corporations that had the power to draw up contracts, fix wages and consider disputes and enforce settlements. In a speech made in October 1926 to celebrate the fourth anniversary of the Fascist March on Rome, the new Minister of Corporations, none other than Benito Mussolini himself, was able to say:

> We have constituted a Corporate and Fascist State, the state of a national society, a State which concentrates and controls, harmonizes and tempers the interests of all social classes, which are thereby protected in equal measure. Whereas previously, labour looked with diffidence upon the State, labour was, in fact, outside the State and against the State, and considered the State an enemy ... there is not one working Italian today who does not seek a place in his Corporation, who does not wish to be a living atom in the great, immense, living organisation which is the Corporate State of Fascism.

In fact, the system had many weaknesses. It was a massive **bureaucracy** in which representation favoured the employers so that any idea of equality was only an illusion. The officials of the Corporations were often inefficient or corrupt or both. Certainly much money intended for economic development found its way into private hands. Overall, the theory of corporations was fine but in practice it was a disaster – even a farce. It was clear that it was just a convoluted way of ensuring the dominance of employers who were 'grateful for the forcible submission of labour' and that the capitalist system survived much as before. As Denis Mack Smith has written, in practice it was 'little more than an unrealised idea'.

KEY ISSUE

The need to eliminate the trade unions.

---

truculent fierce and aggressive

1920	30,560,000
1923	296,000
1924	0

TABLE 23
Number of days lost due to industrial disputes (Source: European Historical Statistics, 1750–1970, B.R. Mitchell, 1975.)

---

bureaucracy a system that employs a large number of officials

C *The Carta Del Lavoro – The Labour Charter of April 1927*

The Labour Charter began with a reaffirmation of the supremacy of the State over the individual – 'The Italian nation is an organisation with objectives, life and means of action superior in power and duration to those of the individuals or groups that compose it.' It then went on to define labour in all its forms as 'a social duty' and confirm the powers of the syndicates – 'only the syndicate which is legally recognised and subject to the control of the state has the right legally to represent the entire category of employers or workers for which it is constituted.' It then emphasised its support for the capitalist system and the private rather than public ownership of the means of production – 'The Corporate State considers private initiative in the field of production to be the most effective and most useful instrument in the national interest. The intervention of the State in economic production takes place only when private initiative is lacking, or is insufficient or when the political interests of the State are involved.' The Charter also included provision for social insurance covering accident, sickness and unemployment, welfare benefits and additional pay for those in dangerous employment or working excessive hours.

> **Q** To what extent did the Labour Charter benefit the workers?

In 1930, a National Council of Corporations was set up to be responsible for policy decisions and give advice in economic matters. Whilst some considered the Corporate State to be at least an interesting and worthwhile experiment, as we shall see it did not succeed in protecting the Italian economy from the depression that was the aftermath of the collapse of the American stock market, the Wall Street Crash (1929). Mussolini next considered a means of bringing together the political and economic aspects of his regime. He said that the fulfillment of the Corporate State now required:

> Three conditions ... a single party, by means of which there shall be effectual political as well as economic control, and which shall be above the competing interests, a bond that unites all in a common faith. Nor is that enough. We must have, as well as a single party, a totalitarian State, that is to say, the State that absorbs in itself, to transform and make them effective, all the energy, all the interests, and all the hope of the people. And even that is not enough. The third ... and most important condition is to live in a period of highest ideal tension. We are now living in this period of high ideal tension.

A major step towards this was The Law on the Formation and Functions of Corporations of 1934 that further revised the structure of the Corporate State and created a new system based on 22 corporations.

Mussolini claimed that the aim of the Law was to 'increase constantly the global power of the nation to further the ends of its expansion in the world' – in other words to prepare for war and colonial expansion. The Law allowed each corporation power, within its own field of competence, to 'fix salary scales for the work and economic services of its producers, as well as prices of customers' goods offered to the public' but these decisions still depended on the approval of the General Assembly of the National Council of Corporations. Since Mussolini had total power over the Council, the final decision was really his.

Mussolini was not yet finished. In 1939, he finally put an end to whatever traces remained of Italian democracy when he passed the Law Creating the Chamber of Fasces and Corporations. The new law declared that the Chamber of Deputies was to be abolished and replaced by the Chamber of Fasces and Corporations and that the new Chamber was to consist of members of the National Council of the National Fascist Party.

Almost without exception, historians have been critical of Mussolini's Corporate State. It has been variously described as 'an elaborate piece of imposing humbug', 'totally irrelevant', 'an elaborate façade behind which corruption and exploitation flourished', 'a sham aimed at suppressing the workers', 'an elaborate fraud', and 'a system noted for bureaucratic bungling'. It did, however, achieve Mussolini's aims of strengthening his own dictatorship and ensuring that industrialists held the whip hand over their employees. In a series of lectures given in Moscow, Palmiro Togliatti, exiled leader of Italy's Communist Party, said:

> Corporativism was organised only after all the democratic liberties had been liquidated, when the workers had been deprived of all representation, when all the political parties had been destroyed, when trade union freedom, freedom of the press, freedom of assembly had been liquidated ... Corporativism is inconceivable without the existence of Fascism as a political dictatorship.

and again:

> What is the structure of a corporation? It is based on equal representation of the employers and of the employees, of the technical experts and of the Fascist Party. This equality is only an illusion, as we have seen, even if the employees' representatives ... were truly representatives of the workers, the upper hand would still be given to the bosses by the representatives of the Fascist Party ... There is only one president of the corporations, Mussolini.

From Lectures on Fascism *by Palmiro Togliatti, 1976*

The view of the British historian Roger Absalom is:

> The Corporations were riddled with careerists and hangers-on … Mussolini had proclaimed, and perhaps even believed, that Fascism would, through its dynamism, be the instrument of Italy's promotion into the league of major economic powers. The real constraints of Fascist economic policy were never identified, far less overcome …

From Italy Since 1800 *by Roger Absalom, 1995*

2 ↜ THE BATTLE FOR THE LIRA

See page 151

As we have seen, the years 1922–5, the period when economic affairs were in the hands of De Stafani, represented a period of relative economic well being during which unemployment fell and there was a recovery in trade. By 1927, this period was decidedly coming to an end and, as the lira came under increasing pressure, its value fell to 150 to the pound (£). Mussolini's reaction was predictably defiant and, instead of following the normal economic response and devaluing the lira, in a characteristic outburst he told the Italian people, 'I shall defend the Italian lira to my last breath – to my last drop of blood'. For reasons based more on national prestige than sound economics, he revalued the lira at a rate of exchange of 90 to the pound (£) and restored the lira to the **gold standard**. His intention was to reduce **inflation** and prove to Italians that the regime was capable of providing economic stability. However, although those industries dependent on imported raw materials benefited from lower prices, it was not a good move since it made Italian exports far more expensive in the world's markets and damaged her export trade. It also reduced the nation's considerable income from tourism. The overall affect was to worsen the **balance of payments** situation and edge the country closer to recession. Italian firms dependent on exports faced severe difficulties and Mussolini thought it prudent to protect industry from foreign competition by increasing **tariffs** on imports by 12%. The countries affected simply retaliated and this made the situation even worse. Between 1925 and 1938, the total value of Italian exports fell by 49% from 44,370 million lire to 21,750 million lire.

	Exports	Imports
1922	100	100
1925	194	100
1929	189	109
1932	142	72
1936	115	52
1938	162	58

(1922 = 100)

TABLE 24

Italian exports and imports (Source: European Historical Statistics, 1750–1970, *B.R. Mitchell, 1975)*

3 ↜ THE STRUGGLE TO ACHIEVE AUTARKY — SELF-SUFFICIENCY

Mussolini's plans for war and colonial expansion made it necessary for him to place the Italian economy on a war footing. Bearing in mind that Germany's defeat in the First World War was, in part, the result of the failure of her economy to adequately maintain her war effort, the Fascist leader was determined that Italy should achieve **autarky**, become self-sufficient and less dependent on foreign imports. To achieve this, the regime would need to make every effort to ensure that the country was able to produce as much of her own food and essential raw materials as possible. Part of this campaign for self-sufficiency was the Battle for Grain.

A *The Battle for Grain*

To achieve self-sufficiency in the production of grain would achieve two aims. Firstly, the imposition of higher tariffs on grain would reduce the amount of grain, particularly wheat, imported and so help reduce the country's balance of payments deficit. Secondly, and even more importantly, it would ensure an adequate supply of food in the event of war. Mussolini launched the Battle for Grain in 1925. Both new and more advanced **intensive** and **extensive methods of farming** were to be used this would mean the use of marginal land, that is land which, because of the additional expense involved, would only just be worth cultivating. To assist hard pressed farmers, the regime made grants available for the purchase of machinery and fertilisers. To add to his prestige, Mussolini sometimes appeared, stripped to the waist, driving a tractor or working alongside the labourers. In order to discourage its import, high tariffs were imposed on imported grain. Whilst the Battle for Grain was successful, there was a downside. Between 1925 and 1938, grain production virtually doubled from 4,479,000 metric tonnes to 8,184,000 metric tonnes but the concentration on grain production meant that the growing of other crops such as vines and olives and the animal husbandry were neglected. During the same time, the import of wheat fell by 75% and this led to an increase in the price of flour and consequently the price of bread and pasta.

B *Land reclamation*

Some regions of Italy were uncultivated marshland unsuitable for cultivation. They were also malarial and a risk to health. The shortage of arable land made it necessary for the government to take action and introduce a programme of land reclamation. In addition to making more land available, the project, known as *Bonifica Intergrale*, would create work and, in the long run, make more grain available. The most ambitious scheme was to drain the Pontine Marshes.

> **KEY ISSUE**
>
> *The problems created by the Battle for Grain.*

1913	5,690,000
1924	4,479,000
1938	8,184,000

TABLE 25
Output of wheat (metric tonnes) (Source: European Historical Studies, 1750–1970, *B.R. Mitchell, 1975.)*

The Pontine Marshes covered an area of 780 square kilometres in central Italy between the Tyrrhenian Sea and the foothills of the Apennine mountains. In pre-Roman days, it had been a fertile and well-populated area but had been abandoned and lapsed into unhealthy marshland. A series of Roman emperors and popes had made plans to reclaim it but none had been successful. The drainage scheme, which required a colossal effort by Italian engineers and labourers, was not completed until the 1930s. Afterwards, the former estates were divided up into smallholdings and given to farmers for permanent settlement. Rural towns such as Littoria (now Latina), Sabaudia, Pontinia, Aprilia and Pomezia were also built in the area.

PICTURE 46

Mussolini symbolically drives a tractor during work to reclaim the Pontine Marshes

The draining of the Pontine Marshes was a spectacular feat that provided Mussolini with yet a further excuse to boast of the achievements of Italian Fascism. Even so, since the regime made no real attempt to introduce land reform, the basic problems facing Italian agriculture remained. The plight of the peasantry worsened since between 1926 and 1934, the **real wages** of farmers fell by over 50%. Thousands of men desperate to find work left their villages and made for the urban industrial centres. Carlo Levi, forced into exile and working as a doctor in a remote village, described the poverty of the Italian peasantry:

> The peasants' houses were all alike, consisting of only one room that served as a kitchen, bedroom, and usually as quarters for the barnyard animals as well … On the one side of the room was the stove; sticks brought in every day from the fields served as fuel, and the walls and ceilings were blackened with smoke. The only light was from the door. The room was almost entirely filled by an enormous bed, much larger than an ordinary double bed; in it slept the whole family, father, mother, and children. The smallest children, before they were weaned, that is until they were three or four years old, were kept in little reed cradles or baskets hung from the ceiling just above the bed. When the mother wanted to nurse them she did not have to get out of bed; she simply reached out and pulled the baby down to her breast, then put him back and with one motion of her hand made the basket rock like a pendulum until he has ceased to cry.
>
> Under the bed slept the animals, and so the room was divided into layers: animals on the floor, people in the bed, and infants in the air. When I bent over a bed to listen to a patient's heart or to give an injection to a woman whose teeth were chattering with fever or who was burning up with malaria, my head touched the hanging cradles, while frightened pigs and hens darted between my legs. But what never failed to strike me most of all … were the eyes of the two inseparable guardian angels that looked at me from the wall over the

> bed. On one side was the black, scowling face, with its large inhuman eyes of the Madonna of Viggiano; on the other a coloured print of the sparkling eyes and the hearty grin of (the American) President Roosevelt. I never saw other pictures or images other than these: not the King not the *Duce* ...

From Christ Stopped at Eboli
by Carlo Levi, 1946

Ironically, at that time the regime was trying to dissuade people from moving from the countryside into the towns by emphasising 'the beauty of rural life'!

4 ⌒ ITALY AND THE WORLD RECESSION OF THE EARLY 1930s

As we have seen, in introducing corporatism, Mussolini effectively turned his back on his own socialist background and the original anti-capitalist views of the Fascist Party and instead looked for the support of the country's industrialists and bankers. In looking for closer ties with industry and banking, he was turning to those best able to ensure the survival of his regime and advance his policies. Although Italy was badly hit by the worldwide depression of the early 1930s, it has to be remembered that the country fared better than some other industrial powers. In Germany, unemployment reached 7 million and the country witnessed the rise of Hitler and the Nazi Party. In the United States, unemployment soared to 17 million and thousands of people were reduced to living in shantytowns or 'Hoovervilles'. In Britain, un-employment peaked at nearly 3 million and this led to hunger marches and the need for a National Government. By comparison, Italian unemployment reached 1,150,000 but there were many more living on reduced incomes caused by part-time employment.

KEY ISSUE

The impact of the Wall Street Crash on world economies.

A *Measures taken to aid Italian industry*

It should be remembered that before the First World War some Italian industries had flourished, won acclaim for their products and expanded into world markets. The Italian motor industry began to expand at the start of the century. In addition to Fiat (*Fabbrica Italiana Di Automobili Torino*) founded by Giovanni Agnelli in 1899, there were Lancia (1906), Alfa Romeo (1907) and Maserati (1914). The Pirelli Company, estab-lished by Giovanni Pirelli in 1872, had become famous for its telegraph cables before turning to the manufacture of tyres, Montecatini for chemicals and ILVA for steel products. During the period 1929 to 1932, as steel production fell by 35%, car production halved and the average national income fell from 3,079 lire to 1,868 lire, Volpi, the Finance Minister, decided to tackle the country's economic problems by follow-ing deflationary and protectionist policies. His first move was to reduce the wages of public employees by 12%. In addition, both direct and indirect taxes were increased. This meant that with lower incomes,

TABLE 26

Italian industrial production (Source: European Historical Statistics, 1750–1970, B.R. Mitchell, 1975.)

Pig iron (m. metric tonnes)		Steel (m. metric tonnes)		Crude oil (metric tonnes)	
1900	0.3	1900	0.7	1900	2000
1930	0.5	1930	0.5	1920	5000
		1940	1.0	1930	8000

Motor vehicles (thousands)		Registered merchant ships (thousand tonnes)		Electricity (m kwh)	
1925	49	1910	1001	1920	4.0
1930	47	1938	2059	1935	12.6
1938	71				

people had less money to spend and, as prices fell, the country began to suffer a deflationary spiral. To cope with the situation, industrialists moved towards creating cartels or, as Charles Delzele says, a situation in which 'the big fish eat the small fish'. A cartel exists when similar companies merge together to gain the advantages of monopoly – control levels of production and drive their competitors out of business. The obvious advantage of a monopoly is that it can control output and thereby influence prices. In 1933, the *Institu Per La Ricosstruzione Industriale*, the Institute for Industrial Reconstruction, was set up to help large firms that were in difficulty as well as some major banks, such as *Credito Italiano*, *Banca Commerciale* and *Banca Di Roma*, that had been supporting them. The following year, in an effort to more evenly distribute the amount of work available, the government reduced the working week to 40 hours. As rates of pay were not increased, the workers effectively suffered a pay cut. The creation of the *Instituto Mobiliare Italiano* was another attempt to help industry. Its function was to buy up worthless shares from the banks and grant long term loans. Between them, the IRI and IMI helped to ensure that Italy survived the depression as well as, if not better than, other European countries.

To provide relief for worker victims of the recession, industrialists and syndicates were made to pay a proportion of their profits and wages to the Agencies for Welfare Activities. The Agency used the money to provide and distribute welfare nationwide.

B *Public works schemes*

The use of public work schemes not only helped to reduce unemployment but also gave the Fascist regime the opportunity to realise some aspects of its ambitious programme for rejuvenating Italy. Some of the schemes are shown in Chart 9.

The building of a system of modern motorways – *autostrada*.	The *autostrada*, which connected most major Italian cities, provided a fast and effective means of travelling in Italy. It was the first motorway system in Europe.	**CHART 9** *Public works schemes*
The electrification and modernisation of the railway system.	Over 5,000 kilometres of the existing railway system were electrified. Other lines were opened and stations and rolling stock modernised.	
The development of hydro-electric power.	By 1935, the country was generating 12,600,000 kilowatts of electricity. An increasing amount came from new hydro-electric power stations situated in the Italian Alps.	
The production of alternative sources of power	A number of oil refineries were built to help counter Italy's chronic shortage of coal.	
A major construction programme.	A great deal of investment went into the building of schools, hospitals, clinics, sports stadia, government and high rise flats for workers.	
The restoration of the buildings that represented the splendour of Ancient Rome.	Plans were made to restore the amphitheatre, the Colosseum, the temples and the columns and triumphal arches of Ancient Rome. Some stretches of the Appian Way were also restored.	

5 ～ STRUCTURED AND ESSAY QUESTIONS

A *This section consists of questions that might be used for discussion (or written answers) as a way of expanding on the chapter and testing your understanding.*

1. What economic problems faced Italy during the years immediately after the First World War?
2. What is meant by *laissez faire* policies?
3. To what extent might the syndicalists be considered extreme in their views?
4. What did Mussolini hope to achieve through the creation of a Corporate State?
5. Why did Mussolini's decision to devalue the lira and return to the gold standard have such dire consequences?
6. What is meant by 'intensive and extensive farming methods'?
7. What advantages did the Labour Charter (1927) bring to Italian workers?
8. Would it be fair to say that Italy suffered less than other European powers during the world recession in the 1930s?
9. Which of the Fascist public works schemes would you say was the most advantageous to the Italian people?

B *Essay questions.*

1. 'They inherited many economic problems and then added others of their own.' Is this a valid assessment of the situation faced by Italy's Fascist regime during the 1920s and 30s?

2. To what extent might Mussolini's Corporate State be considered 'an interesting and worthwhile experiment'.

6 ⌐ DOCUMENTARY EXERCISE BASED ON CONFLICTING VIEWS ABOUT THE FASCIST CORPORATE STATE

Study the interpretations below and answer the question that follows.

SOURCE A

From a speech by Mussolini about the Corporate System, 1934

Corporations are established to provide the wealth, political power and welfare of the Italian people ... It is necessary that at a certain moment these institutions which we have created shall be noticed as institutions through which they can improve their standard of life ... The labourer, the peasant, should be able at a certain moment to tell himself and his dear ones: 'If I am better off, I owe it to the institutions which Fascism has created ...'

SOURCE B

From a lecture given by the exiled leader of the Italian Communist Party, Palmiro Togliatti, in Moscow, 1935

Corporations were organised only after all the democratic liberties had been denied, when the workers had been deprived of all representation, when all political parties had been destroyed, when trade union freedom, freedom of the press, when every possibility of expressing oneself had been eliminated ... Even if corporations had some importance, they would not be able to do anything not approved by the Fascist Party ...

Q

Analyse and evaluate the validity of the two interpretations of the Corporate State. (25 marks)

7 ↩ MAKING NOTES

Read the advice given about making notes on page xix of the Preface: How to use this book, and then make your own notes based on the following headings and questions.

1. *The Corporate State.*
   (a) The doctrine of corporatism.
   (b) The structure of the network of syndicates.
   (c) The role of the National Council of Corporations.
   (d) The significance of (i) the Palazzo Chigi Pact
                            (ii) the Vidoni Palace Pact.
   (e) Would you agree that Mussolini's Corporate State was an elaborate fraud?

2. *Battle for the lira.*
   (a) The consequences of the revaluation of the lira and return to the gold standard.
   (b) Reasons for Italy's balance of payments problem.
   (c) Do you think Mussolini won the Battle for the lira?

3. *Self-sufficiency or autarky.*
   (a) The methods used to increase grain production.
   (b) The purpose of *Bonifica Intergrale*.
   (c) Was reclaiming the Pontine Marshes worthwhile?

4. *Italy and the Recessions of the 1930s.*
   (a) Plans to aid Italian industry.
   (b) Reasons for the creation of cartels.
   (c) Public works schemes.
   (d) To what extent did the Italian working classes suffer during the recession?

11

Imperialist Ambitions and National Prestige – Italian Foreign Policy 1922–40

INTRODUCTION

As we have seen, during the 1910s, Mussolini abandoned his early socialist ideals and turned instead to militant nationalism and imperialism. This was evident by his support for Italian entry into the First World War in 1915 and his subsequent complaint regarding Italy's treatment by the terms of the post-war settlement that denied his country its promised territorial gains and a share in the distribution of the former colonies of Germany and Turkey. It was, so he claimed, a travesty – a 'mutilated victory'. In 1922, once in power, Mussolini assumed responsibility for Italian foreign policy but allowed himself to be influenced by Salvatore Contarini (1867–1945), the existing Permanent Secretary-General at the Italian Foreign Office. Contarini, a skilful professional diplomat, was a moderate and considered to be a restraining influence on the Fascist leader. Although others later held the title of Foreign Minister, Mussolini always exercised overall control of foreign policy decisions.

Although the aims of Mussolini's foreign policy were always clear, his methods of achieving those aims were ever uncertain. They were not based on any well-considered ideas but varied according to Italy's changing circumstances. Basically, his foreign policy decisions were framed to enhance the international status of his country and his own reputation. To achieve his aims, it would be necessary for him to increase Italy's military strength, engage in various forms of political intrigue and enter into favourable alliances. Mussolini would also need to show his skill as an opportunist and be able to recognise and take advantage of chances when they occurred. When in 1923, the British foreign secretary, Lord Curzon, asked Mussolini, 'What is your foreign programme?', he replied, 'My foreign policy is nothing for nothing.' Just how true was this?

1922–29	Benito Mussolini
1929–32	Dino Grandi
1932–36	Benito Mussolini
1936–40	Galeazzo Ciano
1940–43	Benito Mussolini

TABLE 27

Italian Foreign Ministers 1922–41

1 ✍ THE AIMS OF MUSSOLINI'S FOREIGN POLICY

'To advance Italy's strength to the point where the Roman Empire was seen to be reborn' has been suggested as the basic aim of Mussolini's foreign policy. Whilst this is certainly true, this is an over simplification since there were many strands to his foreign policy plans.

Mussolini's Foreign Policy

- Prominent amongst Mussolini's foreign policy aims was the need to achieve great power status for Italy. Although Italy remained on reasonably good terms with her former wartime allies Britain and France, Mussolini was conscious of the fact that they had denied Italy her just reward for taking their side during the First World War. He wanted to raise the status of Italy to at least their level. He held the view that both those countries were decadent and that the future lay with more virile nations such as Fascist Italy.
- Some historians have argued that Mussolini's intention to follow an aggressive and adventurous foreign policy was a direct response to Italy's pressing economic problems. It is their view that, as these problems became increasingly evident, a vigorous foreign policy would distract the attention of the Italian people from the shortcomings and failures of Fascist domestic policies.
- Mussolini recognised the need to promote his country's prestige abroad. Italy emerged from the First World War with her reputation damaged by her failures during the conflict. The wholesale desertions that followed the humiliation of the Battle of Caporetto in 1917 were only in part redeemed by the success at the Battle of Vittorio Veneto late in 1918. Because of the need to support the Italians during the war, the French and British tended to consider the country to have been a liability. Mussolini sought to change this lame duck image and he did this in part through the glorification of war. 'War,' he said, 'alone brings up to their highest tension all human energies and imposes the stamp of nobility upon peoples who have the courage to make it.'
- Bitterness at the terms of the post-war peace treaties that cheated the country of its just rewards remained. Mussolini knew that if he could bring about a revision of those terms it would enhance his reputation both at home and abroad. Consequently, he employed the legend of the 'mutilated victory' to stir up nationalist feelings. Two outstanding issues still needed to be settled in Italy's favour – the future of Fiume and the Dodecanese Islands.

1923	Corfu crisis
1924	Fiume finally became part of Italy
1925	Dodecanese Islands passed to Italy
	Locarno Conference
1926	Albania became an Italian protectorate
1928	Kellogg–Briand Pact
1933	Four Power Conference
1934	Italy intervened in Austrian crisis
	Assassination of King Alexander of Yugoslavia
1935	Stresa Conference
	Italian invasion of Abyssinia
1936	Italian involvement in Spanish Civil War
	Rome–Berlin Axis
1937	Italy joined the Anti-Comintern Pact
	Nyon Conference
1938	Mussolini accepts German annexation of Austria
	Mussolini and Ciano attend Munich Conference
	Albania annexed by Italy
1939	Pact of Steel
	Mussolini declared Italy non-belligerent at time of German invasion of Poland
1940	Italy declared war on Britain and France

TABLE 28

Date line showing Italy's involvement overseas

- Mussolini considered the Mediterranean Sea to be *Mare Nostrum*, or 'Our Sea', and was determined to achieve Italian dominance in that area. This would prove difficult since both France and Britain also had interests there. France was a Mediterranean power and controlled the island of Corsica and the North African coastline stretching across Tunisia, Algeria and Morocco. Her possession of Gibraltar and the Suez Canal gave Britain control of strategic points of the entry and exit to the Mediterranean. Mussolini was clearly aware of the significance of the Suez Canal when, in 1919, he wrote in *Il Popolo d'Italiana* that Italy 'could tomorrow accomplish the task of bringing about the collapse of the British Empire in Asia and Africa'. In addition, Britain also owned the islands of Malta and Cyprus. Mussolini would need to proceed carefully since France and Britain were amongst the world's greatest naval powers.

- Disappointed by Italy's failure to gain control of Fiume and the Dalmatian Coast, Mussolini still sought to extend Italian influence in the region of the Adriatic Sea and beyond, in the Balkans. Particularly inviting was the prospect of annexing Albania, a country that was formerly part of the Turkish Empire and still largely Islamic by religion and culture. In 1921, after a lengthy dispute involving Italy, Greece and Yugoslavia, a regency council was appointed to rule over the country. Albania became a republic under Ahmed Bey Zogu in 1925 who, three years later, assumed the title King Zog. The country was already economically dependent on Italy with even its national bank based in Rome. Mussolini aimed to gain control of Albania and use it as a stepping stone to extending Italian influence in the Balkans. His main adversary in the region was Greece.

- Mussolini was extremely jealous of the great colonial empires of France and Britain and sought to create an overseas Italian empire by conquest. His country already possessed some territories in Africa – Libya, Eritrea and Somaliland – but these in no way matched those of the other two powers. The problem was that there was little scope for territorial expansion in Africa since most of the continent had already been colonised by the European powers. However there remained one opportunity, Abyssinia, where the Italians had already been decisively defeated and humiliated at Adowa in 1896.

- Whatever successes Mussolini might achieve in the realms of foreign policy would clearly reflect on the quality of his leadership and serve as glowing examples of the achievements of Fascism. This, in turn, would help to popularise that political creed abroad. However, there would soon be problems on the horizon. In 1933, another Fascist regime was established in Europe – Nazi Germany. Mussolini was soon to show concern about Hitler's territorial ambitions and their possible affect on Italy.

See pages 27–9

KEY ISSUE

Domestic restraints on Mussolini's foreign policy.

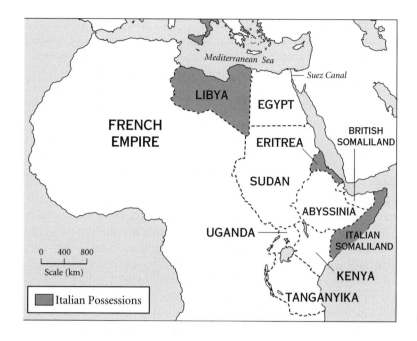

MAP 7
*Italian possessions
in Africa, 1935*

Whatever Mussolini's foreign policy aims, he would face major problems trying to achieve them. To increase his country's military might by increasing the size of the Italian armed forces and equipping them with modern weapons would prove expensive and be a further drain on its already limited resources. Whilst the Fascist leader's drive to achieve autarky had proved successful in limiting the country's dependence on imported grain, Italy remained woefully short and far from self-sufficient in the production of essential war materials – oil, steel and explosives. As for manpower resources, the so-called Battle for Births was in its early stages and was ultimately doomed to failure. Put simply, Italy just did not have the economic or military means to challenge for a place amongst the major powers or become a powerful voice in international affairs.

See pages 156–7

During the 1920s, with no immediate threat from other powers, Italy could concentrate on her own foreign policy ambitions. She enjoyed reasonably good relations with France and Britain although Mussolini was always willing to exploit differences between the two countries. In 1923, at the time when the British were opposed to the French occupation of the Ruhr, he attempted to mediate between the two countries. They realised that he was, in effect, trying to play one off against the other, and Mussolini consequently earned the distrust of both. Italy's northern neighbour, the former Dual Monarchy, had disintegrated into two impotent states, Austria and Hungary. With Soviet Russia experiencing the aftermath of a civil war and the Italian Communist party outlawed, the chances of a revolution had virtually disappeared. To follow an adventurous foreign policy, Italy would need the support of reliable allies. Consequently Mussolini began a stampede into alliances and signed treaties with many European countries –

Poland, Czechoslovakia and Austria (1923), the Soviet Union and Switzerland (1924) and Hungary, Spain, Albania and Greece (1925). The treaties were largely commercial and of little political importance since Mussolini was always prepared to switch allegiances when it was to Italy's advantage. As the British ambassador in Rome, Sir Ronald Graham, commented that Mussolini was always prepared to 'offer Italian friendship to the highest bidder'. In spite of all his efforts, the Italian leader remained a fringe player in European politics and failed in his ambition to win a more influential role.

At home, supporters of Mussolini's aggressive line in foreign policy were easily found. There were the war veterans, those who had enthused over D'Annunzio's exploits in Fiume, nationalists and former members of the *squadristi* looking for further opportunities to indulge in violence and conquest. Of them, the historian Martin Blinkhorn has written: 'The resultant cocktail was a dangerously intoxicating one, especially when composed by someone as vain, capricious, violent and authoritarian as Mussolini.' In the meantime, Mussolini had to tread carefully and appear to be a respectable statesman prepared to achieve his aims through diplomacy. In 1923, he made attempts to settle the issues of Fiume and the Dodecanese Islands that had been garrisoned by Italian troops since 1912. In both instances, discussions with the Yugoslav and Greek governments came to nothing. Later in the year, the Greeks became concerned when the Italians began to strengthen their forces in the Dodecanese since they feared this was a prelude to the formal annexation of the islands. The Italians convinced other European powers that this was not the case. However, the image of Mussolini as a man of peace did not last for long! In 1923, a crisis arose over the Greek island of Corfu.

2 ⌐ THE CORFU CRISIS, 1923

Albania had been independent of Turkey since 1912, and in 1921, the League of Nations entrusted the guardianship of the country's independence to Italy. Since independence, there had been an on-going dispute between Albania and her neighbour Greece regarding the exact location of their common frontier. In 1921, the issue was placed before the League of Nations who, in turn, referred it to the Conference of the Ambassadors of Britain, France, Italy and Japan. They decided to send a commission made up of Greeks, Albanians and Italians to the disputed region to settle the issue. An Italian general, Enrico Tellini, was appointed to lead the commission.

A *The incident*

On 17 August 1923, on the road close to Kakavia in Epirus on the Greek side of the frontier, the car containing Tellini and the other Italian representatives was ambushed and the general and four others murdered. Although there was evidence to suggest that the assassins were Albanian, Mussolini held the Greek government responsible and an ultimatum was sent to Athens. The terms of the ultimatum were extensive and demanded an official apology for the crime, that members of the Greek government should attend the funeral of the victims, that the murderers should be apprehended within five days and executed, a salute by the Greek fleet to the Italian flag and the payment of an **indemnity** of 50 million lire. Later, the French prime minister, Raymond Poincare described the terms as 'extravagant – much worse than the ultimatum after Sarajevo'.

indemnity
compensation for loss or injury

B *The repercussions*

The Greek government was required to accept these terms within a time limit of 24 hours and the indemnity paid within five days. Whilst the Greeks accepted most of the terms, they refused to agree to the automatic execution of the murderers and thought the sum of 50 million lire excessive. They suggested that the amount be set by the League of Nations. On 31 August, an Italian fleet arrived off the coast of the Greek island of Corfu and Admiral Emilio Solari advised the authorities that the island was to be occupied until the Greek government complied with the terms of the ultimatum. He also demanded the lowering of the Greek flag. When this did not occur, the Italian battleships opened fire. Some of the shells landed on an orphanage and refugee camp and some 16 people were killed and a further 30 wounded. Then the Italians occupied the island.

International opinion was divided. Many foreign powers were critical of Mussolini's **gunboat diplomacy** and thought it impulsive and ill advised. However, there was also some support for Italy, particularly in both the British and French press. In London, *The Observer* applauded Mussolini's 'virile direction of his country's affairs'. In Rome, the Italian dictator told British reporters that their government would have acted in exactly the same way if British officers had been murdered in Greece. He also let it be known that he did not want the matter referred to the League of Nations since he considered it outside their jurisdiction. Further, if it was referred, then Italy would resign from the League. Mussolini was truly in a difficult position. This was the first international crisis he had faced and, if he failed to get his way, it would reflect badly on his Fascist regime and public opinion might turn against him. As a British diplomat commented: 'the whole Fascist fabric might collapse like a pack of cards'. That might, in turn, lead to a return to political instability and encourage a reappearance of the threat of Communism. In the end, the League of Nations placed the matter in the hands of the Ambassadors' Conference. The outcome was that the Conference largely supported the Italian case and stated that the indemnity had to be paid. In September, Italian forces were withdrawn from the island.

gunboat diplomacy the use of force in negotiations

The crisis over Corfu ended in a clear victory for Mussolini. It appeared that his display of strength had allowed Italy's Fascist regime to win its first international confrontation. This added further to his popularity at home and his international prestige abroad. In 1924,

KEY ISSUE

The significance of the crisis over Corfu.

Mussolini finally reached agreement with Yugoslavia over the future of Fiume. The port was to pass to Italy whilst the area around was to be retained by Yugoslavia. The Greeks also gave way on the issue of the Dodecanese Islands and the following year they formally became Italian. Significantly, too, the crisis had displayed for the first time the weakness of the League when faced by the aggression of a member state. It was not a good omen for the future. The crisis over Corfu also indicated that Fascist Italy's foreign policy aims represented a threat to peace.

3 ⌁ MUSSOLINI – HONEST STATESMAN AND MAN OF PEACE?

Over the next few years, relations between Italy and Greece improved, as did those with Yugoslavia. Relations with Britain remained uncertain and, in 1925, there was a hiccup in the relations between the two powers when the Albanian government granted the British owned Anglo-Persian Oil Company a concession to search for oil. The Italian government protested strongly since they regarded it as an attempt by the British to become involved in what they regarded as their **sphere of influence**. The issue was eventually settled amicably when the Italians were granted a 33% interest in the concession. Mussolini was also concerned that France continued to offer political asylum to Italian anti-Fascists living in exile. He also disapproved of the French attempt to set up a system of alliances with Poland, Czechoslovakia and Yugoslavia in an attempt to achieve collective security. His reaction was to entertain prominent European leaders in Rome in order to impress them with the achievements of Fascism. In 1924, Mussolini caused some considerable surprise when he recognised the new Communist government in the Soviet Union.

> **sphere of influence** an area in which it is accepted that one nation has the dominating interest

The Corfu crisis over, on the face of it Mussolini reverted to honest statesmanship and being a man of peace. In an effort to ease international tension, in the autumn of 1925 a conference of European powers was called at Locarno in Switzerland.

A *Italy and Locarno Treaties, 1925*

The leading figures at the conference were Aristide Briand and Austen Chamberlain, the Foreign Ministers of France and Britain, and Gustav Stresemann, the Chancellor of Germany. Mussolini, who wanted the conference to be held in Italy, declined to attend and instead his country was represented by Dino Grandi. The conference was successful in that it confirmed as final Germany's western frontiers with France and Belgium and agreed to the continued demilitarised state of the Rhineland. These terms were to be guaranteed by Britain and Italy. The conference was less successful in reaching agreement about Germany's long-term eastern frontiers but Stresemann confirmed that whatever changes were required would be achieved through negotiation and not war. From a distance Mussolini was informed of developments. He was not over concerned about Italian interests since he knew that 'treaties were pieces of paper with no binding force if circumstances changed'. Suddenly he decided to make an appearance.

Q

To what extent did the Locarno Treaties improve the prospects of peace in Europe?

Mussolini finally decided he had better go to Locarno and arrived there in as dramatic a manner as possible – by speedboat and with his usual bodyguard of boisterous Fascists. The Italian press claimed that his arrival at the conference was the critical factor in its success. No mention was made of the fact that he attended only one session for just a few minutes; nor that a hundred journalists boycotted his appearance in protest against Fascist brutality – only a few days earlier another of his murder squads had run amok in Florence, killing many innocent bystanders. He arrived at one press conference escorted by his usual stage crowd of blackshirts, but the journalists refused to attend and waited outside the room to greet him in silent contempt as he emerged from the hotel lobby. This did not stop the *Il Popolo d'Italiana* from describing how a large audience was deeply impressed by what he had to say. But never again did he invite a similar rebuff; henceforth, he preferred to stay at home.

From Mussolini *by Denis Mack Smith, 1993*

Although the agreements reached at Locarno did little more than reaffirm the frontiers agreed in Paris in 1919, the treaties heralded a period of peace based on international co-operation. A new feeling of optimism pervaded the political scene and people spoke of 'the spirit of Locarno'. Mussolini's brief appearance was not without significance. It created an opportunity for him to meet the British foreign secretary, Austen Chamberlain, and discuss their countries' outstanding differences. In fact, they got on well and established a friendship. As with other national leaders, Mussolini thought that Locarno increased the chances of a lasting peace in Europe. Another measure also intended to promote peace came about in 1928.

B *Italy's reaction to the Kellogg–Briand Pact, 1928*

In April 1927, Aristide Briand, the French Foreign Minister, suggested to Frank B. Kellogg, the American Secretary of State, that their two countries should set an example to the rest of the world by openly making a declaration rejecting war as a means of settling international disputes. Kellogg was not in favour of such a limited **bilateral agreement** and suggested that it should be extended to include as many nations as possible. He was particularly keen to involve Germany, only admitted to the League of Nations in 1926, as well as the non-League powers, the United States and the Soviet Union. Representatives to a nine-power conference then being held in Paris signed the Pact on 27 August 1928. The signatories, which included Count Gaetano Manzoni the Italian ambassador to France, solemnly declared that their countries condemned 'recourse to war for the solution of international contro-

bilateral agreement an agreement between two nations

versies', and renounced war 'as an instrument of national policy in their relations with one another'. They further agreed that the settlement of all disputes that arose between them 'should never be sought except by pacific means'. Subsequently a further 56 nations signed an agreement to abide by the principles outlined in the Pact.

At first Mussolini was not keen for Italy to become involved in what he considered 'an absurd proposal'. As with the Locarno Treaties three years earlier, he sought to gain prestige by getting the delegates, then assembled in Paris, to travel to Rome to formally sign the Pact. They refused. Although he had no faith in the Pact and had no intention of keeping to its principles, he was not prepared to oppose it **unilaterally** and finally agreed for Count Manzoni to sign. It made no difference to his preparations for a future war and, in a speech to the Chamber of Deputies, ridiculed it as being 'so sublime that it should be called transcendental'.

unilaterally by himself

In truth, from the start the Kellogg–Briand Pact (sometimes known as the Pact of Paris) was not enthusiastically received and was never to make any meaningful contribution to future settlement of international disputes. Since it appeared to duplicate the undertakings already made in the covenant of the League of Nations, it is possible to question why it was necessary in the first place. Obvious weaknesses were that the Pact neither provided a means of enforcing its principles nor gave any idea of the course of action to be taken against any nation that broke them.

4 ⌐ MUSSOLINI AND THE RISE OF NAZI GERMANY

Most significant for Mussolini's Fascist Italy was the revival of Germany and the rise to power of Adolf Hitler and his National Socialists in 1933. Alarmed by Hitler's decision to withdraw Germany from the Disarmament Conference and the League of Nations, Mussolini called for a Four-Power Conference of the representatives of Italy, France, Britain and Germany in Rome.

A *The Four-Power Conference, 1933*

Little Entente a term used to describe the systems of alliances that developed amongst some of the lesser powers in Europe – Czechoslovakia, Yugoslavia and Romania

It was Mussolini's hope that the Conference, described by some as an attempt to revive the Holy Alliance, would consider and settle the problems of Europe. From the start, progress was slow and then the discussions began to go badly wrong. Whilst France wanted the proposals modified, Britain was suspicious of Mussolini's motives. Was it a ploy to revise the terms of the Paris peace settlement of 1919? Was it an attempt to form an anti-Communist bloc opposed to the Soviet Union? From outside the Conference, the **Little Entente**, an alliance made up of Czechoslovakia, Yugoslavia and Romania in 1929, voiced its opposition since the four powers appeared to be disregarding the interests of the lesser European powers. The truth was that Mussolini was concerned that Fascist Italy might have to share the limelight with Nazi Germany, a development of which he thoroughly disapproved. As usual, at home he exploited the Conference for propaganda purposes. He was keen to imply that Italy was now playing a major role in European diplomacy and the Fascist press referred to the proposed pact between the four powers as the *Patto Mussolini* – 'Mussolini's Pact'. On 7 June 1933, the representatives of the nations attending the Four-Power Conference initialled the proposals for a pact but there the matter rested. In the end, it all came to nothing.

From the start, Mussolini had mixed feelings about Adolf Hitler. Hitler, on the other hand, was flattered when the press made comparisons between him and the Italian leader and claimed that he looked forward to meeting *Il Duce*. It was known that Hitler had a life-size bust of Mussolini in his home and had boasted that once he was in power 'Nazi Germany and Fascist Italy will be friends for tens and tens of years or at least until I die.' When Hitler came to power in 1933, differences arose in the relations between the two men. According to Nazi racial theories, Italians were Mediterranean-types and therefore inferior. Anton Drexler, the original founder of the Nazi Party, did not help matters when he suggested that Mussolini was probably a Jew!

KEY ISSUE

The relationship between Mussolini and Hitler.

In March 1934, Austria, Hungary and Italy signed the Rome Protocols. This was an agreement by which each would provide military assistance to the others if it were needed. At the same time, Mussolini gave an undertaking to defend Austrian independence. Four months later in July 1934, Mussolini had to face the reality of Nazi Germany's territorial ambitions. After the collapse of the Austro-Hungarian Empire in 1918, there were many German-speaking Austrians who favoured union with the new German Republic. Hitler and the Austrian Nazis supported the idea of the *Anschluss*, the incorporation of Austria into Germany. However, the Treaties of St German and Versailles both specifically prohibited an *Anschluss* since it might encourage the revival of a strong, militaristic Germany. It was because of this that France was much opposed to the idea, as were the members of associates in the Little Entente. Mussolini was also against the *Anschluss* since he feared it might lead to a demand for a return of the former Austrian lands gained by Italy after the war. After Hitler came to power in 1933, the Italian leader also had reservations at the prospect of having a powerful Germany as his immediate neighbour. Their common fear of Nazi Germany caused Italy and France to draw closer together. Under Hitler's leadership, the clamour for the *Anschluss* increased and, within Austria, the Austrian Nazis escalated their agitation for union with Germany. In August 1933, Mussolini met the Austrian Chancellor, Engelbert Dollfuss at Riccione in Italy. Dollfuss, a long-time admirer of *Il Duce*, promised to take measures to establish a Fascist-type regime in his own country. Back in Austria, he dissolved parliament and banned both the Communist and Nazi Parties claiming that, 'a Catholic country was better off without Godless Reds and pagan Nazis.' He then formed the

KEY ISSUE

Mussolini's concern about the German threat to Austria.

Vaterlandische Front, Fatherland Front, which was in effect an Austrian Fascist Party. Now decidedly under Mussolini's patronage, the following year he announced his intention of setting up a corporate state based on the Italian fashion. The Austrian Nazis reacted by engaging in a campaign of terror and sabotage. It is thought that Hitler sent his own ***agents provocateur*** to help and encourage them. In January 1934, when Dollfuss issued a decree dissolving the Socialist council in Vienna, the Socialists reacted by calling a general strike. The situation appeared to be getting out of hand when the Austrian army shelled the working class districts of the city and became engaged in street fighting. There was always a chance that Hitler might take advantage of this chaos and use it as an excuse to annex Austria.

In June 1934, Mussolini met Hitler for the first time. The two men met at the Villa Pisani at Stra between Venice and Padua. Afterwards, Mussolini, who described Hitler's appearance as 'like a plumber in a mackintosh', claimed that the German leader had spent much of their time quoting passages from *Mein Kampf*. He thought the book boring and one 'which I have never been able to read'.

agents provocateur
people employed to pretend sympathy and lead others

PICTURE 47
Mussolini and Hitler at their meeting in Venice in 1934

When Mussolini arrived at Venice airport dressed in a well-fitting and bemedalled grey uniform of an Italian general, and Hitler emerged from the plane wearing civilian dress, a rather shabby raincoat and a crumpled hat, they thought that the costume of the two leaders reflected the picture of the powerful Mussolini and the insignificant Hitler. The caricatures in the foreign press showed a giant Mussolini towering over Hitler the pigmy. In fact Mussolini and Hitler were both small in stature, about five feet five inches, but Hitler was marginally taller than Mussolini ... They were alone together and spoke without interpreters in German, the only language that Hitler could speak and one of the foreign languages that Mussolini spoke well. They discussed Austria, and reached a broad measure of agreement, because Hitler agreed to most of Mussolini's demands. Hitler said that he did not contemplate an *Anschluss* between Germany and Austria in the foreseeable future.

From Mussolini *by Jasper Ridley 1997*

B *The Anschluss. Mussolini's reaction to the attempted putsch of July 1934*

In July 1934, the Austrian Nazis attempted a **putsch** in Vienna. They forced their way into the Chancellery building and shot Dollfuss. The

putsch a sudden revolutionary outbreak or attempt to seize power

CONSULTING THE ORACLE.
(As recorded by Mr. Punch's magic microphone.)

Herr Hitler. "WHAT IS YOUR MESSAGE FOR GERMANY?"
Signor Mussolini. "TELL HER SHE MUST BE CAREFUL TO KEEP ON THE RIGHT SIDE OF ITALY."
Herr Hitler. "AND HOW CAN SHE MAKE SURE OF DOING THAT?"
Signor Mussolini. "BY KEEPING ON THE OTHER SIDE OF AUSTRIA."

PICTURE 48
A cartoon by Bernard Partridge, which appeared in Punch *in June 1934, shows Hitler sitting at the feet of Mussolini seeking his advice*

Austrian Chancellor, who was refused medical assistance and the last rites, took four hours to bleed to death. The ringleaders of the putsch surrendered to the Austrian army on the understanding that their lives would be spared but they were all immediately shot without trial. Fearing that the attempted putsch was a prelude to a German occupation of the country, Mussolini ordered four divisions (40,000 troops) to the Austrian frontier and made preparations to help if the country was invaded. At that time, Hitler was in no position to risk a confrontation with Mussolini and the threat of invasion receded. Afterwards, he denied all knowledge of the planned putsch and claimed that if there had been a German involvement then it would have been the work of Ernst Röhm. Röhm, who had been amongst those killed a month earlier during Hitler's infamous blood purge known as the Night of the Long Knives, could not answer for himself!

Mussolini, now regarded as the guardian of Austrian independence, soon had another crisis to deal with.

C *The assassination of King Alexander of Yugoslavia, October 1934*

On 9 October 1934, King Alexander of Yugoslavia was assassinated in Marseilles at the start of a state visit to France. The assassin, under the name of Petrus Kelemen, one of his many aliases, was a professional terrorist with a number of murders to his credit. Macedonia-born, he was employed by Ustasi, a Croat secret society opposed to the domination of their country by Alexander and his predominantly Serb government. Another victim of the atrocity was the French Foreign Minister, Louis Barthou, who had been accompanying the Yugoslav king. Wounded, he had wandered away from the scene and slowly bled to death. Since many of the Ustasi had been living in exile in Hungary, the Yugoslav authorities blamed that country for the murder of their king. Czechoslovakia and Romania supported Yugoslavia, their ally in the Little Entente. Mussolini, still bearing a grudge against Serb ruled Yugoslavia, saw to it that Italy sided with Hungary. The issue was placed before the League of Nations and there Dino Grandi warned that if Hungary was attacked by the Little Entente, Italy would be duty bound to go to that country's defence. Bearing in mind the consequences of an earlier assassination at Sarajevo in 1914, there were those who feared that the crisis might lead to another European war. Fortunately, as negotiations continued, so the tension eased. In the end, Hungary did accept some responsibility for harbouring members of the Ustasi and agreed to keep a closer watch on the activities of Croat refugees in their country. Later, much blame was attached to the French government for its negligence in failing to provide adequate security during the Yugoslav king's visit. It was also discovered that the Italian authorities had subsidised the Ustasi and provided them with training facilities. Whether Mussolini was involved in making these arrangements remains uncertain. Certainly a great deal of double-dealing went on behind the scenes. In *Murder in Marseilles*, the American historian Daniel Leab has written:

KEY ISSUE

The significance of the assassination of the Yugoslav King.

Steps were taken to settle the Marseilles affair as soon as possible. France and Italy apparently came to a secret understanding that France should exercise her influence to prevent Yugoslavia from implicating Italy and to incriminate only Hungary. In return, Italy would do nothing to support Hungary in the League of Nations. To restrain Yugoslavia, France told her that she could not expect military support if she committed any rash acts. With this compromise formula, Hungary was cast as the scapegoat … That King Alexander died a victim of Italian hate and Croat fanaticism seems evident. It remains doubtful if the assassin meant to kill Barthou as well. The fact that Barthou was a staunch supporter of a collective security system to stem German aggression – as was Alexander – has led to the suggestion that the Nazis were involved but there is no evidence to support this. If there ever were powers behind the murders, all efforts to discover them have failed, and they literally got away with murder.

From Murder in Marseilles *by Daniel Leab taken from Purnell's* History of the Twentieth Century

The ending of the Austrian crisis in 1934 did not ease Mussolini's fears of Nazi Germany's territorial ambitions. Following Hitler's announcement that he intended to disregard the limitations imposed on Germany by the Treaty of Versailles and introduce conscription and begin to rearm, Mussolini called for a meeting with the heads of state of France and Britain.

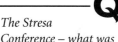

The Stresa Conference – what was its purpose?

D *The Stresa Conference, 1935*

The meeting, held in Italy at Stresa, a health resort on the shores of Lake Maggiore, was attended by Mussolini and Ramsay MacDonald and Pierre-Etienne Flandin, the Prime Ministers of Britain and France together with their foreign secretaries. They protested strongly against Hitler's decision to rearm and discussed the possibility of forming a common front to oppose future German provocation. Ramsay MacDonald writing in *The Times* claimed that 'now nothing could come between the three powers'. Within months the so-called Stresa Front collapsed when Mussolini himself committed an act of aggression by invading Abyssinia.

The Stresa Conference achieved little apart from adding further to Mussolini's prestige by giving the impression that he was now truly a statesman of international standing.

5 ⌐ THE ITALIAN INVASION OF ABYSSINIA

On 3 October 1935, Italian troops crossed from their bases in Eritrea and Italian Somaliland and began the invasion of Abyssinia. The fact that Mussolini had long been preparing for such a war had been known in diplomatic circles for some time.

A *Abyssinia*

Abyssinia, together with Liberia on the west coast, were the two remaining 'unclaimed' territories in Africa. The bulk of that continent had already been claimed as colonies by various European powers. A country that had flourished since biblical times, Abyssinia was a country of contrasting low-lying plains around central highlands. It was populated by a variety of tribal peoples, the majority of which survived on **subsistence farming**. One section of the population were Amharic-speaking people who had centuries earlier migrated from Arabia. Although Abyssinia had earlier attracted the interest of the Portuguese, French and British, it had managed to retain its independence. An earlier attempt by Italy to colonise the country had come to grief at the Battle of Adowa in 1896. Until his death in 1913, the Emperor Menelik II, who claimed direct descent from King Solomon and the Queen of Sheba and took the titles King of Kings and Lion of Judah, had ruled the country. In 1930, the crown passed to Ras Tafari who was crowned at his capital, Addis Ababa, and ruled as the Emperor Haile Selassie. Today there are those, mainly West Indians, who consider Haile Selassie to have been divine. The sect, identified by their style of dress and plaited dreadlocks, are known as Rastafarians. Haile Selassie declined to rule as a feudal king and set about introducing reforms intended to modernise his country.

subsistence farming
farming that will just about support the farmer and leave nothing left over

See page 27

B *The Abyssinian war, 1935–6*

Although a treaty of friendship had been signed between them in 1928, there were frequent border incidents between Italian and Abyssinian troops along their common frontiers in Eritrea and Italian Somaliland. These episodes, which were mainly the result of Italian incursions into Abyssinia, were used by Mussolini to increase tension and provide an excuse for the invasion of the country.

To the outside world, Mussolini boasted that his purpose in invading Abyssinia was to 'bring civilisation to a barbaric country ... unworthy of taking its place amongst civilised people.' Ignoring the fact that many Abyssinians were already Christians, though not of the Roman Catholic variety, he went as far as to claim that he had the Pope's blessing in his mission!

Earlier, in a speech made in March 1934, Mussolini had said:

> There is no question of territorial conquests – this must be understood by all far and near – but a natural expansion which ought to lead to a collaboration between Italy and the people of Africa ... Italy can above all civilise Africa and her position in the Mediterranean gives her the right and imposes this duty on her. We do not intend to demand privileges ... but we do ask and wish to obtain from those who have made good, who are satisfied, who wish to keep their possessions that they should not take pains to block the expansion of Italy

The Reasons for Mussolini's Invasion of Abyssinia

The main reason for Mussolini's invasion of Abyssinia in 1935 was to win imperial status for Italy and prove to the world that Italy was the equal of France and Britain. There were also numerous other reasons:

- The time was right. *Il Duce* assumed that his membership of the Stresa Front would secure, if not the support, then the neutrality of France and Britain for his ambitions in Africa. He hoped that 'if London would not close both eyes as France had done, it would at least close one'. He had also secretly informed Hitler that he intended to change his policy and abandon the Stresa Front and his Anglo-French allies and seek closer ties with Germany. In return, he hoped that Hitler too would give him a free hand in his planned Abyssinian venture.
- To avenge the humiliation of the Battle of Adowa when in 1896 the Abyssinians defeated and inflicted heavy losses on the Italian army.
- To give to the world evidence of the vitality of Italian Fascism.
- To increase Mussolini's prestige in Europe and prove to Hitler that Italy was a power to be reckoned with.
- To exploit the natural resources of Abyssinia. Some thought the country rich in oil.
- To win markets for Italian exports.
- To tackle the problem of overpopulation by providing territory suitable for settlement by Italian emigrants.
- To divert the attention of the Italian people from Mussolini's unkept promises and the regime's mounting economic problems.
- To stir up patriotic fervour that would help guarantee Mussolini the continuing support of the Italian people.
- To further consolidate Mussolini's own position and, of course, add to his personal prestige.

A London correspondent described the excitement as war seemed increasingly inevitable:

The streets are full of soldiers and Blackshirts come from all over the country to embark … For embarkation, the soldiers arrive in military order, well disciplined … They wave their hands and handkerchiefs and shout and sing. Now and again a voice rising above the others cries '*Saluto al Duce*' (Hail Mussolini), and thousands of voices answer '*A noi*' (To us). Then they all repeat the chorus: '*Du-ce, Du-ce, Du-ce*'. Now and then voices rise above the others: '*A chi l'Abyssinia?*' (To whom Abyssinia?) and the soldiers reply comes in chorus '*A noi*'.

From an article by The Times *correspondent in Naples, September 1935*

The crisis that finally triggered the invasion came as a result of a clash at Wal Wal, an oasis some 80 kilometres inside Abyssinian territory, during which 100 Abyssinians and 30 Italians were killed. Mussolini decided to reject League of Nations' mediation claiming that Abyssinia was 'a barbarous and uncivilised state whose conduct placed it outside the Covenant of the League.' At home, Mussolini used his eloquence to stir up his countrymen's patriotic fervour. Italian soldiers were given a hero's send off and their families promised their safe return, 'a war without tears'.

Carlo Levi recalled the reaction of Italian peasants to the invasion of Abyssinia:

From Christ Stopped at Eboli *by Carlo Levi, 1948*

> October 3rd, which marked the official opening of the war, was a miserable sort of day. Twenty or twenty-five peasants, roped in by the Carabinieri, stood woodenly in the square to listen to the historical announcement as it came over the radio … Don Luigi, the local Fascist leader, spoke from the balcony of the town hall. He spoke of the grandeur of Rome … the wolf that suckled Romulus and Remus, Caesar's legions, Roman civilisation and the Roman Empire which was about to be revived … Huddled against the wall below, the peasants listened in silence, shielding their eyes with their hands from the sun and looking, in their black suits, as dark and gloomy as bats.

set-piece battles battles fought according to a prearranged plan

The Abyssinian army was a ragged, largely untrained force of tribesmen equipped with spears or, at best, outdated rifles. Their situation was not helped by a lack of unity amongst their tribal leaders and their willingness to engage the Italian army in **set-piece battles** instead of using guerrilla tactics which would have been more to their advantage. Against them were ranged Italian infantrymen with modern weapons backed by artillery, machine guns, tanks and aircraft.

PICTURE 49
Italian troops bound for Abyssinia display portraits of Mussolini along the side of their troopship

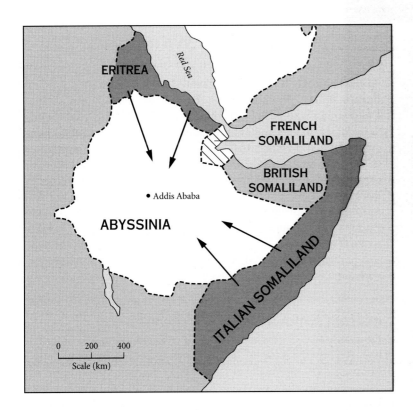

MAP 8
The Italian invasion of Abyssinia, 1935

The Italians' decision to use chemical warfare in the form of flame throwers and mustard gas horrified many. Both sides were guilty of appalling atrocities against prisoners-of-war. At first, the Italian armies were commanded by 66-year-old General Emilio de Bono who advanced from Eritrea whilst forces under Rodolfo Graziani invaded from Italian Somaliland. Indecisive, de Bono allowed the campaign to drag on and seemed more intent on capturing Adowa than ending the war. Consequently a conflict that should have lasted weeks dragged on for seven months. In the end, he was replaced by General Pietro Badoglio and Mussolini ordered him to bring the war to a rapid and successful conclusion.

C *International reaction*

Although Nazi Germany appeared to give Italian aggression against Abyssinia its tacit approval, elsewhere it attracted worldwide criticism. The issue was placed before the League of Nations where only a few months earlier, the British Foreign Secretary, Sir Samuel Hoare, had said:

> The League stands, and my country stands with it, for the collective maintenance of the Covenant in its entirety, and particularly for steady and collective resistance to all acts of unprovoked aggression ... If risks for peace are to be run, they must be run by all.

PICTURE 50
General Emilio de Bono
(1866–1944)

PICTURE 51
General Rodolfo Graziani
(1882–1955)

PICTURE 52
General Pietro Badoglio
(1871–1956)

MUSSOLINI'S WARLORDS

GENERAL EMILIO DE BONO (1866–1944)

Born in Milan, de Bono joined the Fascists and was one of the *Quadrumviri* who planned the March on Rome in 1922. Promoted to major general, he fought in the campaign against Turks in Tripoli (1912) and later, against the Austrians during the First World War. In 1935, he was appointed supreme commander of the Italian forces engaged in the war in Abyssinia, until he was replaced by General Badoglio. A cautious though not a very astute general, he saw no active service during the Second World War. As a member of the Fascist Grand Council, he was one of those who voted for the removal of Mussolini in 1943. Tried for treason by a special court at Verona, he was sentenced to death. De Bono was executed at the same time as Count Ciano, Mussolini's son-in-law (see page 211).

GENERAL RODOLFO GRAZIANI (1882–1955)

From Brindisi, Graziani served in Eritrea and Libya and by 1930 had reached the rank of major general. During the Abyssinian campaign, he commanded the Italian forces advancing from Somaliland. In 1939, he was appointed Chief of the Italian Armed Forces. When Italy joined the Second World War in 1940, he led his country's attempted invasion of Egypt. After a series of humiliating defeats, his forces were reinforced by the German *Afrika Korps* under General Rommel (see page 206). When Mussolini was overthrown in 1943, he was the only leading Italian general to remain loyal to his Fascist leader. He served as Defence Minister of the Salo Republic (see page 211). After1945, he was tried for collaborating with the Germans and sentenced to 19 years' imprisonment. He served less than three months!

GENERAL PIETRO BADOGLIO (1871–1956)

The so-called 'hero of the conquest of Abyssinia' came from Monferrato. He fought in the ill-fated campaign in Abyssinia in 1896, and the Turkish War of 1912. He was one of the few Italian officers to serve with distinction during the First World War and although he was at Caporetto, he emerged from the war with his reputation intact. He replaced de Bono as Italian commander during the Abyssinian campaign and was later appointed viceroy in that country. Following a disastrous campaign against Greece in 1940, he resigned. During 1943, he was one of those who helped to engineer Mussolini's downfall. Afterwards, as prime minister, he arranged Italy's unconditional surrender to the Allies, changed sides and declared war on Germany (see page 210).

These were empty words since neither Britain nor France took any positive action. As Winston Churchill later wrote:

> Mussolini, like Hitler, regarded Britannia as a frightened, flabby old woman, who at worst would only bluster, and was anyhow incapable of making war. Lord Lloyd, who was on friendly terms with him (Mussolini), noted how he had been struck by the resolution of the Oxford undergraduates in 1933 refusing to 'fight for King and Country.

From The Second World War, I *by Winston Churchill, 1948*

The League took the correct course by declaring that Italy had violated Article XII of the Covenant. It declared Italy an aggressor and imposed the only measure it had at its disposal, economic sanctions. This meant that members of the League were debarred from trading with Italy in materials likely to help its war effort. Quite incredibly these did not include coal, steel and oil! Germany, no longer a member of the League, was unaffected whilst other nations continued to trade with Italy secretly. Britain and France might have considered closing the Suez Canal to Italian shipping but chose not to do so. In some ways, too, the imposition of sanctions on Italy proved counter productive since it created a siege mentality which had a unifying effect on the Italian people. They indicated their willingness to accept hardships and as a token of their resolve, women handed in their jewellery and wedding rings to help sustain the country's gold reserves.

D *The Hoare–Laval Plan, 1935*

In December 1935, Sir Samuel Hoare and Pierre Laval, the British and French Foreign Secretaries, secretly put forward a compromise plan which it was hoped would secure peace and maintain the alliance between the members of the Stresa Front. The intention was to partition Abyssinia so that Italy would be allowed to make considerable territorial gains in the north, centre and south. Haile Selassie would then be left to rule a narrow central band that included the capital, Addis Ababa. Whilst Mussolini and the Fascist Grand Council seem to have thought it 'a possible basis for discussion', details of the plan were leaked to the press. International indignation led to an outcry that resulted in the resignations of both Hoare and Laval. Their plan was dropped.

TABLE 29

Date line showing the events of the Abyssinian War

1934	Dec	Italians and Abyssinians clash at Wal Wal
1935	Oct	Italians start invasion of Abyssinia
		Capture of Adowa
		Assembly of the League of Nations declare Italy an aggressor. Economic sanctions imposed on Italy
	Dec	Details of Hoare–Laval Plan revealed
1936	May	Fall of Addis Ababa. End of the war and flight of Haile Selasie to Britain
	June	League ends sanctions

MAP 9

The Hoare–Laval proposals for the partition of Abyssinia

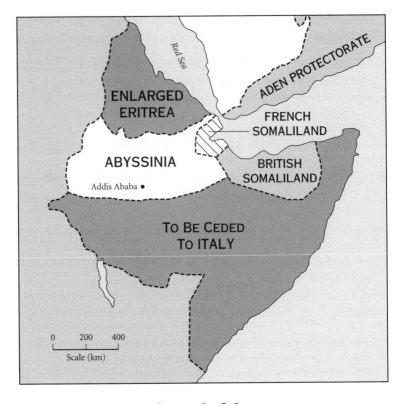

E *The end of the war*

In May 1936, with his country close to being overrun, Haile Selassie, made a personal appearance at the League of Nations. Dressed in his national costume, he said:

> I, Haile Selassie, Emperor of Abyssinia, am here today to claim that justice which is due to my people and the assistance promised to it eight months ago. I assert that the problem is a much wider one than the removal of sanctions. It is not merely a settlement of Italian aggression. It is the very existence of the League of Nations. It is the value of promises made to small states that their independence be respected and ensured. God and history will remember your judgements.

His words were to prove prophetic. On 5 May 1936, victorious Italian troops finally entered Addis Ababa and this virtually brought the war to an end. As guerrilla warfare continued, the Emperor Haile Selassie fled to Britain. As the new colony of Italian East Africa was created, it was clear that sanctions had not worked, the League of Nations had failed and that, on the face of it, the campaign was a triumph for Fascist Italy. Mussolini claimed that his armies had 'won the greatest colonial war known in history'. This view was readily accepted by most of the Italian people and it served to boost *Il Duce*'s reputation even further, but there was a downside.

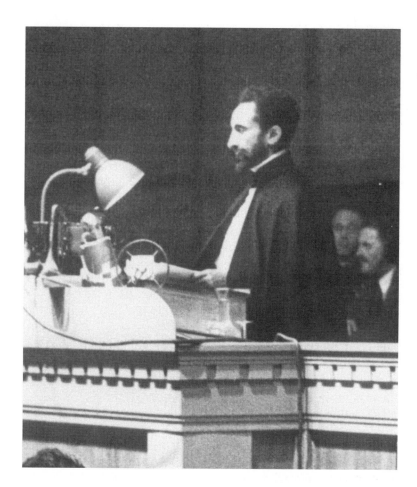

PICTURE 53
*Haile Selassie addressing the
League of Nations in May 1936*

F *The impact of the war on Italy*

● The war had further drained Italy's economic resources. The budget deficit had risen from 2.5 million lire to 16 million lire, a startling 660% As pressure on the lira increased, by 1936 it had effectively been devalued by 40%.

● After the war had been officially won, Italy had to continue to fight a guerrilla war which was made even more costly by the fact that men and materials had to be sent from Italy – over 3,000 kilometres away. The Italian government also faced the prospect of maintaining an army of occupation of 250,000 soldiers to police their colony .

● Abyssinia did not prove to be rich in raw materials. Whilst the country produced quantities of sugar-cane and coffee which with civet hides and oil seeds were its chief exports, it was also subject to invasion by crop destroying locusts. Hopes of finding large quantities of oil proved a pipe dream.

● The settlement of Italians in Abyssinia at government expense also proved expensive. Some 130,000 were encouraged to emigrate but many of those who went quickly became disenchanted with life in East Africa and returned home.

● The war cast Italy in the role of an aggressor and this damaged its reputation overseas. Nations disapproved of the savagery used by the Italian army during the war and their oppressive rule and barbaric treatment of Abyssinia afterwards. Prisoners taken during the period of guerrilla warfare were tortured, and executed often by being publicly hanged.

Even more significant than the impact of the war on Italy was its consequences for the future of world peace. The failure of the League of Nations to deal with Italian aggression provided further evidence of the weakness of the organisation. As we shall see, Mussolini's success was to give encouragement to others intent on achieving their aims through force of arms. The war also brought about a shift in the balance of power in Europe. Italy finally turned away from her traditional allies France and Britain and instead sought an alliance with Germany. Mussolini's Abyssinian venture was to prove a significant step towards the outbreak of another European war since Fascist Italy had set a precedent that Nazi Germany was soon to follow.

See pages 181 and 183

6 ᴗ ITALY AND THE SPANISH CIVIL WAR 1936–9

KEY ISSUE

Mussolini's decision to become involved in the Spanish Civil War.

In 1936, there was a revolt against the Popular Front government of Manuel Azana in Spain. The uprising, led by Generals Jose Sanjurjo and Francisco Franco, aimed to overthrow the legitimate left-wing government. It quickly turned into a full scale, bitterly fought civil war. Since the opposed sides, the Republicans and Nationalists, both attracted support from abroad, Spain became an ideological battlefield. The Republicans made up of liberals, socialists and communists, were eventually to receive support from the Soviet Union. Volunteers drawn from many countries went to Spain to join the International Brigade and fight for the Republicans. The Nationalists, supported by the military, Church, capitalists and right-wing elements, appealed for help and this was soon forthcoming from both Nazi Germany and Fascist Italy.

A *Italian involvement in the civil war*

Whilst Germany contributed 17,000 men and aircraft including the famous Condor Squadron, Italy first sent only 12 aircraft to be used to ferry soldiers from the Canary Islands to the Spanish mainland. As the war progressed, Mussolini increased the Italian commitment considerably to over 75,000 men, who were said to be volunteers, as well as 950 tanks and 700 aircraft. Mussolini's decision to become so involved in the civil war was influenced by a number of considerations. Firstly he wanted to be seen as standing shoulder to shoulder with Hitler in the fight to prevent the advance of Communism in Europe. As he said, 'Bolshevism in Spain means Bolshevism in France which means Bolshevism next door.' Secondly, he was anxious to ensure the

	Men	Tanks	Artillery	Aircraft
Italy (aid to the Nationalists)	75,000	950	1,000	700
Germany (aid to the Nationalists)	16,000	200	1,000	600
Soviet Union (aid to the Republicans)	3,000	900	1,550	1,000

TABLE 30
Italian contribution to the Spanish Civil War – a comparison

establishment of a Fascist-type government in another European country. Thirdly, he wanted once again to demonstrate Italian military strength and the fighting capability of his soldiers. As with the Abyssinian campaign, in 1939 Italy ended up on the winning side but again this was achieved at considerable cost. The war proved expensive and led to the further devaluation of the lira. At times, the performance of the Italian army during the war was far from impressive. In 1937, at the Battle of Guadalajara, Italian regular soldiers faced the Garibaldi Brigade, anti-Fascist Italians serving in the International Brigade. The battle ended in the humiliation of the Italian regulars who suffered over 2,000 dead and 4,000 wounded.

During the course of the war, unidentified submarines began to sink ships in the Mediterranean Sea destined for the Republican ports. The submarines involved were known to be Italian and some of the ships attacked were British and French. In 1937, a conference was called at Nyon in Switzerland to discuss the issue. Mussolini, at his hypocritical best, put on a pretence of being upset and it was agreed that British and French warships should patrol the area. Afterwards the attacks ceased. Italian forces remained in Spain until 1938 and contributed towards the eventual victory of Franco and his Nationalists.

B *The consequences*

There were two significant consequences of the war. Firstly, up to that point Mussolini had been regarded as the senior of the two Fascist dictators. Now a position of parity was reached and this was to turn into a situation where Hitler was the undisputed master. Secondly, it was assumed that since Mussolini and Hitler had made Franco's Fascist regime secure in Spain, he was in their debt and would support them in any future conflict. Surprisingly, this was not to be!

7 ⌐ FASCIST ITALY AND NAZI GERMANY – 'THE BRUTAL FRIENDSHIP'

1936 represented a watershed in the relations between the major European powers. The Italians were completing the conquest of Abyssinia and Mussolini was close to success in his plans to expand his African empire. Whilst at home, *Il Duce* was at the peak of his popularity; abroad, Italian Fascism appeared to be triumphant. Both were ominous developments that diminished the prospects of future peace in Europe. Encouraged by Mussolini's example and the fact that Italian forces were committed to Abyssinia, Hitler seized the opportunity to reoccupy the Rhineland, a demilitarised strip of land to the west of the River Rhine which had acted as a buffer between Germany and France. The German action, which was in defiance of the terms of the Treaty of Versailles and against the 'spirit of Locarno', alarmed the French. On the other hand, some British politicians gave Hitler their tacit approval by declaring that the Germans were merely 'going into their own back garden'. Since France was not prepared to act without British support, nothing was done and Hitler succeeded in bringing off an impressive bluff.

See pages 170–1

A *The Rome–Berlin Axis*

KEY ISSUE

Change in the balance of power in Europe.

During this time, attracted by their common hatred of democracy and Communism, Fascist Italy and Nazi Germany drew ever closer. As we have seen, Hitler refused to apply economic sanctions against Italy and, during the Spanish Civil War, the two countries collaborated to ensure the success of Franco's Nationalists. Both stood to benefit from the emergence of another Fascist-type power in Europe. It was Mussolini who, in a speech in Milan in November 1936, first used the term Rome–Berlin Axis when referring to the new understanding between Italy and Germany. He said: 'This Rome–Berlin line is … an axis around which can revolve all those European states with a will to collaboration and peace.' Part of the Axis understanding was that Italy would concentrate on her foreign policy ambitions in the Mediterranean and allow Germany a free hand elsewhere in Europe.

rapprochement
drawing together or renewal of good relations

In Italy, even amongst the Fascist Party hierarchy, there were those who disapproved of the German alliance. However, Mussolini hoped that Italy's **rapprochement** with Germany would impress, even frighten Britain and France and make them take him more seriously. In part, he regarded the Axis as 'a revolutionary alliance against the West' and, in part, 'an alliance against the continuing Bolshevik menace'. It was known that Italian Fascists were actively engaged in encouraging similar movements elsewhere and, when the opportunity occurred, stirring up anti-British feeling amongst dissidents in parts of the British Empire. In private and sometimes even in public, Mussolini made disparaging remarks about others he considered his enemies – the British 'who think with their bums', the French 'ruined by alcoholism and syphilis', the United States 'a country of Jews and niggers', the Soviet Union, 'a country that only cretins could admire'. In 1937, Italy joined the Anti-Comintern Pact.

B *Italy and the Anti-Comintern Pact*

Comintern, or the Third International, was founded in Moscow in 1919 to encourage Communist-inspired revolutionary activities. It worked to infiltrate and destroy the political systems of capitalist countries and its long-term aim was to bring about world revolution. In 1936, Nazi Germany and Japan declared their opposition to Comintern and agreed to work together to prevent the further spread of Communism. Mussolini's hatred of Communism made it inevitable that Italy would also join the Pact – it did so the following year. In reality, the Anti-Comintern Pact was an alliance against the Soviet Union.

In September 1937, Hitler invited Mussolini to Berlin where Mussolini made no secret of being impressed by German efficiency and military might. In a speech made at the time, he said that Fascism and National Socialism represented 'the most authentic democracies existing in the present world'. In spite of their similar foreign policy interests, Mussolini had reservations about aspects of National Socialism. In private he spoke of his disapproval of Hitler's racial theories, particularly of his anti-Semitism. Even so, with the Italian leader now likely to be more tolerant of his intentions, Hitler revived his plans to bring about an *Anschluss*, the union of Germany and Austria. Mussolini was well aware of the *Führer*'s intentions. The Australian historian, Richard Bosworth, has described the Italian leader's attitude at the time as 'shutting his eyes and hoping that, somehow, the worst would not happen'.

See pages 175–6

C *Mussolini and the renewed crisis over Austria, 1938*

In February 1938, Hitler summoned the Austrian Chancellor, Kurt von Schuschnigg to his home at Berchtesgarden. There he ranted and raved at the Austrian leader and presented him with a list of demands which, if accepted, would bring an end to Austrian independence. Back in Vienna, Schuschnigg recovered his dignity. In an effort to save his country from falling under Nazi control, he bravely called for a **plebiscite** so that the Austrian people could decide their own future. Hitler, who was not prepared to risk the outcome of a plebiscite, made preparations to invade the country. Before this could happen, the dispirited Schuschnigg gave way and on 12 March German troops marched into Austria. Mussolini was advised of Hitler's intentions the day before! This time, *Il Duce*, still unforgiving of the British and French reaction to his invasion of Abyssinia and unwilling to put his new found friendship with Hitler in jeopardy, did nothing. However many Italians were dismayed by his attitude. Concerned at the prospect of having Nazi Germany as an immediate northern neighbour, many Italians thought their leader had blundered and consequently Mussolini's prestige slumped.

Some historians see this event as the **defining moment** when Italy lost its independence and Mussolini's style of Fascism came to an end. It certainly led to a change in the relative status of the two leaders. Since Hitler was the more dominant personality and Germany now had every advantage in terms of population and industrial and military might, the German leader was no longer Mussolini's underling and disciple. In

plebiscite a vote of the people to discover their views on an issue

defining moment a significant or exact moment

fact, the roles were now reversed and, if anything, Mussolini was becoming increasingly Hitler's subordinate. To ensure that at least for the moment he retained a foot in both camps, the following month Mussolini agreed a new pact of friendship with Britain. In 1938, a new crisis arose when Hitler began to threaten Czechoslovakia.

KEY ISSUE

The role of Mussolini in the Czech crisis.

D *Mussolini and the Czech crisis, 1938*

Hitler's immediate demand was the right to annex a border region, the Sudetenland, which had a significant ethnic German population. As the crisis worsened, Neville Chamberlain, the British Prime Minister, asked Mussolini to use his influence with Hitler to arrange a conference to discuss the issue. The Italian leader was taken aback by Chamberlain's request and concluded that Britain must be suffering from '**a menopausal disorder**'. The Italian leader contacted the German *Führer* and' after pledging him Italy's support, persuaded him to call off his threatened invasion of Czechoslovakia. During September, three conferences were arranged at Berchtesgaden, Godesburg and finally Munich. After the first, Chamberlain and Edouard Daladier, the French Prime Minister, prevailed on the Czech government to cede those parts of the Sudetenland with more than 50% German population. By the time of the second meeting, Hitler had raised his demands. With France and the Soviet Union likely to back Czechoslovakia and time running out, a war seemed inevitable. As European powers began to mobilise, a final conference was called at Munich. It was attended by Hitler, Chamberlain, Daladier, Mussolini and his Foreign Minister, Count Ciano. The outcome was virtually a complete surrender to all the German leader's demands. The appeasement of Hitler and the betrayal of Czechoslovakia meant that in October 1938, German troops occupied the Sudetenland. Five months later, in March 1939, Hitler broke all his previous undertakings and, without informing Mussolini, found an excuse to invade the remainder of Czechoslovakia.

menopausal disorder
changes in behaviour that occur in middle age

Mussolini had clearly played a significant role during the Czech crisis and for a time his intervention seemed decisive. Italian propagandists portrayed him as the saviour of Europe. Ironically, he was welcomed home as the champion of peace when he would have preferred to be greeted as a victor in war. The Czech crisis coincided with two other events – one relatively trivial whilst the other brought tragic consequences. In 1938, Mussolini instructed the Italian army to adopt the German goose-step style of marching which he claimed was more militaristic. During a public appearance, he went as far to demonstrate the goose-step which he said would be unsuitable for 'the fat, the stupid and the so-called shorties'. During the same year, he decided to ape Nazi racial policies and passed the Race Law.

See pages 140–2

In May 1938, Hitler made a second visit to Italy during which Mussolini set out to better the reception he had received earlier in Berlin. The military displays arranged were impressive even though the Germans noticed that most of the guns seen were obsolete and some even made of wood! The visit certainly caused embarrassment:

> ... as constitutional head of state, King Victor Emmanuel III was thrust into the *Führer*'s company too often for the contentment of either. It was said that the King asked Hitler unavailingly how many nails could be found in the German infantry boot, and then illustrated his own pedantic knowledge of detail by explaining that in the Italian, there were 74 (22 in the heel and 52 in the sole). Hitler later recalled that he had 'never seen anything worse' than the lugubrious courtiers he met. The Vatican was also touchy about the visit ... Pius XI made difficulties about providing illumination for one he condemned as 'the greatest enemy of Christ and the Church in modern times'. Meanwhile knowing Germans laughed at an Italian military exhibition in Naples where horses outnumbered tanks, whilst police chief Bocchini took the occasion to sound out Nazis whom he thought might be in the know about the exact nature of Hitler's relationship with Eva Braun.

From Mussolini *by Richard Bosworth, 2002*

In November 1938, Mussolini summoned the Grand Council to advise its members of his future foreign policy plans. Referring to them as 'the immediate goals of Fascist dynamism', he said:

> States that cannot communicate freely with the oceans and are enclosed in inland seas are semi-independent ... Italy is bathed by a landlocked sea that communicates with the oceans through the Suez Canal, easily blocked, and the straits of Gibraltar, dominated by the guns of Great Britain. Italy is therefore in truth a prisoner of the Mediterranean and the more populous and prosperous Italy becomes, the more its imprisonment will gall. The bars to this prison are Corsica, Tunis, Malta, Cyprus. The sentinels of this prison are Gibraltar and Suez. Corsica is a pistol pointed at the heart of Italy; Tunisia at Sicily, while Malta and Cyprus constitute a threat to all our positions in the eastern and western Mediterranean. Greece, Turkey, Egypt have been ready to form a chain with Great Britain and to complete the military encirclement of Italy. Greece, Turkey, Egypt must be considered virtual enemies of Italy and its expansion ... The task of Italian policy, which cannot have and does not have continental objectives of a territorial nature except Albania, is to first of all break the bars of the prison.

His aim was to remove the British and French interests as well as the threat posed by Greece, Turkey and Egypt and claim the Mediterranean as an Italian sea. For the moment, however, Mussolini had a more

PICTURE 54
Count Galeazzo Ciano (1903–1944)

COUNT GALEAZZO CIANO (1903–44)

As Italian Foreign Secretary and Mussolini's son-in-law, Count Ciano was one of the key figures in Italy's Fascist regime. Son of a naval officer and a former president of the Italian Chamber of Deputies, Galeazzo Ciano was born at Livorno in 1903. At the University of Rome, he studied law and during this period first became involved in the activities of the Fascist movement. In 1922, at the age of 18, he took part in the March on Rome. After working briefly as a journalist, he joined the diplomatic corps and served in Argentina, Brazil and later China. Following his marriage to Mussolini's daughter, Edda, he rose rapidly through the ranks to be appointed head of the press bureau in 1933 and then a member of the influential Fascist Grand Council. A keen pilot, Ciano led a bomber squadron during the invasion of Abyssinia in 1935 and on his return to Rome was appointed Foreign Minister. Many saw him as the likely successor to Mussolini. Although he first supported Italy's alliance with Germany, he came to distrust Hitler. When Germany invaded Poland in 1939, he urged his father-in-law to follow a policy of non-belligerence. However, early German successes caused him to change his mind and in 1940 he encouraged his country's entry into the war. Once things began to badly for the Axis powers, Ciano was one of a number who wanted to arrange a separate peace with the Allies. It was during this time that he famously said, 'Victory has a hundred fathers but defeat is an orphan'. He aroused Mussolini's suspicions and, in 1943, was dismissed as Foreign Secretary and was sent instead as Italian ambassador to the Vatican. At a meeting of the Grand Council in July of that year he was one of the leading Fascists who voted for Mussolini's removal. For a while his activities were obscure until Italy's new government charged him with embezzlement. Count Ciano fled Rome and in northern Italy fell into the hands of pro-Mussolini partisans. Handed back to Mussolini, he was brought to trial for treason at Verona and executed on 11 January 1944. When Ciano's diaries and diplomatic papers were later published, they provided an interesting insight into Italian diplomacy during that period.

pressing problem. Hitler's successes in Austria and Czechoslovakia and Franco's impending victory in Spain meant that he was in danger of being upstaged. It was urgent for him to prove that Italy was not an inferior member of the Rome–Berlin Axis.

E *The Italian annexation of Albania, 1939*

In March 1939, Mussolini sent an ultimatum to King Zog demanding the right of Italy to annex Albania. The King, who was offered money in exchange for his agreement, refused and the ultimatum was rejected. On 25 March, Italian troops landed in the country and although the small Albanian army offered some resistance, easily overran the country within 24 hours. Altogether three army groups consisting of 30 battalions of infantry and their supporting units were used to carry out the invasion. It was very much a case of using a sledgehammer to crack at nut! King Zog and his family managed to escape and fled first to Greece and then to London. Consequently Victor Emmanuel III assumed the Albanian crown and a Fascist regime was set up under Shefqet Verlaci.

In fact, the invasion of Albania was totally unnecessary. Since 1926, the country had been a vassal state under Italian control and Mussolini's action only confirmed a situation that already existed. Some historians have suggested that the occupation of Albania was intended to show Hitler that Italy was capable of keeping up with Germany as far as territorial expansion was concerned. Others have expressed the view that Mussolini invaded Albania, without first telling Hitler, because he was affronted by the Nazi leader's failure to consult him in foreign policy matters. Whilst the occupation of Albania placed a further stretch of the Adriatic coastline under Italian control and put Mussolini in a position to more easily intimidate his neighbours, the cost of the invasion and of maintaining an army of occupation added further to the drain on Italy's economic resources. Mussolini was also annoyed that his act of aggression led Britain and France to offer military assistance to Greece and Turkey if they were attacked. He regarded this as unwarranted interference in an Italian sphere of influence.

Two months later, on 22 May 1939, the existing understanding between Italy and Germany was replaced by a formal military alliance that Mussolini called the Pact of Steel.

F *The Pact of Steel, 1939*

Of the articles that comprised the Pact of Steel, the most important were:

> **Article 1.** The two contracting Parties shall keep in permanent contact with each other for the purpose of agreeing on all questions regarding their common interests or the general European situation

> **Article 3.** If in spite of the desires and hopes of the two Contracting Parties it were to happen that one of them were to become involved in war with one or more powers, the other Contracting Party shall immediately come to its aid as an ally and shall support it with all its military forces on land, on the seas, and in the air.

KEY ISSUE

The consolidation of the alliance between Italy and Germany.

Article 5. In the event of a war conducted in common the Contracting Parties are committed from this moment on not to conclude an armistice or peace without full agreement with each other.

In effect, Italy had committed herself to following a foreign policy that would be dictated by Hitler and to fight alongside Germany in any future war irrespective of the cause of that war – even if it was Nazi aggression! However, Hitler stated that he had no intention of going to war for at least three years. In spite of this undertaking, Mussolini remained unconvinced since he knew that Germany was currently preparing for a war against Poland.

> Whatever he later pretended, Mussolini signed [the Pact of Steel] in full knowledge that the Germans saw their next move as the invasion of Poland and, despite this, he was quite content to leave them to draft the treaty; moreover he saw no reason to seek any advice from his own ministers and military advisers. Though the Germans had already deceived him more than once, he never bothered to ask them to spell out their intentions over Poland but let them dictate the wording of the alliance that committed Italy to supporting them automatically. The simple fact of an alliance – not its terms – was what mattered to him, as is shown by the fact that he announced its existence before the terms had been decided. A few hours after the pact was signed, Hitler secretly ordered his generals to prepare for an attack on Poland … Diplomacy was, in Mussolini's view, mainly a cover operation, and the reality of foreign policy was better kept out of the hands of professionals.

From Mussolini *by Denis Mack Smith, 1993*

Count Ciano urged his father-in-law to make it absolutely clear to Hitler that Italy was in no position to fight a war until 1942 at the earliest. Mussolini's anxiety was further increased when Germany and the Soviet Union unexpectedly signed a non-aggression pact in August 1939.

The Nazi–Soviet Pact, sometimes known after the two signatories as the Ribbentrop–Molotov Pact, was an agreement between countries representing the conflicting doctrines of Nationalism and Communism. It was clearly a temporary **marriage of convenience** by which each country pledged to remain neutral if the other became involved in a war. This meant that Hitler could now embark on the invasion of Poland without fear of the Soviet Union going to that country's assistance. Further, if Britain and France became involved then Germany would not be faced by the dilemma of having to fight a war on two fronts. Secret clauses of the pact agreed to the partition of Poland between Germany and Russia and allowed the Soviets a free hand to occupy the Baltic States – Estonia, Latvia and Lithuania. Now, for Hitler, the way ahead was clear.

marriage of convenience a union brought about for reasons of self-interest and not for reasons of genuine affection

On 1 September 1939, Germany invaded Poland. On 3 September, a British ultimatum was delivered demanding the withdrawal of German troops. When the ultimatum expired, Britain declared war on Germany. That afternoon, France joined Britain and the Second World War had begun. Hitler had not consulted Mussolini, a sign of his increasing contempt for *Il Duce* and Italy. The Italian leader's immediate reaction was to propose a conference to discuss the situation but Britain and France were in no mood for another Munich. Now he faced a quandary – to fight as he had agreed in the Pact of Steel or to take what Hitler would consider as the cowardly course and find a face-saving excuse to remain neutral.

8 ⌐ STRUCTURED AND ESSAY QUESTIONS

A *This section consists of questions that might be used for discussion (or written answers) as a way of expanding on the chapter and testing your understanding.*

1. What does a nation have to achieve to win 'great power status'?
2. What obstacles were there to Italy becoming the dominant power in the Mediterranean?
3. Why was there little scope for Italian colonial expansion in Africa?
4. To what extent were Italy's chances of becoming a major military power doomed from the start?
5. In what sense was the Kellogg–Brian Pact meaningless?
6. Why did the economic sanctions imposed on Italy fail?
7. Why was there such an outcry against the Hoare–Laval Plan in 1935?
8. For what reasons did Italy become involved in the Spanish Civil War?
9. How important was Mussolini's role at the time of the Munich crisis?
10. Why was the Italian annexation of Albania in 1939 'totally unnecessary'?

B *Essay questions.*

1. With what justification can it be claimed that the need to increase Italy's prestige was the driving force behind Mussolini's foreign policy?
2. 'Fascist Italy will never take the initiative in war.' To what extent was Mussolini true to his word?
3. To what extent did Mussolini's foreign policy contribute to the coming of the Second World War?

9 ⌐ DOCUMENTARY EXERCISE BASED ON THE FOUNDING OF THE AXIS

Read the source below and then answer the questions that follow.

Italian policy was now definitely drawn into the orbit of Nazism. Friendship with Russia was sacrificed, and Mussolini echoed the strident tones of Hitler in his denunciation of Russian Bolshevism as the European public enemy. An elaborate scheme for army, navy and aircraft extension was announced and the self-sufficiency programme developed. In short, Italy was brought into line with the Nazi programme. The formation of the Axis in 1936 thus entangled the policy of Mussolini with that of Hitler. This new political term meant that round the directing policy of either Rome or Berlin, the states of central and eastern Europe should rotate; while retaining their own governments, composed of men sympathetic to Axis policy, their political and economic life was to be controlled from the centre round which they revolved. ... In comparison with the forceful and continuous propaganda of Germany, the efforts of Italy to establish her influence were weak, and the more closely Mussolini identified Italian aims with those of Berlin so much the less could the dependent states rely on her power to protect them against Nazism .... For sixteen years he had declared that Germany on the Brenner meant Italy's doom. In his greed for empire and his hatred of democracy he had scattered his forces, alienated his allies, bound himself to the age-long enemy of his country and brought the Germans to his back door.

SOURCE A

From A Short History of Italy *edited by H. Hearder and D.P. Waley, 1963.*

1. What is meant by
(a) a self-sufficiency programme? *(3 marks)*
(b) Germany on the Brenner? *(3 marks)*
2. According to the source, what did the Axis powers regard as the future role of the countries of central and eastern Europe? *(5 marks)*
3. What evidence is there in the source to suggest that Germany was the senior partner in the Axis alliance? *(5 marks)*
4. How useful is the source to an historian studying the relationship between Italy and Germany during the period 1938–9? *(10 marks)*

10 ⌁ MAKING NOTES

A chapter dealing with foreign policy issues will invariably make references to numerous conferences, pacts and treaties. To make sure that you have understood their significance, complete the chart below:

Date	Conference, Pact or Treaty	Significance
1923	Ambassadors' Conference	
1925	Locarno Treaties	
1928	Kellogg–Briand Pact	
1933	Four-Power Conference	
1935	Stresa Conference	
1937	Nyon Conference	
1938	Munich Conference	
1939	Pact of Steel	
1939	Nazi–Soviet Pact	

12

The Second World War and The Collapse of Fascist Italy

INTRODUCTION

At the start of the war, Mussolini declared that Italy would adopt a policy of 'non-belligerency'. This did not mean that the country would remain neutral but rather that *Il Duce* would bide his time and watch developments before making up his mind. Although public opinion was largely against becoming involved in a war against Britain and France, there was little doubt that Mussolini intended to side with Germany but only when the time was right. Whilst Balbo, de Bono, de Vecchi and other leading Fascists pressed Mussolini to help find a peaceful solution to the European conflict, the pro-Nazi, anti-Semitic Farinacci urged his leader to join on Germany's side without delay.

He referred to those who thought differently as 'honorary Jews' and 'cretinous opponents of the Axis'. Mussolini, who was far from happy with the direction of German foreign policy and was uncertain if Germany could win the war, persisted with his cautious approach. To the annoyance of the Germans, sections of the Italian press were openly critical of the Nazi–Soviet Pact. Following the intervention of the German ambassador in Rome, such articles ceased to appear. On the one hand, Mussolini instructed the Italian press to praise German achievements, on the other they were not to be critical of Britain and

PICTURE 55

J.C. Walker's cartoon which appeared in the South Wales Echo *on 5 October 1939 shows Hitler uncertain as to whether Mussolini will enter the war on Germany's side*

TABLE 31
*Date line covering events from
1939 to 1941*

1939	German invasion of Poland
	Soviet forces occupy eastern Poland
	Finland invaded by Soviet Union
1940	Mussolini and Hitler meet at Brenner Pass
	Denmark and Norway invaded by Germany
	Netherlands and Belgium invaded by Germany
	Italy declared war on Britain and France
	Italian troops attempt invasion of French Riviera
	France and Germany agree terms of an armistice
	Italian invasion of Greece
	Italian forces advance into Egypt
	British counter attack in Egypt
1941	Major British advances in North Africa
	Italian Eritrea and Somaliland fall to British forces
	Abyssinia restored to the Emperor Haile Selassie
	Germans invade Yugoslavia and advance into Greece
	Operation Barbarossa – German invasion of Soviet Union
	Italian fleet attacked off Cape Matapan
	Rommel and the German Afrika Corps drive British back into Egypt
	Italy and Germany declare war on the United States

France. Conversely, whilst Britain and France waged a propaganda war against Germany, no mention was made of Italy. This, they hoped, would encourage Mussolini to stay out of the war.

1 ༈ ITALY'S ENTRY INTO THE WAR

After the German invasion on 1 September 1939, Mussolini watched as the full weight of **blitzkrieg** or 'lightening war' allowed the German armies to advance rapidly across western Poland. As agreed by the Nazi–Soviet Pact, on 17 September Soviet forces moved into eastern Poland. Overwhelmed, Polish resistance finally collapsed and the division of the spoils agreed in the secret clauses of the Pact was put into effect. The conquest of Poland completed, Hitler offered peace terms to Britain and France. These the Allies refused stating that the independence of Austria, Czechoslovakia and Poland would have to be restored before negotiations could take place.

For a time, attention was diverted from the war when, in November 1939, the Soviet Union invaded Finland. In Italy and elsewhere there was great sympathy for the Finns and Mussolini sent aircraft to help their war effort as did Britain! Mussolini found himself in a difficult situation since he was now aiding a country at war with Germany's ally, Russia. Finally, he found the courage to contact Hitler and question the wisdom of the Nazi–Soviet Pact since it contradicted the aims of their membership of the Anti-Comintern Pact. In March 1940, Mussolini and Hitler met at the Brenner Pass. At the meeting, the German leader explained his reasons for the Russian alliance to *Il Duce* whilst Mussolini confirmed his intention of entering the war at the appropriate moment.

blitzkrieg
overwhelming attack by aircraft and tanks

KEY ISSUE

The end of Anglo–Italian friendship.

For months there was little activity along the Western Front but the so-called 'phony war' suddenly came to an end in April 1940 when Hitler ordered the invasion of Denmark and Norway. The following month, German forces invaded Belgium, the Netherlands and Luxembourg and then advanced into France. At this point, Winston Churchill, the new British Prime Minister, authorised his Foreign Secretary, Lord Halifax, to dispatch a letter to Mussolini reminding him of the traditional friendship between their two countries and urging him to stay out of the war. Mussolini's reply stated that Italy's friendship ended when Britain took the lead in imposing sanctions on Italy during the Abyssinian war. In addition, the Italian leader was peeved by the fact that the Royal Navy was blockading German coal exports to Italy. By the end of May, when the British Expeditionary Force had been encircled and forced to evacuate from Dunkirk, France was tottering on the edge of defeat. In a desperate situation, Paul Reynaud, the French Prime Minister, suggested to Churchill that Mussolini might be asked to mediate with Hitler. The British Prime Minister would not hear of it. A German victory now seemed imminent and this meant that Hitler would soon dominate Europe. Mussolini could wait no longer. If he entered the war, it would place him in a situation from which he could eliminate British and French influence in the Mediterranean. He would also be entitled to a say in the post-war treaties. If he hesitated any longer, the war might be over before Italy could play a part. The problem was that the Italian armed forces were unprepared and ill-equipped for war and it was questionable if the country had the capacity to fight a war.

A *The condition of the Italian armed forces in 1939*

bersaglieri regiment of highly trained infantrymen in the Italian army

At that time, the Italian army could call on 73 divisions comprising of 106 infantry regiments, 12 regiments of *bersaglieri*, 10 of Alpine troops, 12 of cavalry, 5 of tanks, 32 of artillery and 19 of engineers, plus a legion of Blackshirts. This was not as impressive as it might appear since only 19 of the 73 divisions were at full strength! Of those, 14 were serving abroad in Abyssinia, Tripoli and Albania. In addition, much of the infantry's weaponry was dated and not suited to the demands of modern warfare. Their tanks were too light and inadequately armed. Although Mussolini boasted of an airforce of 3,000 planes, less than 1,000 actually existed. However, the Italian navy was formidable but, as we shall see, limited by the lack of any aircraft carriers, essential in modern naval warfare. In addition, the fleet only had sufficient fuel to last a year.

B *Italy declares war*

Even though Italian entry into the war seemed inevitable, there were last minute pleas for Italy to remain neutral from Victor Emmanuel III, Pope Pius XII and Franklin D. Roosevelt, the President of the United States. Even some of Mussolini's senior generals advised him against going to war. It was on the 10 June, a day when the French government left Paris and moved to Tours, that Mussolini declared war on Britain and France. Speaking from the balcony of the Palazzo Venezia to an enormous crowd, Mussolini announced:

> Combatants of the land, of the sea, of the air! Blackshirts of the revolution and the legions! Men and women of Italy, of the Empire, and of the Kingdom of Albania! Listen! The hour of destiny is striking in the heavens of our fatherland. This is the hour of irrevocable decisions. The declaration of war has already been delivered to the ambassadors of Great Britain and France. Let us enter into the field opposed to the **plutocratic** and reactionary democracies of the West that, in every epoch, have blocked the progress, and frequently stifled the very existence of the Italian people … Now all this belongs to the past. If we, today, have decided to confront the risks and sacrifices of war, it is because of honour … A great people is really great only if it considers its obligations sacred, and if it does not evade the supreme trials that determine the course of history. We take up arms to settle, after the problem of our continental borders, that of our maritime frontiers: we want to break the restraints imposed by the territorial and military order that suffocates us in our seas, since a nation of 45,000,000 souls is not really free if it has no access to the ocean … The word for our times is but one, categorical and provocative: a word that already flies above and kindles hearts from the Alps to the Indian Ocean: Victory! And we will win and finally gain a lasting peace with justice for Italy, Europe and the World.

plutocratic dominated by a ruling class of wealthy people

The Italian scholar, Filippo Donini, later to be director of the Italian Institute in London, recalled the day:

> Oh yes, enthusiasm there was on the part of Young Fascists, who had been trained for months to sing their outrageous bellicose songs against the French and the English. I well remember my horror and disgust to hear those stupid lads cry out that 'with the heads of the French they would make chamber pots' and that they would go to Nice and Corsica and Tunis 'and show them we are the masters.' As for the English, most songs were built on the theme of Chamberlain missing the bus and being left behind with his umbrella, which obviously meant that the end of England was approaching … From a group of ex-servicemen near us we could hear some angry voices. The discussion was about the difference between today and 1915 when Italy had sided with France and England in the First World War. 'Those were the times!' was shouting a middle aged former captain. 'Then we well knew with whom our heart was! War against the Germans, war to help the French, war to liberate Trento and Trieste.

From Mussolini Goes To War *by Filippo Donini that appeared in Purnell's* History of the Second World War

Oh, the enthusiasm that day! We had no mixed feelings, no divided loyalties, we knew that we were doing the right thing. Today, on the contrary …' They hushed him before the chant of 'Du-ce, Du-ce, Du-ce' drowned his voice.

Mussolini's decision to enter the war was to prove the most ill-conceived of his many blunders. He failed to recognise that the war was being fought to satisfy Hitler's plans for *lebensraum* and to bring a New Order to Europe and not in the interests of Italy. As we shall see, it was to lead to the collapse of Fascist Italy and his own brutal death.

2 ⌐ ITALY'S PART IN THE SECOND WORLD WAR

Immediately the realities of Italy's difficulties became all too obvious. The 'eight million bayonets' of which Mussolini boasted turned out to be closer to three. Many of those 'legions' he spoke of did not comprise of young men bent on acts of heroism but soldiers duped into fighting a war for which they had no heart.

1940

Shortly after Italy's declaration of war, France agreed an armistice with Nazi Germany. Before this, Italian troops just had time to attempt the invasion of the French Riviera and succeeded in occupying two small towns close to the border. These, the towns of Modane and Briancon, were to represent Italy's total reward for supporting Germany and attacking their neighbour! As the Battle of Britain raged and the Germans made plans for *Operation Sealion*, the invasion of Britain, so Mussolini took advantage of the situation to attempt to expand his African empire. Again, against the advice of his generals, Mussolini ordered Italian troops to advance from Abyssinia into British Somaliland. Elsewhere, *Il Duce* became more adventurous as Italian forces moved into the Sudan and Kenya. In September, he ordered the invasion of Egypt and an advance on the Suez Canal. Italian forces advanced as far as Sidi Barrani. In December, the British launched a counter attack during which they advanced 300 kilometres and took 100,000 Italian prisoners.

A *The Italian invasion of Greece*

Envious of Germany's successes and offended by his paltry gains following his invasion of France, in June 1940, Mussolini decided to use

Albania as base for the invasion of Greece. Since he considered the Balkans to be within his own sphere of influence, he did not bother to inform Hitler of his plans. On the morning of 26 October, the Italian ambassador in Athens delivered an ultimatum to the Greek government. The ultimatum accused Greece of adopting a hostile attitude towards Italy and demanded the right to occupy strategic areas of Greece for the duration of the war as a guarantee of Greek neutrality. The Greek Prime Minister and Minister for War, Joannis Metaxas rejected the ultimatum. Later that day Mussolini met Hitler at Florence. The German *Führer* did his utmost to conceal his irritation with *Il Duce* over his unilateral decision to invade Greece. Instead he preferred to discuss the European situation generally. Hitler indicated his intention of crushing Britain by an aerial offensive and, in consideration of the Soviet Union, famously commented, 'My distrust of Stalin is as great as Stalin's distrust of me'. The meeting ended with the usual claim that the outcome was a 'perfect identity of views'.

> **Q**
>
> *Why did Mussolini order the invasion of Greece in October 1940?*

General Visconti Prasca commanded the army that invaded Greece. It numbered six divisions and it had the advantage of total air superiority. They estimated that the Greeks would only offer token resistance and that the occupation of the country would take two weeks. Only four Greek divisions opposed them but these consisted of patriotic soldiers determined to defend their familiar home territory, the high and rugged mountains of the Epirus. In spite of their superiority, after some limited initial success, the Italians found it impossible to make any further headway. The onset of winter meant that the Italian soldiers, with inadequate clothing for the severe weather in the mountains, suffered badly and many opted to surrender. A Greek counter-attack at the end of December drove the Italians back into Albania and a spring offensive planned by Mussolini himself failed to make any headway. The British novelist, Olivia Manning, who was living in Greece at the time, recalled the condition of Italian prisoners of war:

> Then came the halt. The Greeks had advanced along the whole Albanian frontier and were not prepared for such success. They were outdistancing their supply lines. They had to pause to take breath and, having got so far, they had to consider their situation seriously. Italian prisoners trailed through the main roads – a straggle of men in tattered uniforms, hatless, heads bent so the rain could drop from their hair. They were defeated, yet in every batch there were some who seemed untroubled by their plight and grinned at the bystanders as though thankful to be safely out of the fight. They were being sent to camps in the western deserts where they would have sun and food instead of the hardships of the Albanian mountains.

From The Balkan Trilogy *by Olivia Manning, 1960*

Far from winning acclaim for Italian arms, the Greek episode ended in a fiasco that attracted the scorn of other nations and the disapproval of Adolf Hitler. The German leader had far more important plans in the Mediterranean. He aimed to bring Spain into the war on the side of the Axis, to gain possession of Gibraltar and close the western end of the Mediterranean, to destroy the British forces in Egypt and to win control of the Suez Canal.

The failure of Mussolini's invasion of Greece was not his only setback before the end of 1940. In November, the British Fleet Air Arm attacked the Italian fleet based at Taranto.

B *The Battle of Taranto*

Since the Italian navy was considered a threat to their shipping in the Mediterranean, the Allies devised a plan to reduce its capability. On 11 November 1940, planes from the British aircraft carrier *Illustrious* carried out an airstrike against the Italian fleet under Vice-Admiral Inigo Campioni based at Taranto. During an hour-long raid, torpedo-carrying *Swordfish* aircraft succeeded in sinking the battleship *Littorio* and severely damaging the *Conte di Cavour*, and *Caio Duilio*, half the battleship strength of the Italian fleet. This crippling blow to Italian naval prestige ensured the dominance of the Royal Navy in the Mediterranean and made Mussolini aware of the need to have adequate antiaircraft defences and aircraft carriers of his own!

1941

The early months of the new year brought yet more disasters for Italy. Even though faced by an Italian army four times its size, the British advance across North Africa continued as far as Benghazi. To the south, both Italian Eritrea and Somaliland were lost and, in April, Abyssinia was reclaimed from Italy and the Emperor Haile Selassie restored to his throne. The debacle ended when the Duke of Aosta finally surrendered the whole of Italian East Africa and a further 250,000 Italian prisoners were taken. Mussolini's African empire, that he had defied the League of Nations to create, was all but lost. If Hitler was to assist the Italians in Albania, he would need to send German forces across neutral Yugoslavia to reach the Greek frontier. In March 1941, Hitler invited Prince Paul, Regent of Yugoslavia, to Berchtesgaden and pressed him to join the Axis powers and agree for German troops to cross his country. Once home, the Prince was overthrown by a *coup* led by officers sympathetic to the British. Hitler lost patience and the following month ordered the invasion of both Yugoslavia and Greece. Within two weeks both countries had been overrun. As a result of Italian failures, Marshal Badoglio and Admiral Cavagnari were forced to resign their respective commands of the Italian army and navy.

Two other major events took place in 1941 that were, in the long run, to contribute largely the outcome of the war. At the start of the year, in January 1941, without consulting Mussolini, the Germans launched *Operation Barbarossa*, the invasion of the Soviet Union. Ideally Hitler had wanted to begin operations against the Soviets earlier but delayed for six weeks in order to aid the Italians in their war against Greece. Mussolini immediately sent 200,000 Italian soldiers to fight on the Russian Front. At the end of the year, on 7 December, the Japanese attacked the American Pacific Fleet at Pearl Harbor. Consequently, Germany and Italy declared war on the United States. The war that *Il Duce* thought would be short lived and limited to Europe and Africa was now clearly to be a lengthy and worldwide struggle.

C *The Battle of Cape Matapan*

A second major sea battle involving the Italian and British navies occurred on 27 March 1941 at Cape Matipan off the southern coast of Greece. An Italian fleet under Admiral Riccardi was instructed to attack British supply convoys bound for Greece as well as a British fleet anchored at Suda Bay on the island of Crete. Again, the Italian ships were not adequately protected against air attacks and British warships and torpedo-carrying aircraft were able to inflict heavy losses on Riccardi's fleet. In what was later described as 'one of the most sweeping British naval victories since the Battle of Trafalgar', the Royal Navy sank three Italian cruisers and a number of destroyers and again proved its mastery in the Mediterranean.

1942	Axis forces (Rommel's *Afrika Korps*) launch successful offensive in North Africa
	Advance halted at First Battle of El Alamein
	British victory at Second Battle of El Alamein
	Operation Torch – Allied landings in Morocco and Algeria
1943	Axis forces routed at Stalingrad
	Italian and German forces surrender in North Africa
	Allies invade Sicily
	Mussolini dismissed by Fascist Grand Council
	Badoglio forms a new government
	Allied forces land on Italian mainland
	Badoglio asks Allies for an armistice
	Rescue of Mussolini by German force led by Skorzeny
	Establishment of Italian Social Republic (Salo Republic)
1944	Ciano and other former Fascist leaders executed
	Togliatti returns to Italy from exile in the Soviet Union
	Central Committee of National Liberation founded
	Ardentine caves atrocity
	Rome falls to the Allies
	Operation Overlord – D-Day landings in Normandy
	Operation Anvil – Allies land in south of France
1945	Mussolini captured and executed by Italian partisans
	Death of Hitler
	End of the Second World War in Europe

TABLE 32
Date line covering events from 1942 to 1945

However, later in the year the British did suffer some setbacks in the Mediterranean. In November, a German U-boat sank the British battle-ship HMS *Barham*. The following month three Italian midget submarines entered the port of Alexandria and succeeded in damaging two other battleships.

1942

A constant thorn in the flesh of the Axis powers in the Mediterranean was the British-owned island of Malta. Situated to the south of Sicily and opposite Libya, British aircraft on the island were well situated to attack shipping taking supplies to the Axis forces in North Africa. It was equally well situated to act as a staging post for British convoys destined for their forces in Egypt with supplies and reinforcements. Although Italian and German aircraft had been raiding the island during 1941, it was not until the following year that Hitler took the decision to carry out *Operation Hercules* – the occupation of Malta. However, the invasion of the island was cancelled in order to allow the Axis powers to concentrate on developments in North Africa. In Libya, the German *Afrika Korps* had won a series of victories in their desert war against the British. By October, they had forced the British out of Libya into Egypt to a point barely a hundred miles from Alexandria. At last, the capture of the Suez Canal was a distinct possibility. The advance of the Axis forces was finally brought to a halt at the First Battle of El Alamein. The German successes and the eclipse of the Italians upset Mussolini who felt that his generals and armies had failed him. He ordered the Italian commander, Graziani, to appear before a court of inquiry. The German invasion of the Soviet Union had the result of down-grading the importance of the North African campaign. To Mussolini's dismay, units of the German army and airforce were withdrawn from Egypt and transferred to the Russian Front. In October, British and Commonwealth forces in Egypt went on the offensive. At the Second Battle of El Alemein, the Axis forces began a retreat and, in little more than two months, were driven right across Libya and into Tunisia. During November as part of *Operation Torch*, American forces landed in Morocco and Algeria and this meant that the German and Italian forces were trapped between Allied armies advancing from east and west.

On the Russian Front, since the invasion in January 1941 and into 1942 things had gone extremely well for the Axis forces. At one point, the Germans supported by units of the Italian, Hungarian, Romanian and Finnish armies were fighting in the outskirts of Leningrad and were close to Moscow. Unfortunately, the Russians adopted a 'scorched earth policy' which meant that they destroyed everything as they retreated and left no food or shelter for the

1940

Desert war began in September 1940 when 250,000 Italian troops commanded by Graziani invaded Egypt. Three months later, the British counter-attacked, drove the Italians out of Egypt and advanced into Libya as far as Benghazi.

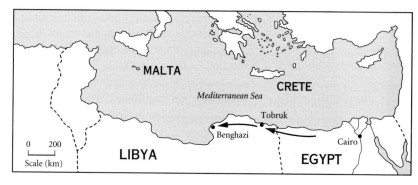

March 1941

Reinforced by the arrival of Rommel and the German Afrika Korps, the Axis forces attacked and forced the British to retreat back into Egypt. The Germans however were unable to capture the port of Tobruk.

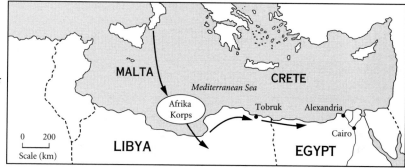

1941–2

In June, it was the British turn to attack and they were able to relieve Tobruk and regain most of the territory lost in March. Fortune next favoured Rommel and in January he more than repeated his success of the previous year when Axis forces advanced as far as El Alamein. He was now in a position to threaten the Suez Canal.

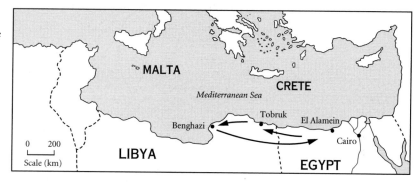

1942–3

In October 1942, the British launched an offensive, the Second Battle of El Alamein. The Germans and Italians were forced into a general retreat across Libya and into Tunisia. In November Allied forces landed in French North Africa and in May 1943. The Axis forces in North Africa surrendered.

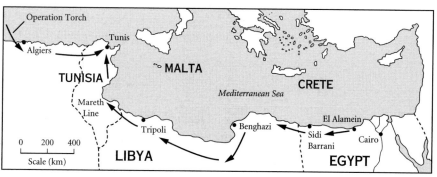

MAP 10   *The campaigns in the North African desert, 1940–3*

invaders. The Russian winter took a heavy toll on the Axis forces since they were unused to and unprepared for the severe weather conditions. The major turning point in the war on the Russian Front came at Stalingrad, a city on the River Volga. Between November 1942 and January 1943, the Russians encircled and destroyed the Axis forces. The Red Army took over 90,000 prisoners. Some of these were Italians destined never to see their homeland again. The Second Battle of El Alamein and the Battle of Stalingrad are recognised as being major turning points in the war.

MAP 11

The invasion and liberation of Italy

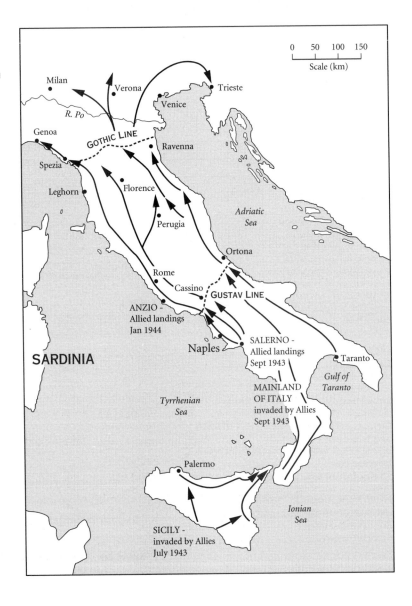

> ## *1943*
>
> On 12 May 1943, the Axis forces in North Africa surrendered. Less than two months later, on 10 July as part of *Operation Husky*, Allied armies landed in Sicily. Although the Italian army put up little resistance and many civilians welcomed the Anglo–American invaders, the Germans fought with great tenacity to hold the island. Even so, after 39 days, Sicily fell to the Allies and the invasion of the Italian mainland now seemed imminent.

3 ⇌ THE OVERTHROW OF MUSSOLINI

The invasion of Sicily and the speed with which the Allies captured the island increased even further the disillusionment of the Italian people and caused unease amongst leading members of the Fascist Party and the commanders of the armed forces. On 16 July, a group of Fascists still loyal to their leader including Scorza, the Party secretary, Acerbo, Bottai, de Bono, de Vecchi and Farinacci requested an audience with their leader. They expressed their concern about the low morale of the Italian people and asked to be better informed about the course of the war. Bottai reminded Mussolini that the Grand Council had not met since December 1939! A full meeting of the Grand Council was arranged for 24 July.

A *Mussolini dismissed by the Fascist Grand Council*

Faced with the prospect of ignominious defeat in the war, at the meeting Dino Grandi drafted an agenda which proposed that the King 'should be pleased to assume the effective command of land, sea and air forces' and 'that the supreme initiative of decision that our institutions attribute to him'. Put simply, this act of open rebellion against Mussolini demanded that the command of the armed forces and the future conduct of the war should be placed in the hands of Victor Emmanuel III. In a long rambling speech, *Il Duce* made excuses and reluctantly gave details of Italian military failures. He ended by reminding those present 'A war that goes badly is one man's war, but it is a people's war when it ends in victory.' At three o'clock the next morning a vote was finally taken and Grandi's proposals were approved by 19 votes to 8 with one abstention. Amongst those who voted for Mussolini's removal were Grandi, de Bono, de Vecchio, Marinelli and *Il Duce*'s son-in-law, Count Ciano. The vote of no confidence made things easier for the King who had already decided to remove Mussolini. When he summoned Mussolini, the Fascist leader boldly claimed that the Fascist Grand Council was only an advisory body and had no power to remove him. Victor Emmanuel replied that the Grand Council's vote was 'absolutely substantial, make no mistake'. Later Mussolini stated that he had been overthrown by a conspiracy involving 'the ex-king, the bourgeoisie and the freemasons'. At the time, *Il Duce* appeared to accept his fate and was placed under arrest. Immediately afterwards, the King invited Marshal Pietro Badoglio to form a new government. In a radio broadcast to the Italian people he said:

> Let us close ranks around His Majesty, the King and Emperor, a living image of the fatherland and an example to all. The charge I have received is clear and precise. It will be scrupulously executed, and whoever deludes himself into thinking that he will be able to hamper the normal course of events, or attempt to upset public order, will inevitably be punished.

martial law to take additional powers needed to cope with an emergency

His first action was to declare **martial law** across Italy and appoint a new cabinet that excluded any Fascists but he let it be known that there would be no mass arrest and trial of the leaders of the former Fascist regime. The resignation of Mussolini was greeted with jubilation since many thought it would bring an immediate end to the war. Fascist insignia disappeared as did the wearing of blackshirts and the *cimice* – the buttonhole badge that indicated membership of the PNF. Then in an extremely confused and dangerous situation, Badoglio played for time by announcing his intention of continuing in the war on Germany's side. Although carried out in secret, the German intelligence was aware that Badoglio had already started peace negotiations with the Allies. If the new Italian Prime Minister had agreed to change sides immediately, the Italian armies might have assisted the Allies in a sweep northward towards Rome. As it was, the Germans were given time to more than treble the strength of their forces in Italy and this was to prolong the war by many months.

The first Allied landings on the Italian mainland finally came on 3 September when British forces crossed the Straits of Messina at Reggio Calabria. Six days later, further Allied landings occurred at Taranto and Salerno. On 8 September, the Italian radio announced that Badoglio had asked the Allies for an armistice. The following day, Victor Emmanuel and his government left Rome and abandoned central and northern Italy to the Germans. Immediately the Italian armies disintegrated. Whilst some servicemen remained loyal to their German allies, others opted to fight with the Allies but most were happy to throw away their arms and make their way home. Uncertain of their loyalty, Italian units in the German controlled areas were disbanded and some 600,000 sent to Germany as prisoners-of-war.

B *Mussolini and the Salo Republic*

From a German viewpoint, Mussolini still had his uses and was needed as a rallying point for those Italian still loyal to their former Fascist dictator. Badoglio's government did its best to conceal his exact position by regularly moving him from one place to another. Meanwhile, Hitler entrusted Captain Otto Skorzeny with the task of locating and rescuing Mussolini. The leader of special troop parachutists followed several false trails and it is said that Himmler even used the services of an **astrologer** to locate him! Finally an intercepted coded message indicated that Mussolini was being held at Campo Imperatore, a skiing centre in Gran Sasso. On 12 September, Skorzeny with 100 airborne troops landed in a light aircraft close to the hotel and succeeded in a most audacious rescue attempt. Mussolini was first flown to Vienna and then on to Munich where he was reunited with his wife. Two days later he met the German *Führer* at Rastenburg. Afterwards, he announced his intention of establishing a new Fascist government in northern Italy. Officially known as the *Repubblica Sociale Italiana*, it is usually referred to as the Salo Republic. Salo, a small town on Lake Garda, was to serve as the capital of Mussolini's new republic. The Salo Republic quickly raised a National Republican Army of 150,000 men, the *Esercito Nazionale Repubblicano* that continued to fight against the Allies and even helped the Germans in their struggle against Yugoslav partisans. Black Brigades, elite groups of loyal Fascist soldiers, were created to enforce law and order within the Republic and wage a campaign of terror against partisans, Jews and army deserters. The Republic also produced its own flag, currency and postage stamps. Although the surrender of the Italian navy was part of the terms agreed with the Allies, it is the opinion of some that Admiral Bergamini planned to send his fleet to Spain and ask for it to be interned. Some ships, the *Marina Nazionale Rebubblicana*, remained loyal to Mussolini and the Salo Republic. Similarly units of the airforce, the most Fascist of all the Italian armed services, the *Aeronautica Nazionale Repubblicana*, continued to fight against the Allies. In the Italian Social Republic, the Salo Republic, Mussolini's puppet regime went through the process of agreeing a constitution. Surrounded by fanatical Fascists and Nazi sympathisers such as Roberto Farinacci, Alessandro Pavolini and Renato Ricci, Mussolini declared Roman Catholicism to be the established religion of the Republic and stated that all Jews were to be considered foreigners. Earlier in January, he had taken his revenge against some of the members of the Grand Council who had voted against him and foolishly remained in the north. Galeazzo Ciano was arrested by the Germans in Munich and flown under guard to face trial at Verona. Those tried included Emilio De Bono, Giovanni Marinelli and Ciano. All were condemned to death and even appeals from Edda Ciano, Mussolini's daughter, did not prevent her husband being shot. Before his execution, Ciano wrote a letter intended for Winston Churchill. In it he described his father-in-law as Hitler's 'tragic and vile puppet' and concluded 'the misfortune of Italy was not the fault of the people but due to the

astrologer a person who claims to be able to foretell the future by studying the position of the stars

KEY ISSUE

Mussolini's aim in setting up the Salo Republic.

Q

To what extent might the Salo Republic have been considered a puppet regime?

shameful behaviour of one man'. The letter was not published until after the war. Edda never forgave her father and said, 'The Italian people must avenge the death of my husband. And if they do not do so – I will do it with my own hands'. Dino Grandi, the leading conspirator in the plot to overthrow Mussolini, fled to Spain where General Franco granted him **political asylum**. In Salo, Mussolini lived in a luxury villa, the Villa Feltrinelli, with his wife, Rachele and his surviving children and grandchildren. However, the apparent domestic harmony was shattered by the arrival in Salo of Clara Petacci, Mussolini's mistress.

For all Mussolini's exaggerated claims, the Salo Republic only managed to encourage the survival of Fascism in a limited area of northern Italy. More seriously, as it helped to protect Germany's southern flank, it turned the region into a battleground.

During this time, Mussolini's health began to decline. He had always suffered from ulcers and gastric problems but now he was clearly losing weight. A strict dietary regime helped him to recover but after a while his old troubles returned. As his condition worsened, he was described as 'reduced to being a walking corpse.'

> **political asylum** refuge granted by a foreign country for political reasons

C *Italian Resistance, 1943–5*

The final stage of the war witnessed the creation of an effective anti-Fascist resistance movement in the German-occupied north. The slowness of the Allied advance from the south encouraged the emergence of groups of partisans prepared to fight behind the German lines. With Italy divided between those who supported Badoglio's government in the south and those who still backed the remnants of Mussolini's Fascist movement, the Salo Republic in the north, the situation risked turning into a civil war. At first, the partisans consisted mainly of ex-soldiers and escaped prisoners of war but the movement grew to include civilians drawn from varied backgrounds. Politically they came from all the non-Fascist parties that had now reappeared. With some 50,000 men at their disposal, the Communists formed the largest group and the Action Party, Christian Democrats, Socialists and Liberals were also well represented.

In 1944, Palmiro Togliatti, the exiled Communist Party leader, returned from the Soviet Union and agreed to collaborate with the King and Badoglio. With the support of the local peasantry, the partisans survived in the mountains from where they carried out acts of sabotage by blowing up bridges and harassing German troop movements. As they grew in number they became more daring and were prepared to engage German units in pitched battles. They also turned on Mussolini's National Republican Army and atrocities and acts of retaliation were committed. Amongst their victims was Giovani Gentile, a Fascist academic and theorist who had been Mussolini's first Minister of Education. Some used the opportunity to settle old scores and long standing family feuds. When the opportunities occurred, the partisans ambushed and killed German soldiers and this brought retaliation. It

> **KEY ISSUE**
>
> *Togliatti's decision to collaborate with the King and Badoglio.*

was made known that for every German soldier killed, 50 local inhabitants would be shot. In one instance alone in disused quarries outside Rome, the Ardentine caves, 335 Italians were executed. One of the victims, Aldo Finz, had served in Mussolini's first government in 1922. He was a Jew! Mussolini complained to Kesselring about the atrocities committed by the Germans but to no avail. In the north, the resistance established in each area a Committee of National Liberation, a *Comitato Di Liberazione*. Eventually a Central Committee of National Liberation, a *Comitato Centrale Di Liberazione Nationale*, was set up which called upon the Italian people 'to struggle and fight for the reconquest of Italy's place among the assembly of free nations'. This Central Committee was recognised as the main co-ordinating body of the Italian resistance movement. The various committees acted independently of the government and, in 1943, the elderly Ivanoe Bonomi was appointed the movement's president. As the end of the war approached, the army of partisans grew to over 250,000 and was strong enough to liberate cities such as Milan, Turin and Genoa ahead of the arrival of the Allies.

KEY ISSUE

The role of Italian partisans in the liberation of their homeland.

1944

The Allied advance was made more difficult by the Apennine mountains, the so-called 'backbone of Italy', that stretches nearly 1,200 kilometres along the length of the Italian peninsula. Moving along the coastal plains to the east and west had to be achieved against German forces that invariably held the high ground. By the winter of 1943, the German armies under Field Marshal Albert Kesselring, a brilliant military strategist, held a defensive line, the Gustav Line, which stretched from the estuary of the River Garigliano to the town of Pescara on the Adriatic. It included the impressively built Benedictine monastery, Monte Cassino. It took weeks of bitter fighting by British, American, French, Indian and Polish troops before the bomb-scarred monastery finally fell. Earlier in January, the Allies tried to by-pass the German strong point by landing further to the north at Anzio. It took four months for the Allies to break out from their bridgehead and begin to push inland. Rome finally fell to the Allies on 4 June, two days before *Operation Overlord* when on D-Day the Allies landed along the beaches of Normandy to begin the liberation of France. Later in August, *Operation Anvil* saw Allied troops land in the south of France. In Italy, the Germans were forced to retreat to another defensive line, the Gothic Line, which stretched across Italy from Spezia in the west to Rimini in the east.

1945

The Allies did not manage to breach the Gothic Line until April 1945. After the capture of Bologna, the Allies began a thrust towards the Alps and the German retreat finally turned into a

PICTURE 56

A sick man and a mere shadow of his former self – Mussolini in 1945

rout. The start of 1945 saw the Germans under pressure on three fronts – in Eastern Europe, the Red Army was advancing through the Balkans, in the West, the Allies were moving towards the River Rhine, and to the south, the Germans had been driven from Italy. The war was virtually over.

4 ∽ THE LAST DAYS OF BENITO MUSSOLINI

About to be hunted down by his own countrymen, Benito Mussolini, pale, exhausted and a shadow of his former bombastic self, looked older than his 62 years. Hitler had promised that secret weapons were being developed that would change the course of the war but *Il Duce* recognised that this promise was no more than an illusion. Unaware that the Central Committee of National Liberation had ordered that leading Fascists were to be executed without trial, he left his villa at Salo and made for Milan. He said, 'I am close to the end ... I await an epilogue of this tragedy in which I no longer have a part to play. I made a mistake and I shall pay for it'.

For a time, he considered negotiating with the resistance. He was told that if he surrendered, he could only expect the 'ordinary guarantees given to prisoners of war'. When he was made aware that the Germans had been secretly negotiating their own safe passage from Italy, he raged, 'They have always treated us like dogs, and in the end they have betrayed us.' On 25 April, together with other leading Fascists and protected by German armoured cars, Mussolini reached Como where he spent the night. There he wrote a final letter to his wife:

> Here I am on the last lap of my life, at the last page of my book ... I ask your forgiveness for all the harm I have done you without wishing to. But you know that you are the only woman I have really loved ...

He advised his wife and children to either seek refuge in Switzerland or give themselves up to the Allies. He did not mention that Claretta Petacci was travelling with him! The next morning the convoy of vehicles left for Menaggio and joined with other German vehicles heading north. At the village of Dongo, the convoy was halted by partisans who insisted on searching the vehicles. Although dressed in German military uniform and pretending to be asleep, he was recognised. At first his captors seemed uncertain what to do with him but eventually he was taken to Azzano and there spent the last night of his life with his young mistress. The next morning, 28 April 1945, they were bundled into a car and after a short drive reached the front gates of the Villa Belmonte. There gunmen led by Walter Audisio, also known as 'Colonel Valeria', shot them. Claretta Petacci, who refused to be separated from Mussolini, was also executed. Elsewhere, groups of leading Fascists were executed in groups, 15 or more at a time. The next day, the bodies of *Il Duce* and his mistress were taken into the centre of Milan to be further mutilated by local bystanders. Finally they were strung up by their feet from the girders of a garage roof in the Piazzale Loreto.

In an interview with a journalist eight days before partisans shot him, Mussolini appeared to remain convinced that Fascism would survive:

KEY ISSUE
The need to execute Mussolini.

> Only an Axis victory could have entitled us to lay claim to our share of the world's resources, of resources which are in the hands of a small number of greedy nations who are the cause of all the evils, all sufferings, and all wars. The victory of the so-called Allied Powers will give the world only an **ephemeral** and illusory peace. For this, you have remained faithful to me, must survive and maintain faith in your hearts ... I was not bluffing when I declared that the Fascist idea will be the idea of the twentieth century. An eclipse of five years, or even ten, has absolutely no importance. It is partly events, partly men with their weaknesses which today are bringing about this eclipse. History will vindicate me.

ephemeral short lived

From an interview with Gian Gaetano Cabella which appeared in Testamento Politico de Mussolini, *1948*

Two days later, Adolf Hitler and his mistress, Eva Braun, committed suicide in their Berlin bunker, and on 8 May, the German armies surrendered. The Second World War in Europe was over.

As for the fate of Mussolini's family – his wife, Rachele, as well as his son and daughter, Romano and Anna-Maria, were arrested. They were cared for by the Allies and later released. Vittorio had earlier escaped to

PICTURE 57

The bodies of Mussolini and Claretta Petacci hanging in the forecourt of a garage in Milan

PICTURE 58

The mutilated bodies of Il Duce and his mistress

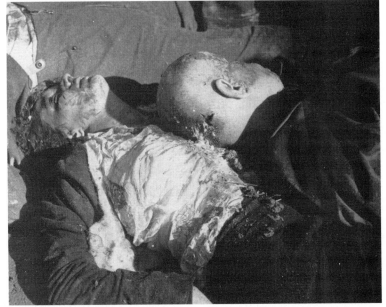

Switzerland whilst, the war over, Romano remained in the hope of reviving his musical career. After the execution of her husband, Edda had also made her way to Switzerland where she rejected any attempt at reconciliation with her father. Ten years passed before she agreed to meet her mother and visit her father's tomb.

5 ∽ ITALY AND THE SECOND WORLD WAR – OTHER CONSIDERATIONS

A *To what extent was Italy the 'Achilles heel' of the Axis powers?*

During the course of the war, the mass surrender of Italian soldiers led the Allies to make comparisons with Caporetto in the First World War and claim that *Il Duce*'s soldiers surrendered in large numbers because of their lack of fighting spirit and for reasons of cowardice. In reality, this was far from the truth, but the myth was widely circulated and provided excellent propaganda. As we have seen, most Italians had been forced into a war of which they really wanted no part and for which they lacked both the economic and military resources. Poorly trained, equipped with inadequate and outdated weapons and led by incompetent commanders, it was disillusionment rather than cowardice that caused them to surrender in droves. Some Italian units fought alongside the Germans with distinction, particularly on the Russian Front. When, towards the end of the war, Italy changed sides, Italian partisans operating behind the German lines fought bravely and won the admiration of their Anglo–American allies.

As the war progressed, it became increasingly clear that Italy was involved in a conflict it could not afford and for which most of its people had no enthusiasm.

Despondency increased as it became evident that the Axis powers could not match the material and military might of the United States, the Soviet Union and Britain and her Empire. By backing Nazi Germany, Mussolini had backed the wrong horse and drawn his country into the war on the losing side. With Italy clearly unable to achieve much on her own, Hitler now openly expressed a view that he had previously only confided in private, Mussolini's Fascist Italy had become a liability and was the '**Achilles heel**' of the Axis.

See page 44

See pages 212–13

'Achilles heel' the most vulnerable point

PICTURES 59 (LEFT) AND 60 (RIGHT)
The two faces of Italian military prowess. Left: the mass surrender of Italian soldiers in the Western desert in 1941. Right: an Italian cavalry charge on the Russian Front in 1942 where they fought with great courage.

B *The home front – the impact of the war on the Italian people*

As we have seen, one of the most obvious impacts of the war was the decline in the morale of the Italian people. Signs of disillusionment were the result of the failure of their armed services to live up to Mussolini's extravagant bombast and gain any notable victories. Although censorship of the media prevented the people from knowing the truth of the extent of their military defeats, rumour abounded. From the start of the war, Italy lacked the essential raw materials and foodstuffs to back their war effort or supply the people with basic necessities.

- Previously dependent on German coal, a fall in imports from her Axis partner had a knock-on effect on her production of iron and steel. By 1942, production had fallen by nearly 20%. This not only limited armaments production but also ensured that no iron and steel-based consumer goods were available to the general public.
- There was also an acute shortage of oil. Of the limited quantity imported from Romania, military needs took precedence and there was little left for public and privately owned transport.
- In addition to the shortages of raw materials and power, industrial production was adversely affected by the Allied bombing of Italian towns and cities that increased during the latter stages of the war. This led to the destruction of factories and workers' housing.
- Shortages of artificial fertilizers and machinery together with the fact that so many peasant labourers had been recruited into the armed services resulted in a significant fall in agricultural production. This led to food shortages and the introduction of rationing. The projected level was a meagre 1,000 calories a day per person, less than 20% of the average peacetime food consumption. The daily bread ration was limited to 150–200 grams per person.
- The government introduced legislation to control the price of foodstuffs and essential consumer goods. It proved difficult to enforce. As luxury goods disappeared from the shops and there were shortages of such things as coffee, shoe leather and clothing, so a black market developed in which profiteers thrived and amassed fortunes by overcharging for scarce goods.
- The financial demands of the war led to increases in taxation which offended the middle classes who, in the past, had been prominent amongst Mussolini's supporters. It also made the lives of the rural peasants even more difficult.
- Although previously unheard of in Fascist Italy, in 1943 100,000 workers went on strike in northern towns and cities. During 1944 industrial unrest increased and in March 1944, 119,000 took strike action, and this eventually grew to 350,000. The Nazis threatened to shoot or deport strikers and this led Mussolini to intervene. He asked those involved to return to work and appealed to their patriotism. He claimed that the strikes were communist inspired and schemed by Palmiro Togliatti who had recently returned to Italy. It worked, and the industrial unrest temporarily subsided.

● As the war progressed, the Fascist Party became increasingly remote from the people and appeared to show insensitivity to their suffering. Mussolini seldom appeared in public and his sloganeering came to an end. The people who had previously been unaware or turned a blind eye to the corruption and inefficiency in the Party, now became less tolerant. Anti-Fascist leaflets and graffiti appeared in the streets and Mussolini became the butt of crude humour.

● Bluff and propaganda no longer worked. As casualty rates soared, so grieving families joined those demanding peace, bread and an end to Fascism. The truth of what was happening in the war became increasingly apparent since many Italians now listened to overseas radio broadcasts.

Less recognised was the suffering of the many thousands of Italians who had earlier emigrated abroad. They had lived in adopted countries for decades and had become thoroughly integrated within their communities. Many were well known and much respected figures. Italy's entry into the war in 1940 changed that for those living in Britain. Branded as 'enemy aliens', they were classified according to the threat they were thought to represent. Some were interned, some had to appear before tribunals and had their freedom of travel curtailed, some were allowed to remain at liberty. There were anti-Italian riots in London, Liverpool, Manchester, Edinburgh, Belfast and elsewhere and mobs threw stones at Italian-owned property and ransacked and looted their shops. The irony was that some had taken British nationality and had sons and husbands serving in the British armed services! Then in what was later deemed 'a blind act of panic', all Italian males aged between 16 and 70 were interned. A most tragic incident occurred on 2 July 1940 when a German U-boat operating in the waters off the coast of Ireland torpedoed the *Arandora Star*, a Blue Star liner carrying German prisoners-of-war and Italian internees to Canada. As a result, 486 Italians and 175 Germans were drowned. Following the United States' entry into the war in 1941, tens of thousands of men of Italian origin volunteered to serve in the American armed services.

C *Pope Pius XII and the Holocaust*

An on-going controversy amongst historians relates to the attitude of Pope Pius XII to the treatment of the Jews in Germany and Nazi-occupied Europe. The charge is that he appeared indifferent to their suffering and, when asked, refused to speak out against Nazi atrocities and the genocide then taking place across Europe.

Most damaging to Pope Pius XII's reputation was a play, *The Deputy*, by the German Rolf Hochhuth that had its premiere in 1963 and, much more recently, the disclosures in the book by the British historian John Cornwell, *Hitler's Pope – The Secret History of Pius XII*, published in 1999. Not surprisingly, many Catholic historians have written in the pontiff's defence. In his book, Cornwell describes Pope Pius XII as 'arguably the most insidiously evil churchman in modern history …

PICTURE 61
Pope Pius XII (1876–1958)

POPE PIUS XII (1876–1958)

Eugenio Pacelli was born in Rome in 1876. One of four children, his father was a lawyer. He studied for the priesthood and was ordained in 1899. Astute, hard working and considered a high flyer in Vatican circles, promotion came rapidly and in 1917 he was appointed Apostolic Nuncio, the Vatican's representative, in Bavaria. For much of his life, he was concerned with German affairs and, after the First World War, he took up a similar post in the German Weimar Republic. In 1929, Pope Pius XI created him a cardinal and the following year he was appointed Secretary of State for the Vatican City. He witnessed the rise of Hitler and the Nazis at first hand and played a major role in the negotiations that led to the Concordat of 1933. By this agreement, Hitler guaranteed Roman Catholics in Germany 'freedom of belief and of public worship' and to 'administer its own affairs'. In return, the Catholic Church agreed to stay out of politics. In 1939, Pacelli was elected Pope and took the title Pius XII. Many assumed that the new Pope would continue with his predecessor's anti-Nazi stance, particularly where it applied to the treatment of the Jews. During 1939, he made every effort to prevent war and even offered to mediate between the two sides. The following year he urged Mussolini to stay out of the war. His attitude during the war, particularly as in relation to the Holocaust, remains a matter of debate and disagreement (see below). After the war he worked to relieve distress amongst prisoners and refugees but was nevertheless criticised by numerous post-war European governments. He died in 1958.

who did more than fail to speak out against Nazi crimes – he supported Hitler's final solution.' On the other hand, Robert Graham, editor of an American Jesuit magazine, describes Cornwell's allegations as 'malicious', and an 'obscenity'. Wherein lies the truth?

The Jewish historian, Shira Schoenberg, is of the view that earlier, as Cardinal Pacelli, he had spent so many years in Nazi Germany he must have been well aware of the nature of Nazi anti-Semitism. Unlike Pius XI, up to 1939 he never once criticised Hitler's racial policies although he did speak out against aspects of Mussolini's racial laws of 1938. In 1939, the Pope used his influence to obtain 3,000 visas for European Jews to emigrate to Brazil, but they were all Jewish converts to Catholicism! During the war numerous political and religious leaders including representatives of President Roosevelt, the Chief Rabbi of Palestine and the head of the Polish government in exile, pleaded with the Pope to be more outspoken. He refused insisting that the Vatican must remain neutral and that it was impossible to verify rumours about crimes committed against the Jews. In 1940, Pope Pius XII did speak out against 'the horror and inexcusable excesses committed on a helpless and homeless people' but did not mention the Jews by name. It should however be remembered that in Germany and Nazi-occupied Europe there were many Catholic priests, most famously Alfred Delp and Clemens von Galen, who did speak out against Nazi excesses and that a great many Jews were given sanctuary by Catholic families and institutions.

In 1943, following the invasion of Sicily, the Pope attempted to use diplomatic channels to get Rome declared an 'open city' – a city that would not be defended and therefore should not be attacked. Nevertheless, on 19 July, American aircraft bombed the city. With 500 civilians killed and many more injured, Pius II appeared in the rubble to pray and offer the people money and sympathy. Italian Jews were placed in peril when in September 1943, the Germans occupied northern and central Italy. Rome had a Jewish community of some 8,000 and these were immediately threatened with deportation. Major Herbert Kappler, head of the SS in the city, cynically used the situation to hold the Jews to ransom by demanding a payment of 50 kilograms of gold in 36 hours in order to call the deportation off. With the help of a loan of 15 kilograms of gold from the Vatican, the amount was paid in full and on time. Despite this, the round up of Roman Jews went ahead. Assembled in a barracks before being transported to a railway station, one train alone containing over 1000 women and children headed for Germany and then Poland and Auschwitz. Of these only 15 returned after the war. Although nearly 500 Jews were hidden in the Vatican and a further 4,200 taken in by monasteries and convents, at no time did the Pope protest against the roundup and deportation of Rome's Jews.

Several theories had been put forward to explain the Pope's silence or at best his unwillingness to speak out more forcibly. Cornwell is of the opinion that the Pope was an admirer of Hitler, 'Hitler's Pope' and was himself anti-Semitic. Less harsh is the conclusion that Pius XII feared that if he spoke out, Hitler would next turn on the Catholic Church and victimise Roman Catholics. Towards the end of the war there was some indication that he intended to do just that. The *1996 Grolier Multimedia Encyclopedia* may be close to the truth when it states:

> Wishing to preserve Vatican neutrality, fearing reprisals and realising his impotence to stop the Holocaust, Pius nonetheless acted on an individual basis to save as many Jews and others with church ransoms, documents and asylum.

Is it perhaps the case that Pope Pius XII has been denied credit for the achievements of his quiet diplomacy and behind-the-scenes activities. Then there is the view that faced with the threat of Communism, the Pope regarded the Nazi and Fascist regimes of Germany and Italy as Europe's bulwark against the further advance of godless Bolshevism. In other words, he simply sided with what he regarded as the lesser of two evils.

6 ∽ MUSSOLINI'S FASCIST ITALY – AN OVERVIEW

Because of his appearance and behaviour, Mussolini is an easy person to ridicule and lampoon. Whilst Winston Churchill referred to him 'as the bullfrog of the Pontine Marshes' and A.J.P. Taylor as a 'vain blustering, boaster', many historians have regarded him as little more than a buffoon. It is often claimed that his only achievement was 'to get the Italian trains to run on time'. Are these estimates of Italy's Fascist leader a fair assessment of his character, achievements and legacy? In retrospect, how have some leading historians assessed Mussolini's Fascism?

From The Origins of the Second World War *by A.J.P. Taylor, 1964*

Fascism never possessed the ruthless drive, let alone the material strength, of National Socialism. Morally, it was just as corrupting – or perhaps more so from its very dishonesty. Everything about Fascism was a fraud; the social peril from which it saved Italy was a fraud; the revolution by which it seized power was a fraud; the ability and policy of Mussolini was fraudulent. Fascist rule was corrupt, incompetent, empty …

From Italy 1915–1945: Politics and Society *by Paul Corner that appears in* The Oxford Illustrated History of Italy *edited by George Holmes 1997*

Ironically, Mussolini had succeeded in uniting Italians briefly – but against Fascism rather than for it. None the less the legacy of Fascism was to be far reaching. Quite apart from a disastrous war fought on Italian territory, Fascism bequeathed poverty, and inefficiency … and a political practice which had generalised petty corruption and made the use of public office for private gain the norm … The attempt to form a nation, to give Italians a single identity in the Italian State had proved a total failure. This was perhaps inevitable in an authoritarian state which attempted to achieve mobilisation through myths of past greatness and illusions of future conquest. Fascist pretensions were ultimately beyond the means available to the regime. Many had known this all along but it took a world war to burst the bubble and make it obvious to everyone.

In sum, then, it may be agreed that Mussolini was, in some sense, 'a man for all that', a personage who reflected his gender, class, region and nation, a tyrant of course, but not so vicious that history should relegate him, frozen, to the bottommost circle of some Dantesque hell … In the final analysis, the problem with Benito Amilcare Mussolini was that, for all his aspirations to exercise power, he turned out to be no more than an ambitious intellectual from the provinces who believed that his will mattered and who thought, as did others, that he was a *Duce* and could lead a state like Italy towards a special sort of modernisation. His propagandist declared that he was always right. However, in the most profound matters which touch on the human condition, he was, with little exception, wrong.

From Mussolini *by Richard Bosworth, 2002*

Did Adolf Hitler regret his alliance with Mussolini?

Judging events coldly, leaving aside all sentimentality, I have to admit that my friendship for Italy and for the *Duce*, could be added to my list of mistakes. It is visible that the Italian alliance rendered more service to the enemy than ourselves. The intervention of Italy will only have bought us the minutist advantage in comparison with the difficulties which it created for us.

From Hitler's Political Testament, *1945*

And a warning from the present:

A mayor in northern Italy is struggling to stop his town from becoming a mecca for Fascists from all over Europe amid signs that Italian right-wingers are rehabilitating the legacy of Benito Mussolini. Predappio, near Bologna, the birthplace and final resting place of *Il Duce* has long been a place of pilgrimage for Mussolini apologists. More than 100,000 people have visited in the past year ... On Predappio's main street, souvenir shops enjoy a burgeoning trade in Mussolini paraphernalia despite a law banning the public glorification of Fascism. In addition to *Il Duce* flags, badges, posters and calendars, the shops also sell CDs of Fascist songs ... A woman buying a 2003 Mussolini calendar said his only fault was that he lost the war.

From an article in British newspaper, The Independent, *by Kate Goldberg, July 2002*

7 ∽ STRUCTURED AND ESSAY QUESTIONS

A *This section consists of questions that might be used for discussion (or written answers) as a way of expanding on the chapter and testing your understanding.*

1. How well prepared for war were the Italian armed forces in 1940?
2. What finally made Mussolini decide to enter the war on Germany's side?
3. Why did the Italians attempt the invasion of Greece in 1940?
4. How close did the Axis forces in North Africa get in their bid to reach the Suez Canal?

5. Explain the strategic importance of the island of Malta during the war.
6. Why did the Fascist Grand Council vote for the removal of Mussolini in 1943?
7. What major obstacles did the Allies face as they advanced northwards through Italy?
8. Is it possible to justify the criticisms made of Pope Pius XII's conduct during the war?

B *Essay questions.*
1. With what justification can it be claimed that Italy made a substantial contribution to the Axis war effort?
2. To what extent was the civilian population of Italy affected by the war?
3. Explain the reasons for the rise and fall of the Salo Republic.

8 ⌁ MAKING NOTES

Read the advice given about making notes on page xix of the Preface: How to use this book, and then make your own notes based on the following headings and questions.

1. *Italy's entry into the war.*
   (a) Reasons for Mussolini's hesitation at the start of the war.
   (b) His decision to declare war.
   (c) To what extent might Mussolini's decision to become involved in the war 'a most ill conceived blunder'?
2. *Italy's part in the war.*
   (a) To what extent was Italy ill-prepared for war?
   (b) The reasons for and the consequences of the Greek campaign of 1940.
   (c) The fortunes of the Italian armies in North Africa.
   (d) The reasons for the German involvement (Rommel and the *Afrika Korps*).
   (e) The stages of the Italian campaign (from landings in Sicily to surrender).
   (f) The part played by Italian partisans in the liberation of Italy.
3. *The collapse of Fascism.*
   (a) The decision by the Fascist Grand Council to dismiss Mussolini.
   (b) Skorzeny and the rescue of Mussolini.
   (c) The Italian resistance movement.
   (d) The fate of Mussolini and other leading Fascists.

Post-War Italy 1945–70

13

INTRODUCTION

The war had been costly for Italy. The country had suffered 330,000 military and 80,000 civilian casualties including over 17,000 who had died fighting with the resistance. In addition, Italy had been turned into a battlefield and this had resulted in massive structural damage and dislocation. The fact that their partisans had played an important part in the final stages of the liberation of their country went a long way towards restoring Italian self-respect. Although the future was uncertain, the end of the war was greeted with great celebration and euphoria. As we have seen, soon after the Allied landings on the Italian mainland in September 1943, political activity began with the re-creation of political parties as well as the first moves towards the restoration of political democracy. The dominant political parties immediately after the war were the Christian Democrats, (*Partito Democrazia Cristiana* or DC), the Italian Communist Party (Partito Communista Italiano or PCI), the United Socialist Party (*Partito Socialista de Unita Proletaria* or PSU), the Italian Liberal Party (*Partito Liberale Italiano* or PLI), the Italian Social Democratic Party (*Partito Socialista Democratico Italiano* or PSDI) and the Action Party (*Partito d'Azione* or PA). There was also a revival of trade unionism. Whilst many of the leading members of the former Fascist regime had already been dealt with, many remained at large. Some took refuge in the Vatican whilst others fled abroad. Dino Grandi made his way to Portugal and others found refuge in sympathetic dictatorships in South America. Giuseppe Bottai, who in spite of having a Jewish mother had been prominent in supporting Mussolini's race laws, joined the Foreign Legion! However, the government did not carry out a vindictive campaign against lesser Fascist officials. Indeed, many who had served the Fascists in the foreign ministry, civil service, judiciary and local government continued to hold positions of responsibility. Sabato Visco, another of the sponsors of the race laws, was allowed to continue as the president of the Faculty of Science at the University of Rome. Former military leaders were also treated leniently. Even Marshal Graziani, commander of the armed forces of the Salo Republic, was put on trial but only received a short prison sentence. However, the Yugoslav government listed him with others as guilty of war crimes and pressed for his re-trial.

KEY ISSUE

The revival of party politics.

TABLE 33

Date line showing major post-war events in Italy

1944	Badoglio's government replaced by a coalition under Bonomi
1945	Bonomi's government gave way to a new coalition under Parri
	Fall of Parri's government. Succeeded by new coalition led by de Gasperi
1946	Victor Emmanuel III abdicates in favour of his son Umberto
	First democratically held elections for 20 years.
	De Gasperi coalition continues
	In referendum, Italian people vote for a republic
1947	De Gasperi resigns then forms new government with Communists excluded
	Peace Treaty agreed
1948	New constitution introduced
1949	Italy joined NATO
1950	Fund for Southern Development set up
1951	Founder member of European Coal and Steel Community
1957	EEC founded by the Treaty of Rome
1958	New coalition under Amitore Fanfani
	Angelo Roncalli elected Pope (Pope John XXIII)
1963	Sweeping Communist gains in election
	New coalition under Aldo Moro
1969	*Autunno Caldo* – 'Hot Autumn'
1970	Workers' Act
	Referendum approves of divorce

1 ✎ FREE ELECTIONS AND THE END OF THE MONARCHY

In 1944, the government formed by Badoglio after the overthrow of Mussolini was replaced by a coalition of Christian Democrats and other parties led by Ivanoe Bonomi. Togliatti's Communists, profiting from their prestige as leaders in the resistance, had a membership of over two million and were to become the largest Communist Party in Western Europe. In retrospect, the Communists might have used their numerical strength and popularity to seize power through revolution. However, such a move would almost certainly have provoked the intervention of the United States and Britain as had already been the case in neighbouring Greece. Italian governments of the immediate post-war period faced the daunting task of establishing political stability and overseeing recovery and reconstruction. The achievements of the resistance stirred enthusiasm for a period of renewal. This 'wind from the north', as it was called, kindled a genuine desire amongst Italians to abolish all traces of Fascism and make a fresh start. In June 1945, Bonomi's government was replaced by another coalition led by Ferruccio Parri (1890–1981) leader of the Action Party. An opponent of Fascism, in 1942 Parri had been imprisoned but managed to escape and afterwards became an outstanding resistance leader. He showed less skill as a political leader and seemed unable to cope. He soon offended the Christian Democrats and after six months his government fell and he was replaced by Alcide de Gasperi (1881–1954).

KEY ISSUE

The 'wind from the north'.

Heads of State	Prime Ministers	
Provisional Head of State	**Prime Ministers (Presidents of**	
1946 Alcide de Gasperi	**the Council of Ministers)**	
	1944–45 Ivanoe Bonomi	No party
Presidents of the Republic	1945 Ferruccio Parri	PA
1946–48 Enrico de Nicola	1945–53 Alcide de Gasperi	DC
1948–55 Luigi Einaudi	1953–54 Giuseppe Pella	DC
1955–62 Giovanni Gronchi	1954 Amintore Fanfani	DC
1962–64 Antonio Segni	1954–55 Mario Scelba	DC
1964 Cesare Merzagora	1955–57 Antonio Segni	DC
1964–71 Giuseppe Saraget	1957–58 Adone Zoli	DC
	1958–59 Amintore Fanfani	DC
	1959–60 Antonio Segni	DC
	1960 Fernando Tambroni	DC
	1960–63 Amintore Fanfani	DC
	1963 Giovanni Leone	DC
	1963–68 Aldo Moro	DC
	1968 Giovanni Leone	DC
	1968–70 Mariano Rumor	DC
	1970–72 Emilio Colombo	DC

TABLE 34
Italian Heads of State and Prime Ministers 1944–70

A *Elections and a referendum*

In June 1946, Italians took part in the first democratic general elections for over 20 years. The electorate, which for the first time included women, were not only asked to choose a new government but also decide the future of the monarchy.

(i) **The parliamentary elections of June 1946**
In the elections, the Christian Democrats gained 35% of the vote and won 207 of the seats in the Chamber of Deputies. However they had far from an overall majority since the Socialists gained 115 seats and the Communists 104. The other parties were largely also-rans.

(ii) **Monarchy or republic – the referendum of June 1946**
The other major issue to be settled was the future of the Italian royal house, the House of Savoy. In 1922, Victor Emmanuel III had failed to prevent Mussolini and his Fascists coming to power. Although the relationship between the King and *Il Duce* had been uneasy, in the eyes of many Italians Victor Emanuel had become tainted by his association with Fascism. The fact that the King had played a part in the Fascist dictator's downfall was not sufficient to deter the government from considering the future of the monarchy. In an effort to ensure the future of the House of Savoy, in May 1946 Victor Emmanuel III abdicated in favour of his 41-year-old son, Umberto. This was far from a shrewd move since the new King, who was married to Princess Marie Jose of Belgium, had served in the Italian army, appeared with Mussolini and was said to be homosexual. There was also other unsavory gossip about his

See pages 77 and 113

KEY ISSUE

Reasons for the unpopularity of the monarchy.

family life and the fathering of his four children. The issue was put to the Italian people in the form of a national referendum. The outcome was close-run. On 2 June 1946, 12,718,641 (54%) voted in favour of a republic and 10,718,502 (46%) for retaining the monarchy. The **referendum** emphasised the divide between the north and centre that were predominantly republican and the monarchist south. Afterwards Umberto II, sometimes referred to as the 'King of May', the month that approximately covered of his 34-day reign, was banished together with the rest of his family and went into exile. He lived the remainder of his life in Portugal, and died in Geneva in 1983.

referendum putting an issue to the vote of the entire electorate

B *A new constitution*

Under the chairmanship of the socialist leader, Giuseppe Saragat, the Constituent Assembly planned a new constitution that was finally agreed by 453 votes to 62 in December 1947. The constitution, which came into force on 1 January 1948, described Italy as 'a democratic republic founded on work' and emphasised that constitutional **sovereignty** belonged to the Italian people. Other significant Articles included:

sovereignty supreme power

Article 2. The Republic recognises and guarantees the inviolate rights of man, both as an individual and in social formations, in which he expresses his personality, and asks to fulfill his political, economic and social responsibilities ...

Article 3. All citizens have equal social dignity, and are equal before the law regardless of sex, race, language, religion, public opinion, personal or social condition ...

Article 5. The Republic ... recognises and promotes local autonomy; it practises broad decentralisation in services that depend on the state ...

Article 10. The Italian judicial structure conforms to the generally recognised norms of international law. The legal status of a foreigner is regulated by the law, in conformity with international norms and treaties.

Article 11. Italy repudiates war both as an instrument that offends the liberty of other peoples and as a means of resolving international controversies ...

centralisation the tendency for the administration of all the nations affairs to be hands of the central government

Article 5 represented a move towards regional government and away from Fascist **centralisation**. Italy was divided into 92 provinces, each under a prefect. There were also to be four special regions each under a government commissioner – Sicily, Sardinia, French-speaking Val a'Aosta and German-speaking Trentino Alto Adige. The constitution also guaranteed freedom of religious practice, of thought, speech and writing and stated that no person could be deprived of his citizenship on political grounds. The press was also to be free of control and censorship. In courts of law, the accused was to be considered 'not guilty' until otherwise proven and the treatment of criminals was to be directed at their re-education and rehabilitation. In addition, the death penalty was abolished except under martial law. However, not all the measures were liberal in their content. Any attempt to resurrect the Fascist Party was forbidden and the male descendants of Victor Emmanuel were to be excluded from all public offices, banned from Italian territory and their estates confiscated. In addition, the titles of the Italian nobility were no longer to be recognised.

The new system of government was similar in outline but differed in detail from the old. The parliament would continue to consist of two houses, a Chamber of Deputies and a Senate but as a republic, Italy would no longer have a hereditary monarch as nominal head of state. Instead, a president was to be elected jointly by the Chamber of Deputies and Senate together with delegates from the regional councils.

See page 10

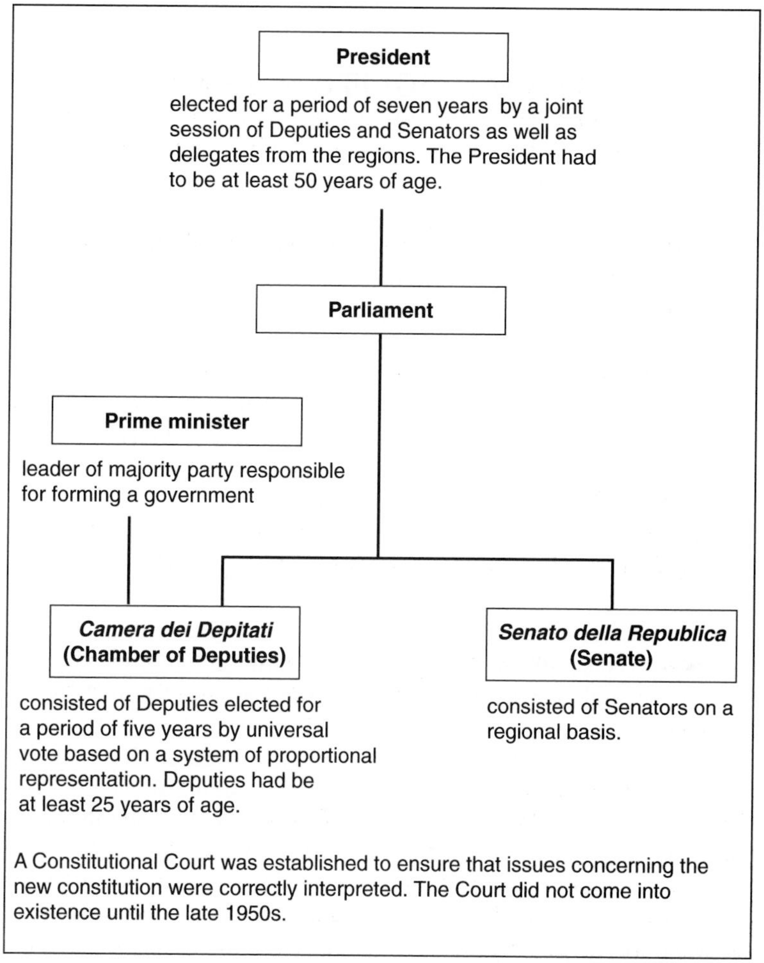

DIAGRAM 4
The System of Government based on the Constitution of 1948

President

elected for a period of seven years by a joint session of Deputies and Senators as well as delegates from the regions. The President had to be at least 50 years of age.

Parliament

Prime minister

leader of majority party responsible for forming a government

| *Camera dei Depitati* (Chamber of Deputies) | *Senato della Republica* (Senate) |

consisted of Deputies elected for a period of five years by universal vote based on a system of proportional representation. Deputies had be at least 25 years of age.

consisted of Senators on a regional basis.

A Constitutional Court was established to ensure that issues concerning the new constitution were correctly interpreted. The Court did not come into existence until the late 1950s.

To what extent might the terms of the Italian peace treaty be considered severe?

2 ∽ THE PEACE TREATY 1947

After much deliberation, in February 1947 a peace treaty was finally signed between Italy and the Allies. The severity of the treaty came as something of a blow to de Gasperi. The main terms agreed were:

● Italy was to lose all her colonies, even those gained before the First World War. Abyssinia (now called Ethiopia), who had already regained her independence, received Eritrea whilst Libya and Italian Somaliland became independent.

● Italy was also to lose the much-disputed Istrian peninsula and Trieste was to become a free territory under international supervision.

● Italy was to pay reparations totalling $360 million to the Soviet Union, Greece, Yugoslavia, Albania and Ethiopia. Other Allied powers declined to claim a share of the reparations.

From an Italian point of view, the most distressing feature of the treaty was the loss of the Istrian peninsula, an area whose ownership they had earlier contested so vigorously. The treaty also finally shattered what had once been Mussolini's dream of an Italian empire.

See page 30

3 ∽ ITALIAN POLITICS 1948–63

De Gasperi, a stern yet conciliatory politician and a devout Catholic, faced a difficult time. Inter-party feuding and disagreements within his own Christian Democrat Party hindered his attempts to deal with the economic and social problems facing the country. Nevertheless, he continued to lead a coalition government dominated by his own party. Life was made even more difficult by the appearance of new extremist right-wing political parties. These included two monarchist parties, the *Partito Nazionale Monarcho* (National Monarchist Party) and the *Partito Popolare Monarcho* (Popular Monarchist Party) and the neo-Fascist Italian Social Movement (*Movimento Sociale Italiano* or MSI). Members of the *Missini*, as it came to be known, adopted the old style Fascist salute and indulged in street violence.

A *The election of 1948*

The elections of 1948 were bitterly contested. De Gasperi's overriding need was to ensure the defeat of the Communists and in this he had the support of both the United States and the Catholic Church. Italian post-war recovery was dependent on aid provided by the American sponsored **Marshall Plan** and the United States warned that such aid would come to an end in the event of a Communist victory. The promise to return Trieste to Italian rule was offered as an additional incentive. The American cardinal Francis Spellman, an ardent anti-Communist, said 'I cannot believe that the Italian people will chose Stalinism against God'. As a further inducement but with an implied threat he added, 'America has done so much and stands ready and will-

Marshall Plan an American plan to assist European post-war recovery

ing to do so much more, if Italy remains free.' The Communist leader, Togliatti, forecast that intelligent Italians would vote for de Gasperi because 'he's obtained free from America the flour for your spaghetti as well as the sauce to put on it'. In his *History of Contemporary Italy* (1990), Paul Ginsborg describes a more personal exchange between the two men. When De Gasperi accused the Communist leader of 'having the cloven feet of the devil', Togliatti replied that he had perfectly normal feet but that 'one of them, heavily shod in a studded boot, would be firmly implanted in de Gasperi's backside once the elections were over'. It was much to the disadvantage of Togliatti that the election coincided with a Communist *coup* in Prague, the capital of Czechoslovakia. In the election, the Christian Democrats did impressively by winning nearly 49% of the vote and 305 out of the 574 seats in the Chamber of Deputies that gave them an overall majority. The Socialists and Communists, even though they combined and contested the election as a Popular Front, only won 140 seats between them. The Communists with 106 seats had the lion's share with the Socialists gaining a paltry 41.

De Gasperi wanted Italy to once again become part of the international community. It was impossible for his country to stand aside from the Cold War in the relationship between the Soviet Union and the Western democracies and in 1949 Italy became a member of the North Atlantic Treaty Organisation (NATO). A staunch European, in 1948 de Gasperi negotiated Italy's membership of the Organisation for European Economic Co-operation (OEEC) which was to administer Marshall Aid, the Council of Europe, set up in 1949 to encourage political co-operation, and in 1952, the European Coal and Steel Community.

B *The election of 1953*

Driven by his fervent anti-Communism, prior to the elections of 1953 de Gasperi proposed a change in the electoral law that would allow any two parties who between them received more than 50% of the vote to automatically be allocated two-thirds of the seats in the Chamber of Deputies. The purpose of the measure seemed similar to that of the Acerbo Law of 1923 and the Communists described it as *La Legge Truffa*, 'the cheating or swindle law'. They failed to prevent the law being passed. This time it was the Christian Democrats who agreed an election pact with the Liberals, Social Democrats and the Republicans. Even so, the four-party alliance did badly. The Christian Democrats lost 80 seats as well as their overall majority in the Chamber of Deputies. The other parties of de Gasperi's intended coalition also lost ground. With insufficient support to form a government, he resigned and retired from political life. De Gasperi died the following year at the age of 73. Italy was set for a ten-year period of political instability during which there were to be no less than twelve changes of government (see chart on page 227).

See page 89

PROFILE

PICTURE 62
Alcide de Gasperi (1881–1954)

ALCIDE DE GASPERI
(1881–1954)

Born in 1881 in the Trentino, then under Austrian rule, Alcide de Gasperi was educated at Vienna University. Before the First World War, he represented the city of Trento in the Austrian Congress in Vienna. Once the war was over, he represented the same area in the Italian parliament. In 1925, he became leader of the *Partito Popolare*, the forerunner of the Catholic Democratic Party. De Gasperi was imprisoned by the Fascists and, following his release in 1939, worked in the Vatican library. He took no further part in political life until after the downfall of Mussolini. After the war, he became leader of the Christian Democrat Party and served as Foreign Minister during the ministries of Bonomi and Parri (see page 227). In 1945, he became Prime Minister. Altogether, he led eight consecutive coalition governments. Alcide de Gasperi supervised his country's transition from a monarchy to a republic, the introduction of a new constitution and negotiated a peace treaty with the Allied powers. He worked to restore his country's economy after the devastation of the war years and was responsible for introducing a programme of land reform. Through his close co-operation with the United States and Italy's membership of NATO, he went a long way towards restoring his country's international status. A staunch Catholic and lifelong opponent of Communism, de Gasperi was a shrewd politician who led his country's transition from a Fascist dictatorship to a democracy. He resigned in 1953 and retired from active politics. He died the following year. Alcide de Gasperi has been described as 'undoubtedly the most outstanding figure in Italian politics in the immediate post-war era'.

TABLE 35
Elections to the Chamber of Deputies 1948–68 (Based on statistics in A History of Contemporary Italy 1943–1988 *by Paul Ginsborg, Penguin Books 1990.)*

	% of votes gained				
	1948	1953	1958	1963	1968
Christian Democrat Party (DC)	48.5	40.1	42.4	38.3	39.1
Italian Socialist Party (PSI)		12.7	14.2	13.8	
Italian Social Democratic Party (PSDI)	7.1	4.5	4.6	6.1	
Popular Front (left-wing alliance)	31.0				
United Socialist Party (PSU)					14.5
Italian Liberal Party (PLI)	3.8	3.0	3.5	7.0	5.8
Italian Communist Party (PCI)		22.6	22.7	25.3	26.9
Republican Party	2.5	1.6	1.4	1.4	2.0
Monarchist Party	2.8	6.9	4.9	1.7	1.3
Italian Social Movement (neo-Fascist MSI)	2.0	5.8	4.8	5.1	4.4
Italian Social Party of the United Proletariat (PSIUP)					4.4
Others	2.3	1.8	1.5	1.3	1.6

The elections of 1958 saw only marginal gains and losses by the various political parties. There was a hint of a partial revival in support for the Christian Democrats whilst the extremists lost ground. Even so, the Christian Democrats could only muster 42% of the vote and this meant that the new party leader, Amitore Fanfani (1908–99), had to seek the support of one or two other parties in order to form a workable coalition. A more promising development of that year was the election of Angelo Roncalli as Pope John XXIII following the death of Pius XII. A former army chaplain and papal nuncio to liberated France, he was a popular figure and a man of great humility.

In the elections of 1963, the electorate of the so-called 'Red Belt' in central Italy ensured that the Communists won a record 166 seats in the Senate. For the first time, the Christian Democrat vote fell below 40%. A new centre-left government came into being that included the Christian Democrats, Francesco Nitti's Socialists and Giuseppe Saragat's Social Democrats. The leader of the coalition was Aldo Moro (1916–78). Moro, a Christian Democrat who had been in politics since 1946, was an impressive orator. As Minister of Justice between 1955 and 1957 he had acquired a reputation as a reformer. During this time, he improved prison conditions and made the purpose of imprisonment more character reforming than punishment. He also abolished capital and corporal punishment. As Prime Minister, he brought some stability to government. Importantly, after a 19-year rift between the Socialists and Social Democrats, the two parties united. Even so, between them they could only muster 95 seats in parliament, far fewer than the Communists. In 1964, the death of Palmiro Togliatti came as a blow to the Communists. He had seen his party grow from a handful of left-wing activists to the largest Communist Party in western Europe. Widely respected, throughout his life he had sought to achieve a peaceful transition to socialism rather than revolution. Over a million attended his funeral. He was succeeded by Luigi Longo. In spite of early promise, Moro's government failed to deal with the urgent problems facing the country. In 1968, the year of the next election, the Communists took advantage of the growing discontent amongst workers and students to increase their representation to 177 seats and become the second largest party in the Chamber of Deputies. The following year, the alliance between the two socialist parties collapsed and the Social Democrats formed a new party, the Unitarian Socialist Party (*Partito Socialista Unificato* or PSU). The period witnessed increased unrest amongst Italy's students as they copied their French and German counterparts and sought to form an alliance with the workers. In 1970, during the acting premiership of Mariano Rumor, the divorce bill was passed. During this period, a time when the Fascist MSI was gaining in popularity, Italy witnessed an increase in violence and terrorism made evident by street crime, bomb outrages and kidnapping. In the south where the condition of the people remained neglected, the country was close to open civil war.

PICTURE 63

A Christian democrat election poster emphasising their belief that Italy weathered the storm and is on the path to peace

4 ⌐ ITALY'S ECONOMIC MIRACLE

By the later 1940s, most of the countries of western Europe were already making steady progress towards economic recovery and, with West Germany leading the way, by the early 1950s this had turned into a boom. The economic recovery of Italy began much more slowly but this accelerated until, by the late 1950s and into the 1960s, she too was enjoying an exports-led 'economic miracle'.

A *Reason's for Italy's 'economic miracle'*

The reasons for Italy's 'economic miracle' were many:

- Between 1945 and 1950 Italy received 3,500 million dollars in Marshall Aid.
- The activities of the resistance towards the end of the war ensured that much of the industrial plant in northern Italy escaped unscathed.
- During the period 1953 to 1960, investment in Italy's manufacturing industries increased by 14%. Cheap government loans were made available, particularly to firms considered to have potential for growth.
- As with other countries, Italy was in a position to take advantage of a worldwide expansion in international trade encouraged by a surge in the demand for manufactured consumer goods.
- The influx of workers from the south meant that Italy had a plentiful supply of cheap labour. On the other hand, unemployment was kept to a minimum by the migration of many Italian workers to Germany and elsewhere.
- After years of acute shortages of energy, in 1949 oil was found in the Po valley and, in 1953, in Sicily. In addition, natural gas was discovered at Lodi near Ferrara. This was exploited by the state-sponsored ENI, *Ente Nazionale Idrocarburi*, the National Agency for Hydrocarbons.
- Overseas competition, particularly from the Far East, was not yet a threat. Between 1958 and 1963 Italian exports increased by 14% with the vast majority of this going to other EEC countries. Her most popular exports included inexpensive Fiat family cars, Olivetti office equipment, Zanussi and Candy domestic appliances and Ignis optics.
- The loss of her colonies did have a beneficial effect since it rid Italy of the expense of being a colonial power. Britain and France, on the other hand, were facing the expense of the struggle to stop their empires disintegrating in the face of calls for independence from their colonial peoples.
- Italian membership of the EEC brought her many advantages. By the late 1960s, Italy was selling more cars in the Common Market than any other member.

During this period, evidence of Italy's prosperity was apparent in the successful completion of several national projects. In 1962, the *Autostrada*

Del Sol, the 'Highway to the Sun' which connected Milan with Naples, was completed and 1964 saw the opening of the road tunnel through the Italian Alps, the Great St Bernard Pass.

Italy's economic miracle also brought some economic benefits to her people. With the growth of the national economy increasing annually by an average of 5.5% and inflation as low as 2.5%, standards of living improved and between 1952 and 1970 average income per head increased by over 13%. There is no better indicator of the new prosperity than the fact that between 1960 and 1970 the number of private cars in use had increased from just under two million to over ten million. Unfortunately there was also a downside to the new prosperity. Across the country, the boom in manufacturing was not matched by investment in public services such as hospitals, schools and public transport. It also increased even further the differences between north and south so that by 1971 the average income of a northern worker was twice that of a man in the south. As men from the south migrated northwards, so towns and cities became overcrowded. It was not unusual for men to work 10 to 12 hours a day and live in doss houses, four or five to a room.

B *The plight of the southern peasantry*

The period also witnessed changes in distribution of workers between agriculture and industry. By 1964, only 26% were employed on the land with 41% in manufacturing and heavy industry. Even so, the wide discrepancies in living standards between central and northern Italy and the south remained. Although de Gasperi had attempted some land reform, the overall condition of the majority of the peasants in the south had barely changed and some would say even worsened. Housing remained primitive and lacking in amenities. Few had adequate sanitation or running water and less than 7% had electricity. There were still a goodly number who lived rough. Wages for those in employment were half those paid to workers in the north. The land reform had broken up some of the large estates and the land had been allocated to the peasants as smallholdings. Altogether 700,000 hectares had been distributed amongst 120,000 families. Sadly this barely scratched the surface of the problem since it affected so few. In addition, financial help and advice had also been offered but this too was slow to materialise. When subsidies became payable, it led to corruption since the main recipients were supporters of the Christian Democrats and it was simply a case of money for votes, and the peasants repaid the party officials on polling day. For the peasant families who received neither land nor money there were three options – to migrate to the towns, emigrate abroad or resort to banditry. Some of those who sought work in the towns did reasonably well and for the first time in their lives received regular wages. However, the majority merely joined the ranks of the unemployed and destitute. The situation came to a head in 1970 when riots occurred in Reggio Calabria that threatened to turn into an open revolt.

> **KEY ISSUE**
>
> *The extent to which the Italian people shared in the new prosperity.*

5 ⌒ YEARS OF INCREASING UNREST 1968–70

The benefits of the new-found Italian prosperity during the early and mid 1960s were not shared by all the Italian people. This led to dissatisfaction and unrest that came to a head in 1968. In Italy, as in other European countries, it became increasingly fashionable to be critical of capitalist materialism. This was particularly true of university students who had their own reasons to be dissatisfied and used the situation to openly reject discipline and authority.

A *Revolutionary activity amongst students*

Students first openly protested about overcrowding on university campuses, the poor standard of lecturing and the lack of maintenance grants. It was also true that there was a surfeit of graduates and on leaving university many failed to get suitable work. Student organisations tried to unite with workers in their efforts to change the system, claiming that their problems could be blamed on the capitalist society that they despised. Many appeared to think that that Europe was on the verge of revolution. Politically active Leninist/Stalinist groups abounded. These included *Potere Operaio* (Workers Power), *Lotta Continua* (Unending Struggle), *Servire Il Popolo* (Serve the People), *Avanguardia Operia* (Workers' Vanguard) and *Momento Studentesco* (Student Movement). Their **icons** were Mao Zedong, the revolutionary, Che Guevara, and the North Vietnamese leader, Ho Chi Minh, and they tried to win over the masses with leaflets, calling for demonstrations. They were also prepared to use violence to achieve their aims.

icons portraits. In this case, images of revolutionaries they admired

B Autunno Caldo, *the 'Hot Autumn' of 1969*

It was late in 1969 that discontent amongst Italian workers led to them taking industrial action. During what became known as *Autunno Caldo*, Hot Autumn, there were strikes, demonstrations, and factory occupations. They had many reasons for complaint.

consumerism promoting and protecting the interests of buyers of goods and services

From A Concise History of Italy *by Christopher Duggan, 1994*

The causes of unrest were both economic and social. Unemployment had declined during the boom years and yet industrial wages were still the lowest in western Europe and the quality of housing, transport, education, and health care was for many Italians abysmal. Furthermore expectations had risen, fuelled by the glittering images of **consumerism** dangled before growing audiences in television advertisements, in films and the glossy weekly magazines that had become so popular in the 1960s. There was certainly a strong political dimension as well to the labour unrest, in that the workers were voicing dissatisfaction not just with their material conditions, but also with the parties and trade unions of the centre and left, which, they understandably felt, had failed them.

There were strikes across Italy with the most serious at the Pirelli works in Milan and the Fiat factories in Turin. In one demonstration in Turin, some 300,000 workers took to the streets and there were violent clashes between the strikers and the police.

In an attempt to defuse the situation, the government introduced a number of reforms. In 1969, government pensions to those who had been in regular employment were increased. It was a measure that did not help those in irregular employment or the unemployed. The *Statuo Dei Lavoratori*, a Workers' Act, of 1970 settled more important grievances. It guaranteed the right to organise trade unions, allowed appeals against unfair dismissals, and provided improved protection to those employed in dangerous occupations. In the same year, a campaign led by the *Lega Italiana per L'Istituzione del Divorzio*, the League for the Institution of Divorce or LID, was finally successful. In a Catholic country such as Italy, the issue of divorce was contentious and strongly opposed by the Church and the Christian Democrats. In parliament, the measure was passed by 325 votes to 283, and when put to a referendum, 60% voted in favour.

C *The re-emergence of the* mafia

During the years of Mussolini's Fascist dictatorship the *mafia* were suppressed. It might cynically be claimed that former *mafia* members merely transferred their allegiance to Fascist organisations such as the *squadristi*. During the post-war period, the *mafia* again appeared, firstly in Sicily and then across Italy as a whole. To the government's embarrassment, they used political connections to become involved in 'a higher culture of corruption and racketeering than before'. Apart from running protection rackets, controlling gambling and prostitution and the marketing of drugs, they also ran apparently legal businesses that they used to **launder money**.

> For most Italians the *mafia* were, of course, simply criminals who had to be suppressed by the actions of the police ... Those unwilling to pay for 'protection' continued to be murdered by the traditional method (shooting with a sawn-off shot gun in order to inflict massive mutilation), as did the policemen who proved too zealous and sought to reach beyond the small fry towards the bigger fish ... In the 1970s, the average murder rate by the *mafia* in Palermo city was almost one a day and later it more than doubled. Most victims were typical *mafia* targets: 'awkward' politicians, trade-union leaders and policemen, although there were often lengthy periods when these murders were suspended during bloody settlements of accounts between rival 'families'.

By 1970, Italy's economic, social and political problems were far from over. Both student and industrial unrest continued and there were

PICTURE 64
Militant students at the University of Pisa gathered under a banner of the Potere Operaio *(Workers' Power). Note the pictures of Ho Chi Minh, Mao Zedong and Che Guevara*

Q *Why did divorce become such a major issue in Italy?*

launder money to use a legal business as a means of transferring money from an illegal source so that its origins can not be detected

From Italy Since 1800 *by Roger Absalom, 1995*

appalling bomb outrages. In 1978, terror struck at the highest level when Prime Minister, Aldo Moro, was kidnapped in Rome in broad daylight. The government rejected demands made by his kidnappers, members of the *Brigate Rosse* (Red Brigade). On 16 May, his body was found in the boot of a car significantly parked between the headquarters of the Christian Democrat and Communist Parties.

During the previous hundred years, the Italian people had survived the duplicity of *transformismo*, the ravages of two world wars, the rule of Mussolini's Fascist regime, and periods of major political social and economic upheaval. There could be little doubt that, in the long run, they would also have the fortitude to survive the problems they faced at the start of the 1970s.

6 ⇜ STRUCTURED AND ESSAY QUESTIONS

A *This section consists of questions that might be used for discussion (or written answers) as a way of expanding on the chapter and testing your understanding.*

1. What action was taken against former leading Fascists at the end of the war?
2. Who were the main supporters of the Christian Democrats?
3. In what ways did the system of government adopted in Italy in 1948 differ from that of Britain?
4. For what reasons did Italians vote against the monarchy in 1946?
5. Why did Italians consider the loss of the Istrian peninsula a 'distressing feature' of the peace treaty?
6. Account for the increase in the popularity of Togliatti's Communist Party during the 1960s.
7. Why was divorce such a controversial issue in Italy?
8. What were the main reasons for student unrest in Italy during the 1960s?

B *Essay questions.*

1. How successfully did Italy's post-war governments deal with the problems facing the country?
2. To what extent might the recovery that occurred during the period 1950–60 be regarded as an Italian 'economic miracle'?

7 ⇜ SYNOPTIC QUESTIONS

The main skills required in answering synoptic questions are those of being able to identify from the content of your study that which is relevant to a topic or theme and the extent to which this provides evidence of change and continuity. In addition you may be required to provide historical explanations, make judgements and evaluate evidence. The questions may take the form of open-ended essay questions or questions based on one or a number of sources. The sources may be prima-ry or secondary and cover areas of historical debate. In this case you will need to bear in mind the basis upon which the authors of the sources reached their conclusions. Remember that you will be required to take an overview and cover a range of perspectives including politi-cal, social, economic, cultural and religious. Some topics covered by this book that might be used as the basis for synoptic questioning include:

- relations between the Catholic Church and the State
- the quest for colonies and imperial status
- foreign policy
- agriculture and the condition of the peasantry
- industrial developments
- the struggle to establish democratic government
- the impact of war and the peace treaties that followed
- constitutional developments – from monarchy to republic

Let us consider what might be included in a response to a possible synoptic question based on the relations between the Catholic Church and the State.

> *'A period of continuous disharmony and tension.'* How valid is assessment of relations between the Catholic Church and the Italian State during the period 1870–1970?

- The aftermath of unification – the issue of Rome
- The Papal States and the Pope as a spiritual leader
- The Doctrine of Papal Infallibility (1870)
- Catholic reaction to The Law of Guarantees (1871)
- Pope Pius IX – 'the prisoner of the Vatican'
- Pope Leo XIII – a more moderate 'working men's Pope'.
- The Church's attitude to liberalism, socialism and Marxism
- The Catholic *Popolari*
- The significance of the encyclical *Rerum Novarum* (1891)
- Luigi Sturzo and the *Partito Democrazia Cristiana* – the Christian Democrat Party
- Mussolini's early atheism (*The Cardinal's Mistress* etc.)
- Attempts at reconciliation with the Church
- Fascism – champion of moral and family values?
- The Lateran Treaty and Concordat (1929)
- The issue of 'Catholic Action'
- The significance of the encyclical *Non Abiamo Bisogno* (1931)
- Religious teaching in schools
- Pope Pius XI and Italy's Fascist regime
- Church's attitude to Italian involvement in the Second World War
- The Church and the Salo Republic
- The controversy relating to Pope Pius XII
- The Church during the post-war period. Divorce and other issues.

Bibliography

Although the number of texts covering Italian history from 1870–1945 in no way matches the sheer avalanche of books about Germany during the same period, there are some excellent and accessible books available. Whilst the years of Mussolini's Fascist Italy 1922–45 are well covered, there is a relative scarcity of books about the periods prior to the Fascist *coup* in 1922 and following the overthrow of Italian Fascism in 1945. As far as AS/A2 level texts are concerned, amongst those currently available are *Italy: Liberalism and Fascism 1870–1945* by Mark Robson (Hodder & Stoughton Education 2000), and the relevant sections in *Italy Since 1800* by Roger Absalom (Longman 1995), *A Concise History of Italy* by Christopher Duggan (CUP 1994), *Modern Italy 1871–1982* by M. Clark (Longman 1984), Denis Mack Smith's *Italy, A Modern History* (Univ. of Michigan 1981), *History of the Italian People* by Giuliano Procacci (Pelican Books 1968), and *The Oxford Illustrated History of Italy* edited by George Holmes (OUP 1997). The years of Fascist Italy are well covered in:

Blinkhorn M., *Mussolini and Fascist Italy* (Methuen 1984)
Bosworth R.J.B., *Mussolini* (Hodder Headline 2002)
Gallo M., *Mussolini's Italy* (Macmillan 1974)
Hite J. & Hinton C., *Fascist Italy* (John Murray 1998)
Jones D.M., *File on Fascism* (Univ. of Wales, Aberystwyth 1990)
Knox M., *Mussolini Unleashed 1939–41* (CUP 1982)
Mack Smith D., *Mussolini* (Weidenfeld & Nicholson 1981)
Mussolini B., *My Autobiography* (The Mayflower Press 1928)
Palla M., *Mussolini and Fascism* (Interlink Books 2000)
Payne S., *History of Fascism 1914–45* (UCL 1995)
Pollard J., *The Fascist Experience in Italy* (Routledge 1998)
Ridley J., *Mussolini* (Constable 1997)
Williamson D., *Mussolini from Socialist to Fascist* (Hodder & Stoughton 1997)

Also only available in French but full of interesting and unusual photographs:

Legrand J., *Mussolini* (Editions Chronique 1997)

Books covering interesting aspects of the period include:

The Last Days of Mussolini After the Battle series number 7 (1975)
Cornwell J., *Hilter's Pope – The Secret History of Pius XII* (Penguin Books 1999)
De Grand A., *Women under Italian Fascism* (The Historical Journal XIX 1976)
Ginsborg P., *A History of Contemporary Italy 1943–1988* (Penguin Books 1990)
Griffin R. (ed), *Fascism* (OUP 1995)
Hughes C., *Lime, Lemon & Sarsaparilla – the Italian Community in South Wales 1881–1945* (Seren Books 1991)
Levi Carlo, *Christ Stopped at Emboli*, a novel about life amongst the peasantry in southern Italy (four Square Books, 1946)

Glossary

Index